THE PEACEABLE KINGDOM

Denise:
Let's tear down
some walls,

Stan

Adweek Books is designed to present interesting, insightful books for the general business reader and for professionals in the worlds of media, marketing, and advertising.

These are innovative, creative books that address the challenges and opportunities of these industries, written by leaders in the business. Some of our writers head their own companies, others have worked their way up to the top of their field in large multinationals. But they share a knowledge of their craft and a desire to enlighten others.

We hope readers will find these books as helpful and inspiring as *Adweek, Brandweek,* and *Mediaweek* magazines.

Published

Disruption: Overturning Conventions and Shaking Up the Marketplace, Jean-Marie Dru

Under the Radar: Talking to Today's Cynical Consumer, Jonathan Bond and Richard Kirshenbaum

Truth, Lies and Advertising: The Art of Account Planning, Jon Steel

Hey, Whipple, Squeeze This: A Guide to Creating Great Ads, Luke Sullivan

Eating the Big Fish: How Challenger Brands Can Compete Against Brand Leaders, Adam Morgan

Warp-Speed Branding: The Impact of Technology on Marketing, Agnieszka Winkler

Creative Company: How St. Luke's Became "the Ad Agency to End All Ad Agencies," Andy Law

Another One Bites the Grass: Making Sense of International Advertising, Simon Anholt

Attention! How to Interrupt, Yell, Whisper, and Touch Consumers, Ken Sacharin

THE PEACEABLE KINGDOM

Building a Company without Factionalism, Fiefdoms, Fear and Other Staples of Modern Business

Stan Richards

with David Culp

John Wiley & Sons, Inc.

New York • Chichester • Weinheim • Brisbane • Singapore • Toronto

Published simultaneously in Canada.
Published by John Wiley & Sons, Inc.

Library of Congress Cataloging-in-Publication Data:
Richards, Stan, 1932–
    The peaceable kingdom: building a company without factionalism, fiefdoms, fear and other staples of modern business / Stan Richards, with David Culp.
        p. cm.
    "An adweek book."
    Includes index.
    ISBN 0-471-39116-6 (cloth : alk. paper)
    1. Advertising agencies—Management.   2. Advertising agencies—Case studies.
3. Richards Group.   4. Corporate culture.   5. Decentralization in management.
6. Office politics.   I. Title: Building a company without factionalism, fiefdoms, fear, and other staples of modern business.   II. Culp, David, 1959–   III. Title.

HF6178 .R53 2001
659.1'068—dc21   00-064919

Printed in the United States of America.

10 9 8 7 6 5 4 3 2 1

This book is dedicated to my wife, Betty, with whom I've enjoyed every minute of this exhilarating ride. She embodies all the characteristics of Texans that first enthralled me when I decided to stay here some 40-odd years ago.

I also want to acknowledge the extraordinary people of The Richards Group, who are the real creators of this "Peaceable Kingdom." For without their steadfast guardianship, this culture would long ago have vanished.

—Stan Richards

Contents

Introduction:
Tearing Down the Walls

My company is an advertising agency (or a branding agency, as we could more accurately be called). But that doesn't mean this is a book about the advertising business.

It's about the culture and company organization that my colleagues and I have built at the agency. I believe that the nontribal ethic we've devised over the years could be instituted in any other industry, in any size company—*if* the people in charge are serious about doing away with internal politics and equity-focused management.

Companies, especially creative companies like mine, reach success because their people are motivated not so much by the bottom line as by their will to win and their desire to bring something new and valuable into the world. That's what I believe we've done at The Richards Group. And I believe we've done it because of our somewhat oddball way of valuing work, highlighting performance, and conducting relationships within the organization and with our clients. If we've succeeded at that, then you can, too, whether you're in a manufacturing concern, a dot-com, a professional practice, the hospitality field, retailing, nonprofit work, or education. I'm convinced that the principles apply to any enterprise that involves getting two or more people to try to work together in a productive way.

Mine, I must admit, is a strange company. Oh, on the surface there's nothing too peculiar about us. We're based in Dallas and have a staff of around 600 people (Groupers, we call ourselves), along with a constellation of related businesses such as an interactive group, a sales promotion agency, a PR firm, and RBMM, the design firm. We've got a pretty good reputation within our industry—four-time Agency of the

Year in *Adweek*, lots of awards, lots of appearances on magazines' lists of the most creative agencies in America, that kind of thing.

There's nothing flaky about our client list, either—brands like Corona, Motel 6, The Home Depot, Nokia, Chick-fil-A, Fruit Of The Loom. Real A-list companies. And we're growing. The milestone of half a billion dollars in billings is in our rearview mirror, and a billion is starting to look like a real possibility.

Not bad credentials. Nothing unconventional looking. But when you start getting to know the part of our company that can't be summed up in a few bullet points, that's when questions begin to arise. Questions like, "What is *up* with these people?"

It's our company culture. It's odd. It takes a lot of explaining, sometimes even to people who work here, who wonder how this company got to be so different from the places where they worked before. So we produced a little culture piece, a 12-page booklet that became the seed of this book. Here's how it begins.

> Remember that painting we've all seen called "The Peaceable Kingdom," where the lion and lamb, bear and ox, leopard and child, et cetera and so forth, all coexist in perfect harmony?
>
> That's basically the setup we're trying for at The Richards Group.
>
> We're working toward a utopian realm where people of wildly different personalities and highly varied—some would say naturally hostile—roles in the business all mingle in mutual esteem and selfless common labor, the end of which is personal happiness for each individual and fame, fortune, and universal admiration for our agency and our clients. . . .
>
> In other words, we've made it our mission to tear down walls. . . .

So that's what visitors find on all the reception-area coffee tables. We get a lot of visitors. There's the usual stream of clients, media and production reps, job candidates, and so forth, that you'd expect. And then there are the Seekers. They're here to find out what *It* is—this strange but apparently desirable *thing* that has made The Richards Group that rarest of creatures, the unpolitical ad agency.

To say that we're unpolitical compared to other ad agencies doesn't necessarily mean much. Compared to the average advertising agency, the Medicis' palace wouldn't seem political. But even people from companies that truly aren't very political think we're unpolitical. So I guess we are.

In retrospect, we've always been a little, well, different, starting back in the 1950s when I came to Dallas straight out of school in New York and began doing work like they weren't used to seeing around here. One creative director at a staid, old (and long since defunct, I might add) agency even suggested that I pack up my little black portfolio case and move on; they didn't cotton to that kind of *design* —his lip curled in contempt as he said it—in this town. I stayed. He's gone. End of that story.

Over the years, we started to get noticed for our work. Awards and new accounts rolled in. A lot of great minds came to work here. Most stayed. We concentrated on practicing our craft together, found that we could make money doing so, treated our clients and each other the way we'd like to be treated, and generally minded our own business. Billings climbed into nine figures. The number of Groupers climbed into the hundreds. And that's when I noticed that, without ever trying, we were starting to get nearly as much attention for our *workplace* as we were getting for the work that came *out* of the place.

That's just about the last thing I ever would have expected to become known for. All we've ever really, truly concentrated on around here is doing the best work we can do. *Ad* work. Not office-politics-removal work. Now, obviously, if we weren't producing notable work in our chosen field, nobody would care what a swell workplace we had. But I guess it just so happens that a lot of the practices we've picked up along the way to help us do the work—not to mention a lot of the practices we've avoided like the plague along the way because they'd be detriments to the work—have inadvertently made us an organization that people think is worth studying *as* an organization.

We didn't plan it that way. But there are enough dysfunctional organizations in the world, so if we can help somebody discover what *It* is and make their organization more functional, we're happy to try.

Some of the seekers after *It* are from other industries. I guess they figure, "If an *advertising agency* can get flat and unpolitical, for crying out loud, then surely *we* can do it."

Others are ad people themselves. Typically they're talented up-and-comers who, like my colleagues and me, are doing this work for the love of the craft and aren't yoked with the silly competitive paranoia our industry is famous for. If they're secure enough to call, then we're secure enough to give them a peek at how we do things. We're not sharing trade secrets anyway; we're trying to make the world (or at least the ad agency piece of it) a little better. And if they should end up competing against us someday (and that has happened before), well, that's okay. We never mind pitching an account against a worthy competitor; it's when we're in a pitch against a lightweight agency that we wonder if we've given the client a terrible misimpression.

So this book, like the little seed it grew from, is all about what those visitors see and how it got that way. Some of it is my story, as much as I'd prefer for it to be about the whole agency—the Group—and the people who make it successful. I've never even been a diarist, and I'm not *about* to come a memoirist. But I am, after all, the Richards in the Group, so tell my story I must. Hopefully, it will also dispel some of the wild stories I've heard about us over the years.

Some of the impressions that I've heard floating around out there (mostly at other agencies) are real lulus. Small facts morph into fabulous tales. Here are some genuine facts about The Richards Group:

- The agency structure is very flat.
- We have no manager caste, no officer titles.
- I'm very close to a lot of the agency's work.
- My colleagues, even the juniors, consult me a lot because I make myself available.

Okay. Now here's how the story comes back to me: I am, I have learned to my great surprise, a complete autocratic control freak, controlling the agency's output and closely enforcing order among the staff—something along the lines of Tito ruling Yugoslavia.

It's also still widely thought in creative circles that I see and approve every piece of work that goes out the door. Ridiculous, of course, for an agency this size (and I'm flattered that anyone could think I'm such a superman), but this particular exaggeration is understandable. Years ago I did approve practically everything, but that was when we were much smaller and I wasn't surrounded by a whole squad of world-class creative directors, any of whom could be running an agency if they wanted to. And to this day I still confine all the boring administrative stuff to about 10 or 15 minutes a day so I can spend the rest of my time doing the fun part, helping my associates create and present great work.

People hear that I'm directly involved in all the work. They can see that this is, in all likelihood, far from true of their own boss. And so they come up with the Tito theory to explain it.

Another favorite fable out there—and if I'm exaggerating about this, I promise it's not by much—is that the The Richards Group maintains a relatively calm (for an ad agency) workplace and keeps itself largely free of the typical infighting by operating as something akin to a for-profit religious cult. I play the guru in this picture, getting people from otherwise hostile tribes, such as art directors and account executives, to cooperate with each other by exercising some kind of nefarious mind control. Okay, the mind control part I'm making up, but the guru-and-disciples image turns up a lot in the folklore.

I think I know a couple of the supporting facts behind this particular myth: We never have parties, and we used to have a dress code. Well, actually I can't say we *never* have parties. We did have a party once, to celebrate our twentieth anniversary and introduce the new office we'd just moved into. But families were invited and nobody got wasted, so it wasn't a *real* agency office party. And the dress code part is (or was) absolutely true—ties on the guys, the whole thing. We used to have a very talented, funny young copywriter who had been a Mormon missionary before coming to work here. Somebody once joked that he could have gotten a job anywhere but picked The Richards Group so he wouldn't have to change his wardrobe. He didn't disagree.

Thus, between the dearth of parties and the dress code, we picked up a reputation in certain quarters as the ascetic sect of the advertising industry. "Let's see . . . no tequila in the office, neckties on copywriters—yep, there's definitely something spooky about these people."

For what it's worth, the dress code, which had once served a pragmatic purpose that I'll get into later, outlived its usefulness. So we killed it. And it was never exactly the Marine Corps anyway. The guideline was, "Dress like you're going to the bank for an eighty-thousand-dollar loan." Now we just say, "Dress like you're going to the bank for an eighty-dollar loan."

As for the parties, I suppose we could, theoretically, have another one someday. The subject comes up just about every November: "Hey, do you guys want to have a Christmas party this year, or should we just kick the cash into profit sharing again?" So far, it's been profit sharing by acclamation every time.

As an organization, we behave strangely. When young writers and art directors call up wanting to interview, it's always been our policy (unwritten, of course—we *hate* written policies) for a creative group head to see them even when we don't have any positions. We'll look at the portfolio even if it's lousy, give some constructive criticism, try not to crush the kid's spirit. That probably doesn't make much sense to the creative directors I keep hearing about who like to shred the novices. But it makes all kinds of sense when you see how many 200-karat diamonds in the rough we've found that way, some of whom I'll tell you about.

Generally—almost universally, judging by what I hear from interviewees—agencies just don't do that kind of thing. Nor do you find copywriters humbly accepting headlines suggested by account executives, even if the line is *good*. Come to think of it, account executives don't suggest headlines, if they know what's good for them. Little things like that are just not done. Tribal boundaries forbid it. But we'll let it happen here. Not that I ever really see AEs sitting around dreaming up headlines. But sometimes it happens. Smart people get ideas. Why stifle them?

It gets weirder. We give money back to clients. Do it all the time. The agency and client agree on a profit goal up front, and if we go over the target amount I write them a check. Seems fair to me. But when I mention this in talks to advertising groups, I see the agency people start to sweat, as they say in Texas, like a hooker at a church rally.

I could go on—and will. But this being the introduction, suffice it to say that my fellow Groupers and I have managed (mostly by *not* managing) to put together a fair-sized and very successful company, in a high-strung, often vicious business, with very little tribalism, fear, or sub-rosa shenanigans to show for it. And that's odd.

People (like, say, the kid with the crummy book whom we didn't mistreat) have a brush with the oddness. It makes an impression. They tell somebody. The stories morph. The wacky mythology grows. And it grows, I think, because when people hear that it's possible to work in a company without factionalism, fiefdoms, fear, and all the other toxic staples of modern business, they don't think it's possible without something *funky* driving it. Tito, hypnotism—*something*. To them—maybe to you—tribalism, politics, and self-aggrandizement are the way of the world, normal life at work, no way around it, is now and ever shall be. (But at least *Dilbert* lets us enjoy a bitter laugh about it, right?)

In other words, a company without tribalism seems too good to be true. Well, I'm here to tell you it's possible. Hard, but possible.

If your company's just starting out, if you're still small, then you'll have it easier. You don't have to erect the barriers that would divide your company into warring factions, an Ulster with regular business hours. Chances are, everything from your industry's time-honored custom to several of this hour's best-sellers on Amazon will try to get you to do it, to tribalize your company. But you don't have to. You're lucky.

If your company is more "mature," as they say, if you've already got all the trappings of success—caste systems, ruling juntas, dissident parties, guerrilla insurgencies, feudal estates, peasants and suzerains, all that good stuff—then you've got a trickier task ahead of you, one that calls for subtlety and cunning on the one hand and barefaced, unabashed pollyannaism on the other.

But don't worry, you can do it. In fact, it's going to be fun.

Think of it along the lines of a remodeling job. The house is fine; you're just going to rearrange the floor plan. Sure, it's going to be messy. But there's no emotional release quite like the feeling of picking up a nine-pound hammer and taking it full force to a wall that needs to come down. Chances are, people will line up to help. Because tearing down dividing walls is fun—and you'll probably be amazed to see how few of them are load-bearing.

So are you ready? Then let the demolition begin.

THE PEACEABLE KINGDOM

CHAPTER 1

Tribalism Is Alive and Well—Let's Kill It

Invisible barriers in your company sap your energy and spoil your fun. And visible barriers only exacerbate the problem. It doesn't have to be that way.

THE ZILLIONAIRE'S LAMENT

> *... office politics represent a science derived from two words: "poli," meaning many, and "tics," meaning small, blood-sucking insects.*
> —George Pitcher

We recently had a visitor come to The Richards Group to see how we work. If I said the man's name, there's a pretty good chance you'd know who he is. He runs a tech company, a fairly large one, and his personal net worth is, I would guess, roughly equivalent to the gross domestic product of France. And if not France, Belgium.

The guy is a zillionaire. More important, he's a zillionaire who does not rest on his hefty green laurels but works for his very considerable living. And on this particular day his work had brought him to The Richards Group for the nickel tour.

Clients do that all the time, of course, but he wasn't a client. In fact, as we conversed over coffee in the area that passes for my office, it became clear that the reason for his visit had nothing to do with marketing or advertising at all. Like most agency heads, I can smell a prospect at 300 paces, and the gentleman in question had no such whiff about him.

What he did have about him was an air of perplexity and frustration, and an idea that touring the agency might help him come up with a solution for both.

His problem—or, rather, his company's problem—was tribalism. Soul-polluting, productivity-robbing divisions between individuals and groups of individuals in the company. Tribalism is what happens when formal or de facto divisions between individuals, departments, ranks, task groups, or disciplines within the organization create destructive competitive behavior. Factionalism, cliquishness, a caste system, ramified office politics—call it what you may, tribalism is one trait of the workplace that's common to all industries, all regions, the public and private sectors, the sacred and the profane. My guest had heard that The Richards Group was relatively unafflicted by tribalism, and he had heard that said freedom from fracture had something to do with the physical arrangement of the office itself. That's what he came to see.

Notice, please, that I said we're *relatively* unafflicted. Let it be clear right up front that my company is not perfectly apolitical. We are not unblemished by tribalism, not innocent of cliquishness or immune to petty turf battles—not, in other words, unaffected by the foibles of human nature as manifested when you try to get a bunch of people to work together. I have yet to hear of, let alone be part of, any institution that *is* immune. So don't think I'm trying to paint The Richards Group as Utopia, Incorporated.

However, I do have to say that we have it a whole lot better than most. I'm sorry, but we just do.

Factionalism, sneaky little maneuverings for personal advantage, power plays, and the fear that rides with them aren't the constants around which we 600 or so Groupers order our days. They happen, but they're the exception.

Usually, when the blood-sucking little "poli-tics" do find their way into part of the office, some of the agency's self-appointed Guardians of the Culture (and there are a lot of those) will exterminate the bugs while they're still in the petty annoyance stage, before they have a chance to multiply into a true infestation that would really screw up the culture. Work groups usually settle their own relational problems; I rarely have to put on my judge's wig and hand down a ruling.

Little frictions and breaches in relationships, if left unsettled, as they are in most workplaces, wreck productivity and poison the atmosphere for everyone around. Yet they're usually not that hard to settle. Recently, for example, an account executive, in a moment of irritation, made a derogatory remark to a coworker about another AE in her group, who—

wouldn't
you know it—just
happened to be in earshot. Uh-oh,
serious discord brewing—and between two people on the
same account, to boot. After a brief exchange of words, none too
kind, the offended party went to their group head, one of the agency
principals, and poured out her complaint to him: "Do you know what so-
and-so just said about me?" At that moment, he, the group head, became
the culture guardian. "Hang on a second," he said. "We need to talk about
this *together.*" So he asked the other AE to join them. You see, when we say
we have an open workplace, we aren't referring to just the floor plan.
Direct interpersonal communication is the bedrock of our company
culture.

Down the hall to a conference room they went, all three of them—
the principal and the two rankled coworkers. They spent 15 minutes
talking and getting to the root issues of the conflict, at which point the
senior guy stood up. "All right," he said, "I'm leaving. You two stay in
here and work things out. See ya later." And with that, he strolled out
of the conference room and closed the door behind him. When the
door opened again 20 minutes later, out walked the two AEs. Together.
They had indeed settled their differences, and they have been working
together peaceably and productively ever since.

I can't tell you how they reached their rapprochement. Their group
head, who told me the story, didn't know, either. What he knows is that
the whole incident—the kind of ordinary little misunderstanding that
can mushroom into an ongoing feud—was over in less than an hour,
simply because they took care of it on the spot. No formal complaint
procedures, no taking of sides. And no getting *me* involved. The only
reason I heard about it at all was because I was asking people around
the agency for stories that illustrate the point about how we settle little
problems before they become big ones.

As a rule, then, we find ourselves in a pretty nice place to work.
Genial, nonhierarchical, productive, well regarded in our field, and, at
least so far, handsomely profitable. Stress-free, no. But nice.

That's what the zillionaire had heard about. And he had come to see it for himself because he wanted that kind of atmosphere in his own company. He'd tried to create it, and it hadn't worked. He was a world-class corporate leader with more power than God, as his employees would say, yet he couldn't make all the little fiefdoms and factions within his company go away and stay away.

"I'll visit one of our departments or facilities," he told me, "and find all these competing groups. Engineers arrayed against the marketing people. Or managers who set up their little personal kingdoms with all their coworkers in a subservient role."

"Normal business, in other words," I said.

"Normal, yes, but not right. So I do what obviously needs to be done. Mix things up, physically reorganize the whole facility to get managers out of their ivory-tower offices, tear out walls, create cross-functional work groups. Something more like this," he said, making a circular gesture in the air to indicate our surroundings.

We were sitting in my conference area, a square glass coffee table surrounded by low swivel office chairs. A few feet away, separated from us by neither a door nor a wall, agency staffers were hurrying back and forth, maybe pausing for an impromptu meeting, unbothered by the fact that my guest and I were having a meeting of our own. Just beyond the passing people, my closest neighbor, a young AE, was writing creative briefs, taking phone calls, talking with colleagues who stopped by her desk. Next to her, an art director hunched over his computer keyboard, squinting at the monitor, respacing the type in a mechanical, oblivious to the media planner's animated phone conversation about target gross rating points coming from another desk.

"We try to make it more like this, more crossover between groups, fewer badges of status," the visitor said. "It looks like it should work, and might for a short time. But I go away for a while— a few weeks or months—and the next time I visit, things are exactly the way they were before. This group hates that group, managers have their fiefdoms again, we don't really have much to show for all the upheaval."

My visitor straightened his tie (Hermes, of course). "Stan," he asked, "what are you guys doing that I'm not? I feel like I've been beating my head against the wall."

"Yet you've been knocking down walls like crazy," I said.

"That's true, we have," he said. "But ours have a way of putting themselves back up."

I appreciated his honesty, not to mention his acuity for exposing the kind of office dysfunction that people can be very good at camouflaging when *el Jefe* comes calling.

Here was a guy whose company was riding the tsunami of high tech. A well-established company, well thought of, obviously thriving. The analysts certainly weren't suggesting that he needed to make Dibble and Snodgrass out in the Tacoma office get along better. Nothing, in other words, was *making* him attack tribalism. Too many managers in his position would have ignored it. "Well, now," they'd aver, "if you're going to have a company full of go-getters, you've just got to live with a certain amount of political nonsense."

Most of the others, if they did anything at all, would make the physical changes—tear out the Sheetrock, put in the cubicles, get their company looking like the New Age, running-and-gunning, tech-savvy outfit is *supposed* to look, and then leave it at that. Status quo with a fresh coat of whitewash.

One agency I know conducted no less than four physical reshufflings in three years, with no apparent effect (at least no apparent *positive* effect) on either their work or the people doing it. Rejiggering like that happens all the time. Surface appearances change. The decorators make a mint. But the *real* landscape, the psychological landscape where the people live, gets jolted by about 0.9 on the Richter scale. Not enough vibration even to make the squirrels nervous, but enough for those in charge to say they shook things up.

This guy in charge, though, wasn't going to be happy with that, which must be how he got to be a zillionaire in the first place.

"I don't want any more superficial changes," he said. "I want to make some changes that will stick."

"I admire your resolve," I said. "More power to you."

And what I was thinking was, "You're going to need it."

IF THIS ISN'T A WALL, THEN WHY DO I KEEP BUMPING MY HEAD?

As my zillionaire guest had learned, the walls that cause trouble in a company aren't necessarily the ones that define interior spaces and hold up picture frames. Those walls can sometimes contribute to tribalism, and we'll get to that. But the *real* dividing walls are invisible.

They're the barriers, perceptual and procedural, that partition your workforce into competing interest groups, the unintentionally divisive effects of attitudes and practices so woven into the fabric of your organization that it probably hasn't even occurred to you to question them. It's possible for your organization to be honeycombed with barriers and for you to never even know it. At least not until you bump into one of them.

For example, I just took five minutes and jotted down, off the top of my head, some of the points of potential systemic conflict that you might very well find in a hypothetical mid- to large-size advertising agency. Here is my unscientific and by no means complete list.

Creative	versus	Account service (the classic battlefront)
Agency	versus	Client
The highly paid	versus	The lower paid
Longtimers	versus	Newcomers
People in the know	versus	People in the dark
Supervisors	versus	The supervised
Buyers	versus	Vendors
Managers	versus	The managed
Hipsters	versus	Traditionalists
Diligent people	versus	Slackers
Conformists	versus	Iconoclasts
Females	versus	Males
Gifted people	versus	Average people
High-budget work	versus	Low-budget work
Headquarters	versus	Branches
Older people	versus	Younger people
Symbolic thinkers	versus	Literal thinkers
Verbal people	versus	Visual people
People with perks	versus	People without perks
People on sexy accounts	versus	People on ordinary accounts
Consumer work	versus	Trade* work
Award winners	versus	Non-award-winners
Spenders	versus	Conservers
Optimists	versus	Pessimists
Risk takers	versus	The risk averse

*Usually called "business-to-business" nowadays because of the silly and unjust stigma attached to the term "trade." But, of course, the same bigots who equate "trade" with being dull, uncreative, and second class attach the same judgment to "business-to-business," so why not just go back to using the shorter word?

Techies	versus	Nontechies
Well-known people	versus	Obscure people
Homegrown talent	versus	Acquired talent

So that's where I ended up after five minutes of stream-of-consciousness scribbling—a couple of dozen ways for agency people to draw up lines of us-versus-them.

Some of my ideas of tribal lines might not make a lot of sense to you because they were suggested by my organization's particular experience. The last item, for example, came to mind because for many years The Richards Group almost never hired senior people from the outside. We have a tradition of hiring talented pups, often straight out of school, training them, and steadily giving them more responsibility. We still do that all we can, but fast growth has overwhelmed our ability to fill the majority of senior positions with homegrown talent. Nothing wrong with that; if anything, introducing new blood to the agency has had a refreshing effect on our work and our culture. However, the mere presence of a homegrown-is-best tradition raises the possibility that a subtle caste division could sneak into the agency. It's something we've had to be alert to, lest it catch us unawares. In any case, it's easy to see how barriers spring up, as one group defines its interests in terms of another's.

For example, the Tribe of the Obscure may say of their more visible colleagues (the ones, say, who happen to win a lot of big awards), "If those glory hounds [the bad guys] gain more visibility, then we [the humble, good guys] will sink deeper into the shame of our undeserved obscurity. Therefore, we must subvert them."

That's tribalism. It's a zero-sum game: Any gains for your tribe must come at the expense of mine, and vice versa.

It's dumb; it's wrong; it's nasty; it's wasteful. And unless you're one of the lucky and the few, it's robbing your company of productivity, robbing your clients of the best work they could get, and robbing you of the fun you ought to be having.

Tribalism is alive and well.

So here's an idea. Let's kill it.

Touring the Peaceable Kingdom

You be the zillionaire now and let me show you around the office. It's as good a snapshot of our culture as any.

The Agency with a Hole in the Middle

When you got off the elevator, no doubt you noticed the stairs suspended through a big hole in the middle of the building, from the fourteenth floor down to the eleventh. You might also have noticed—at least I hope you did—a kind of energy or kinetic vibe in the atmosphere of the place. The two are connected, the stairwell and the vibe. Stand here at the stairwell railing, if it won't make you dizzy, and I'll tell you about it.

It goes back to a decision I made in the 1980s. At the time, The Richards Group was maybe a tenth the size we are now. That was changing fast, though. Motel 6, Pier 1 Imports, and some other nice-sized advertisers had brought us on to handle their business, more new accounts were knocking, and we were just about to outgrow our office space, one floor of a high-rise about a mile north of where we are today. For the first time we were about to need multiple floors. This was not an altogether welcome notion.

Maybe you've been around an agency or dot-com company or studio organization of some sort with a tight-knit group of 50 or 60 people doing terrific work together and there's this wonderful, exciting intensity, an electricity in the air. There's a dynamic efficiency in a company like that, but it's not a mechanical efficiency, with every part bolted into place doing its one little job. It's more organic, less hierarchical and structured. Nobody's too hung up on what job function you're supposed to be performing; it's all about how the different functions flow together to produce a cool outcome. That's what The Richards Group was like. Quite a few agencies start out that way. It's a beautiful thing to see, and exhilarating to work in a place like that.

But then they grow. The 50 or 60 people become 125 or 150. They get layers, they get structured, they get ponderous, they get expensive, they get very, very serious about themselves, and the electricity just goes away. It always seems to happen somewhere around that magic number of 125 to 150. That's the danger zone. And once the electricity goes away, it never comes back. I had observed the phenomenon in agency after agency, and it scared me. We were small, we had the electricity, and we had the opportunity to grow right into the danger zone, where we could lose it.

Now, given the choice between being good and being big, I could give you my answer in about six nanoseconds. If I had thought we needed to stay small to maintain our culture, to keep the electricity, I would've been happy to do it. So I thought long and hard about it, and I concluded that we didn't have to stay small to stay good. I came to that conclusion after a careful study of the agencies I *didn't* want to be like, the ones who had lost the electricity.

They had all done one thing exactly alike. When they hit that 125-to-150 range, they moved into new quarters, spread across multiple floors, broke the agency down into "manageable" chunks. They would have a creative floor, an account management floor, a media floor, a research floor. And what had been a tight-knit group of fellow travelers who knew each other, worked shoulder to shoulder, and recognized each other's contributions, suddenly became divided. The group—people with different functions and gifts working harmoniously—is now partitioned into categories, blocs, a series of departments, each with its own territory. Incidental contact ceases. Tribalism takes root.

The elevator is Checkpoint Charlie in this scenario, your portal into a hostile culture. When an account executive steps off on the creative floor, she's an outsider. The people here think differently. They dress differently. They have different rituals. She feels a little like a friend of mine who once ran afoul of the wrong people in a provincial city in Japan and suddenly needed to make himself inconspicuous until he could get out of town. So here he is, a six-foot-two-inch, blond Westerner trying to blend in as he sneaks toward the train station through crowds of Japanese. To make matters worse, he's wearing an orange sweater while the season's local fashion craze is black, head to toe. That's kind of how the AE feels on the creative floor—like a sore thumb sticking out. And the creatives feel the same way about her. They're thinking, "She doesn't belong here, and I hope she'll go back to wherever she does belong, as quickly as possible."

Even if the agency was segregated into clearly delineated departments all along, it wasn't so bad as long as they shared one floor. People could still run into their fellows from other departments at the coffeepot; overhear shop talk in the washroom; learn, without really trying, at least a little about what the others do with their 8 or 10 or 13 hours a day. As long as there's plenty of contact, you can create some of the old electricity. Shut off contact and it's like throwing the circuit breaker. The electricity just stops.

I don't think it matters how long people have worked together, either. As soon as physical barriers go up, people in one department cease to know what the people in another department are doing all day. Barriers encourage ignorance. And ignorance, as Melville's Ishmael said, is the parent of fear. A sudden suspicion can grow even between old colleagues. The creative team *says* they're working on the ad you promised your client you'd have on Tuesday, but when they're stuck off in Creativeville and you're confined to Account Service Land, you don't really know, do you? There's no memo, status meeting, or conference report that can substitute for actually witnessing the work of others.

It was the same story in every agency I studied. I was committed to preventing it from happening here. So my colleagues and I made ourselves guinea pigs in an operational experiment, one that continues to this day. The day we said yes to growth, we made a major change in our operation. When we moved into our new building, we abolished departmental divisions and simply jumbled up where everybody sat. (Accounting remains the only exception, so we can lock up the sensitive information at night. Even guinea pigs have *some* brains.)

Having people from different disciplines arranged in clusters all around the office worked beautifully. If you're an art director and you're crashing to make a deadline, you can peek over the top of your cube and see next door an account supervisor or print production person or account planner or media buyer working just as hard and caring just as much about his or her end of the craft. To know them is to respect them. (I feel safe in saying that because our kind of setup offers the lazy and incompetent no place to hide.) We doubled and redoubled and re-redoubled in size without losing the essence of what made us successful in the first place.

Which brings us back to the stairwell. When we made that first move to a multifloor office, we knocked a hole in the floor and put stairs right through the middle of the agency. Later, after another expansion, we had to knock *another* hole—much to the displeasure of the landlord—to tie in yet another floor. Several years and another move later, we're up to our present four-floor stairwell. It's the focal point of the agency, the literal center of our culture, and the symbol of our no-barriers philosophy.

There's an unwritten rule here: Don't use the elevator. It's just something we ask, not a hard-and-fast policy you can get sacked for violating. But since practically everybody buys into the reasoning behind it, the stairwell is a beehive of activity during the day. Chance encounters create little impromptu meetings all up and down the way.

Same thing in the flat spaces of the building. We prefer, if you have something to say to a colleague, that you get out of your chair and walk to the person's desk, say what you have to say, get a reaction, see the body language, read the expressions. It may take an extra minute or two, compared to using the phone, but something important happens. Communication is cleaner. Everybody understands each other a whole lot better because of the manner in which information is conveyed.

Plus there's this: On my way to my coworker's desk, I'm going to pass four or five people, some of whom may have a useful word for me, or vice versa. And even if not, at least I get to say hi. And when you want a collegial atmosphere, there's a lot to be said for saying hi.

That's the idea behind the stairwell. Once we had it, we found that it serves another handy purpose, too. It's the one place where the whole staff can gather all at once. Anytime there's important news to share or someone such as a new client to be introduced, we ask somebody to get on the paging system and "call a stairwell." Five or ten minutes later, the whole agency is gathered on and around the stairs. By standing in the right spot on the twelfth- or thirteenth-floor landing

Addressing the Groupers at a stairwell meeting. We'll call a stairwell to introduce clients, celebrate wins and mourn losses, honor colleagues' achievements—anytime there's news worth sharing with everybody all at once.

and speaking in a slightly elevated voice, you can be a regular Cicero addressing the citizens.

Once, a stairwell meeting turned into a hootenanny. Being great champions of radio as an advertising medium and having created memorable campaigns for Motel 6 and many other clients, The Richards Group enjoys very cordial relations with the radio networks and radio stations. On one occasion a few years ago, Charles Osgood, the CBS Radio newsman, was in Dallas on some network business, so he dropped by to meet us.

To this day I'm not sure why be brought a banjo. Maybe he always travels with it, like Linus with his blanket. More likely, Larry Spiegel, our media director and a bit of a showman himself, alerted Charlie that banjo playing was part of my own checkered past. As a student in New York in the early 1950s, I was a disciple of Pete Seeger and his folkie ilk. A few years later, while getting established in the ad business in Dallas, I cohosted a daily half-hour show called *Variety Fair* on one of the local TV stations. Each day I sang two songs, one performed with my banjo or guitar and the other accompanied by—I promise this is true—the staff organist. I'm glad the ad gig worked out, bringing an end to my television career. The viewing public would probably agree.

In any case, Charles Osgood shows up at the agency one afternoon and he's carrying a banjo. Not something you get to see every day, so we call a stairwell. He's a charming man and also—as you know if you listen to his daily commentaries—one of the nation's leading practitioners of doggerel. Larry prevails upon him to read one of his classic verses, written when the census bureau announced a new official term for someone with whom one is shacking up. The term was POSSLQ—Person of Opposite Sex Sharing Living Quarters—and it's pronounced "possle-queue." So Charlie reads his composition, a love poem, which has lines like, "There's nothing I wouldn't do / If you would be my POSSLQ." The Groupers are delighted. And that warms them up for our big banjo sing-along.

Maybe you have a lot of group singing in your office. We don't, so it took a little coaxing. What marks this in my mind as our most unusual stairwell meeting ever wasn't the sing-along per se. It was the bemused looks on the faces around me as the entire staff, from the most ultrahip to the most ultradignified, joined in on "This Land Is Your Land." Several of them wouldn't make eye contact with me for several days afterwards. Pete Seeger, however, would have been proud.

The stairwell comes in handy in other ways, too. When new clients and prospects come calling, one of our favorite stunts is to post a lookout in the parking lot to alert the staff, who have assembled at the stair-well, that they need to shut up and be still. The clients emerge from the elevator into a silent office, to be greeted moments later by an ovation from several hundred people. It makes a powerful impression. (Thank-fully, no one so far has had to reach for the nitroglycerin pills.) It's also the only way most clients get to meet, or at least wave to, all the men and women who work on their behalf.

All right, let's continue our little tour.

Cube, Sweet Cube

All this walking around and bumping into one another that I mentioned happens not in the vast, open-concept labyrinth of cubicles that you often see these days but in an easier-to-navigate and, I think, friendlier network of studio spaces. Some people call them neighborhoods. Most of the neighborhoods have eight individual work spaces, four cubes per side, running from the center of the building outward toward the win-dows. A long, built-in, studio-style worktable runs down the middle of each studio. Fax machines, printers, presentation materials in progress, the thousands of free magazines our media people always get—that stuff goes on the studio tables. Walk around a few minutes and you can usually find a birthday cake or bag of bagels that the locals will let you share.

We don't worry about grouping people according to accounts much more than we try to group them according to function (which, as I've said, we don't worry about at all). You might work on some of the same business as the person in the next cube, but if you do it's a coincidence. Generally you'll be on the same floor as your creative director or account service principal, but if you end up with a desk a floor or two away, that's okay.

Douglas Coupland, the author of *Generation X* (St. Martin's Press, 1992), calls cubicles "veal fattening pens." If you're treated like a prole laboring away in a rat maze while your betters occupy finely appointed offices, I can see how you'd feel that way. Here if we're veal, at least we're all veal. We don't have offices (except, as I mentioned, the accounting folks, whose cubes are in an area that can be closed up after hours). My own work space, in an odd-shaped corner of the building, is fairly large. It has wooden cabinets where we display clients' products and interest-ing memorabilia such as props from TV shoots, and it has a chat area with audiovisual equipment for the short meetings that happen 10 or 14 or 22 times a day. It's spacious but open, practically in a hallway; you can wan-der right in. Privacy, I have none.

Which, of course, is exactly the point of this floor plan: so we can eavesdrop on each other.

We want everybody to know everything—that a client called with a question, that we're still negotiating with a certain station, that a creative team is concepting a certain print campaign, that a creative brief is taking a particular shape. Everybody's making decisions all day on behalf of our clients. We want no secrets. We want the hard work every person does to be plainly visible to their counterparts. And if it's your spouse or a head-hunter or the IRS on the phone with an urgent personal matter, feel free to take it in a conference room.

Stick Around and You'll Get Your Name on the Door

Speaking of conference rooms, as we walk around the agency you'll see them by the dozens. At last count we had 50. When you want to hole up with your partner and pin ideas up on the walls, when you want to interview a candidate or meet with a rep, when you want to discreetly return that call from the IRS agent, here's where you come.

Each conference room is named after somebody, one of the 50 Groupers with the longest tenure. The two biggest rooms are named in

The 50 longest-serving Groupers (other than me) each have a conference room named for them.

honor of Jim McGhee and Gary Gibson because they've been here the longest. Jean Howe, my coordinator, has a conference room named for her; so does the senior woman from word processing, Joyce Henry. At least half a dozen people from accounting have conference rooms named for them. The new creative hotshot from L.A. can wait. If one of the honorees leaves the agency, off will come his or her name, to be replaced by whoever is next on the tenure list. Fair is fair.

Once, however, there was some confusion on this fairness point. At the time we were moving into our current building and first naming all the conference rooms after agency employees, Continental Airlines was one of our accounts. One of the clients at Continental, Sam Coats, was an old friend of mine and of the agency. Sam and The Richards Group went way back together, to his days as president of Muse Air when we gave mighty Southwest a run for their money. It just so happens that Sam's son David is a talented young copywriter, and he had just come to work for us.

One lunch hour, a few days before our move, a couple of Groupers went by for a look around the new space, figuring out which desks would be theirs, that sort of thing. Everything was finished, including the nameplates outside each conference room door. They read the names as they walked around: Gibson . . . McGhee . . . Howe . . . Coats. *Coats?* Yep, there it was, in a prominent spot near the stairwell and one of the reception desks. They rushed to the nearest phone and angrily called a coworker, a member of our employee Moving Committee. "This is not right," they protested. "Just because his dad's a client, we suck up and name a room after David Coats. Why, *we've* been here a lot longer than he has, and *we* don't have conference rooms."

Vile politics, it seemed, had found its way into The Richards Group. Except there was one thing the offended parties had not checked out. They hadn't opened the door of the room named Coats. If they had, they would have seen that it is a closet.

A Disclaimer

Let me repeat: This whole peaceable kingdom concept is an ideal. Tell me if you achieve it, because we haven't yet. Naturally I want to believe that the organization of my founding is the best yet devised by human ingenuity, just spitting distance away from perfection. I don't believe it, though, being reminded daily as I am of the foibles that keep that hole through the middle of the agency from being our little stairway to heaven. There's plenty of tension around here—let's just admit it.

"Whoops. I guess we should've looked inside."

Recently, for example, I was in a meeting with several clients and agency people, including Brad Todd, one of our principals in account management. Now, Brad is a highly cultured man—head of the Dallas Symphony Association, went to cooking school in France, doesn't slurp his soup. Very civilized. But he's also very passionate about his work. In this particular meeting, in which we were discussing what to do about an especially knotty problem involving dissident pricing activity in the client's dealer network, Brad grew, shall we say, *poco agitato,* shouting about these SOBs in the field and how advertising was powerless to deal with the problem they were causing. He half-rose from his chair. He pounded his fist on the conference table. I thought he might start hitting it with his shoe like Khrushchev at the United Nations. Fortunately, Brad was in safe company. We've worked with this client for years, so all of us knew about his sometimes operatic ardor. Hey, it beats indifference. And we were agreeing with him. But if you were a stranger just passing the conference room, you might have started dialing 9-1-1 on your mobile phone.

As you walk around our office, you'll pass some grim faces in the halls, hear some tense exchanges coming from those cubes. Advertising, need I remind you, is a high-stress way to make a living. Deadlines, great emotional investment in the work, being constantly subject to judgment by people who have *no idea* how much we've bled into our work—it can make you grumpy, for sure, and can sometimes incite displays of defensiveness and snits of passion.

We even have a special word at The Richards Group for intensely stressful situations: *grom.* "How's that assignment going?" "It's a grom." Someone who's under pressure or stressed out is "in a grom." The term was coined years ago with reference to the tufted leather sidechairs in my office and a meeting that did not go well for a team that was presenting work to me. Their gluteal muscles grew so tense, the story went, that they plucked the grommets right out of the upholstery.

So I'm not promising nirvana. In the ad business, *peaceable* is a relative term. Okay, let's keep walking.

A Copy Room with a View

As we continue our little tour, note that some of the best views from our office are in the workroom on each floor where we keep the photocopy machines, report-binding gadgets, mail bins, all that support stuff. Now, maybe this is silly, making a big point about our workrooms. It seems like such a minor detail, but I think it says something important about the agency's culture.

Every business has workrooms and every place I go they're all the same. They're linoleum-floored dungeons. No windows, bad light, toner fumes—a really crummy place to pull an all-nighter collating the leave-behind for your boss's meeting the next day. That sends the wrong signal about the relative importance of what is, in fact, a vitally important function within the company.

If we're going to be the kind of agency we aspire to be, then we've got to make it clear that there are no unimportant functions here, that everyone must receive all due respect, that every task is of supreme importance in the long run. Every day there's somebody who's going to be standing there feeding pages to that photocopy machine for a long time at a stretch. It's not the most pleasant job, probably not the one that's going to help them achieve their bliss. But it matters. It matters a lot. So the least we can do is give them a pleasant view of the city across the top of that document feeder.

As I said, it's a silly detail. To date, nobody has ever stopped me in the hall and said, "Hey, Stan, I just wanted to say thanks for that clear northern light in the copy room." But I'm convinced that small gestures

Giving prime window space to our support areas is a deliberate signal about the importance of the work that goes on there.

of respect for every person, every function in the agency, have a cumulative effect beyond our imagining.

It's the effect I hope you felt when you stepped off that elevator in the first place, the effect of a palpable fervency in the air. I think it was Astor Piazzolla, the great Argentine musician, who said that in order to compose his marvelous tangos he needed the very *smell* of Buenos Aires to inspire him. Since Buenos Aires smells mostly like diesel buses and grilled beef, you'd think he would have been able to work just as well in downtown Fort Worth. But he meant, of course, that he was moved to creativity by a certain ineffable *something* he encountered in that place, a certain spirit. Well, I want a certain spirit in *this* place that will inspire creativity like the smell of B.A. did for Astor Piazzolla. The degree to which we've had it, and still do, is the degree to which we've torn down barriers between the functional groups within the agency and kept them down.

We encounter more of our own creative potential the more we encounter one another. And that's why the unconventional office.

FENG SHUI À LA RICHARDS: CLOSED DOORS ATTRACT EVIL SPIRITS

Fear has many eyes and can see things underground.
— Cervantes

Before we leave the topic of the physical work space, let me add this: Never underestimate the power of human paranoia.

The energy your people waste wondering about what's happening behind the closed doors of their bosses' and coworkers' offices could fuel an aircraft carrier on a round-the-world cruise. There's something about being outside a closed door that conjures a little demon who whispers, "They're talking about *you* in there." You know that it's probably not true, but it still makes you wonder: What *is* going on in there, and why do they feel compelled to keep it private?

The stairs are the literal center of The Richards Group culture and the symbol of our no-barriers philosophy. Promoting incidental contact in the office helps us keep the energy we had as a small company.

Why put up with the distraction? Abolishing office doors and, later, walls at The Richards Group was probably the most profound act of cultural liberation we've ever undertaken.

Eavesdropping on each other is beneficial in a couple of ways. A lot of actual, productive communication takes place—the transfer of useful information overheard from those around you that they wouldn't deem urgent enough to be worth knocking on your door to tell you. Call it accidental sharing. That's probably what the Skunk Works engineer had in mind when he hung a sign on his cube that said "Privacy Sucks." The other benefit we gain is a general understanding that most of our little encounters and conferences—which would be intriguing if they were happening behind closed doors—are, in fact, as dull as dirt to the uninvolved bystander. So you learn to tune them out and go on about your business, unburdened by fears of a plot being hatched against you next door.

Fears and insecurities are potent creative forces, but that is not the kind of creativity we're after. An acquaintance who works at another company in town was talking about her most recent annual review. Although this woman is a highly capable and dedicated person, she still wrestles now and then with just a smidgen of self-doubt. So by the morning of her review she was braced for the inevitable: a humiliating roll call of her flaws and failings, followed by a blunt dismissal from the company. She knew it was coming, and, worse, that she deserved it. She couldn't have been more shocked when the supervisor spent the whole meeting praising her valuable work and solid leadership, then offered her a handsome raise. You've probably got lots of people just like her around your place. Don't give them something else to worry about by cultivating an air of secrecy in the office. They'll come up with plenty of worries without your help.

WHISKEY IS BLENDED, MILK IS HOMOGENIZED

Let's be clear about something. There's nothing wrong with tribes per se. They're part of the natural order. If you flip back a few pages and look at my stream-of-consciousness tribes list, you'll notice that half or more represent perfectly legitimate—indeed, necessary—distinctions between job functions, degrees of experience, and so forth.

You don't have to get rid of tribes to get rid of tribalism.

Your organization needs the differences, the distinct and disparate gifts, that exist in your workforce and around which groups of people naturally coalesce. Different personalities, different ages, different cultural backgrounds, different priorities in life—they're volatile ingredients for a company culture, to be sure. But then who really wants a company composed of inert ingredients anyway? Give me volatile.

Flakes, suits, bean counters, geeks, graybeards, greenhorns—I want them all. I want them all influencing one another, sure, but I don't want them pureed into a workforce of utter uniformity. The image of the classic *Esquire* cover shot of Andy Warhol comes to mind. You've seen the photo: the artist as a drowning man pulled down in a maelstrom inside a gigantic can of Campbell's tomato soup. That's what it would be like to lose your distinctiveness in a homogenized workforce. Sucked into the soup.

Creative work is what put my agency on the map. But I don't know how far we would have gotten without some very strong people in disciplines that are supposed to be somehow opposed to the artsy shenanigans of creative-driven agencies. Our chief financial guy, Scot Dykema, is a great example. Fifteen years in a studio-like creative shop have in no way diminished his money-guy chops.

Six mornings a week around six o'clock, Dykema (nobody ever calls him Scot, for some reason), David Gravelle, and I, along with a constantly rotating roster of other Groupers, clients, and friends, meet at the Cooper Aerobics Center for a four-mile run. One morning as we huffed our way around the track I mentioned that I was going to be writing this book.

"I know (huff) . . . what Chapter 1 (puff) . . . should be," Dykema said. He's always been good for advice, so I listened, which was easier than talking anyway. He continued, "If you can't (huff) . . . bill it (puff) . . . then you shouldn't (huff) . . . be doing it."

We all laughed as best we could with the breath available. Later, though, I started thinking about the grain of truth in his joke. There actually *is* a little bit of that attitude at The Richards Group. The hard-nosed, dollars-and-sense work ethic of strong leaders like Dykema has seeped into the agency in a lot of little ways, helping balance the notoriously undisciplined, loosey-goosey world of the writers and artists who have gotten the more public credit for our success. I want a dyed-in-the-wool money person to be the money person, dyed-in-the-wool creative people to be the creative people. Put them together and bits of color rub off in nice ways.

The floor plan does most of the putting together for us, with different job functions sharing the same real estate. A copywriter recently told me about listening, transfixed, as the woman in the next cube, a senior media negotiator, did battle on the phone with a TV network salesguy. "You won't see negotiating like that in an Arab market," the writer said with admiration. "She was relentless. I want her to go with me the next time I'm buying a car." Not only did the writer gain new appreciation for how a colleague did her job, but who knows how her hard-nosed tenacity might inspire him the next time *he's* the one spending the client's or the agency's money.

Having the opportunity to witness valid contributions by colleagues different from oneself is a powerful blending influence for the diverse groups within the company. It doesn't make them any less diverse, but it provides some unity.

Now, maybe uniformity sounds good to you. Theoretically it might seem appealing to create congruity, a consistent corporate gestalt. But once your company has grown to a certain point (which I would estimate to be two people), trying to homogenize your workforce makes them unhappy and your company bland. I say "trying" because no policy yet devised — no dress code, no dogma, no code of practices — has ever fully managed to do it anyway.

Kathleen Norris is a Presbyterian woman who hangs out a lot with Benedictine monks and has written two best-sellers about it. If there were ever a group that I would expect to be homogeneous, it would probably be Benedictine monks. But, no, nothing of the sort. "One monk," Norris writes, "when asked about diversity in his small community, said that there were people who can meditate all day and others who can't sit still for five minutes; monks who are scholars and those who are semiliterate; chatterboxes and those who emulate Calvin Coolidge with regard to speech. 'But,' he said, 'our biggest problem is that each man here had a mother who fried potatoes in a different way.' "

If you want a potent company (or monastic order, for that matter) — if you want what Boston adman Jim Mullen calls a "dangerous workforce" — then you've got to blend all the volatile ingredients without suppressing their distinct characters. And, as Norris points out, considering the tensions that naturally arise in our efforts to blend, we're better off when we retain our ability to laugh at ourselves.

Company cultures need to allow some room for everybody's quirks. I say "everybody" because if someone *doesn't* have quirks, that in itself is quirky. Albert Camus once said, "Nobody realizes that some people expend tremendous energy merely to be normal." That being the case, I don't particularly want "normal" in my company. I want those people expending their energy on whatever it is that they're good at: writing brilliant copy, making recalcitrant computers work, negotiating spot buys, what have you. Some people are like the stealth fighter in Operation Desert Storm: Only 2 percent of the force, they knock out 40 percent of the targets. And they're the oddest-looking birds in the air.

Blending wildly divergent types of people, helping them work together without suspicion, is more art than science. That's hard for some managers to accept. It would be nice if you could bring people together to create a stronger workforce, like Luther Burbank breeding plants to create fatter, juicier peas. "A" leads to "B." If this, then this. One of these deep-rooted ones, one of these leafy ones, add 10 pounds of manure, and there you have it. But it's not that simple. You can't formulate this into an action plan, reduce it to a PowerPoint presentation, and watch your company hit the heights. Blending tribes is messy. When you plunge into this business of managing tribes without tribalism, you've simply got to reconcile yourself to the inexactitude, confident that you're just the fearless leader to pull it off.

TOO GOOD TO BE TRUE?

I'm of the opinion that people — like the ones who work for you, for example — generally like the idea of different types of people, different tribes, being thrown together for some common purpose. They like the idea of working with colleagues who are unlike themselves, working out the frictions, having a good laugh about it later, and getting some spectacular stuff accomplished. Or they *would* like it if they thought it were possible. Experience has taught most of us that the world doesn't really permit that sort of thing. If there's a peaceable kingdom at all, it's out yonder.

There's something inside people that's wishing for a peaceable kingdom. At some level, we all understand that human enterprises are more colorful, potentially more successful, and in many ways a whole lot more fun when you get contrasting types and talents involved.

Yeah, sure we do.

Yes, *sure* we do.

Just look at the kind of stories people choose for entertaining themselves. Some of the most popular ones revolve around people (or, in the case of cartoons and sci fi, species) unlike one another who get together for a common purpose. Having markedly different types is important. Any 10-year-old knows that if your comic book has a team of superheroes, it can't have two of them made out of fire; that would be lame. Everybody on the team has to be made out of a different element: a flame guy, a rock guy, a water woman — that's much cooler.

Comedy teams, buddy movies, picaresque novels, the lame sitcoms that go into syndication forever—it's all the same. *Mismatched partners work through differences to make it all come out fine in the end.* It's a gimmick that sells.

Take the *Lethal Weapon* movies. Two cops. One is young (at least in the first couple of movies), rebellious, hotheaded, single, and white. The other is middle-aged, a team player, cautious, a family man, and he's black. Audiences have a great time watching these mismatched partners work, fuss, and shoot people together. The studio has been making *Lethal Weapon* sequels for so long, it's just a matter of time before they have to merge their idea with another series and do *Grumpy Old Lethal Men with Weapons.* I bet it'll still make money.

We'll gladly plunk down eight bucks at the multiplex to watch fictional people use their differences to get the job done. In practice, though, people and the companies that employ them just don't trust that mixing the tribes can work. Tearing down the barriers and laying down our arms will leave us too vulnerable. Something's bound to go wrong. If we start to disarm, we'll be slaughtered. Or if we, as managers, take any of our well-reasoned strictures off people, surely order will dissolve into wanton selfishness. And if we revoke any of the privileges of rank, an uprising is inevitable; feudal lords stripped of their noble titles will quit.

The heart may wish to dismantle tribalism, but the mind conceives unacceptable upheaval from any attempt. "A disaster of biblical proportions . . . Human sacrifice! Dogs and cats, living together! Mass hysteria!" as Bill Murray's character portends in *Ghostbusters.* Trying to get rid of tribalism—well, it would just be weird.

And so we persist. As bad as factionalism is, at least it's familiar. It feels safest to hang out with the people we think are like us. Even though we may recognize that there's huge power in bringing different styles and viewpoints to a project, we shrink from the unruliness and untidiness of such radical admixture. We sort into "manageable" sets. We segregate along tribal lines. We choose facile and weak over challenging and strong. We hitch our plows to poodles because an ox, we think, would be just too messy.

My client Lars von Kantzow told me a story not long ago. Lars is president of Pergo, Inc., the Swedish company that makes the world's leading laminate floor. In their largest region, the company has a factory and, a few miles away, a marketing and sales operation. Production and marketing, two tribes as traditionally at loggerheads in manufacturing businesses as creative and account service are in ad firms.

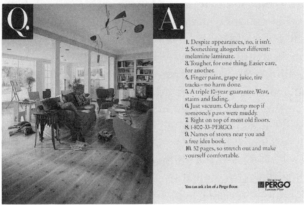

Pergo dominates its category because the company is unafraid to challenge the status quo. When they demolished a barrier between the manufacturing and the marketing tribes, they gained an immediate payoff in productivity and morale. Art director: Dennis Walker; writer: David Culp.

When Pergo established these two facilities (it's a relatively new region), they naturally established the lines of communication in the traditional manner, with the manufacturing people reporting to the production executives at corporate headquarters and the regional marketing group reporting to the headquarters marketing group. It would be analogous in the agency business to having the creative director in your Chicago office be answerable to the worldwide creative director in New York, while the chief suit in Chicago answers to the chief suit in New York.

It's very clean that way, and safe. You want manufacturing people to deal with manufacturing people, marketers with marketers. After all, when a company has grown large and successful as a manufacturing concern, it's wise to keep production at a safe remove from those crazy marketing and sales people, who should never be allowed to touch expensive machinery. Their $100 cravats might get caught in the gears, strangling the wearers—which would not, in itself, be such a bad thing, except for the annoying delay in production that would result.

So, as our story opens, the plant is answering, quite logically, to the nabobs of manufacturing back at HQ. Only there's a flaw in this setup. The nabobs are far away—several time zones away, in fact—and the plant is not, at this juncture, exactly running on autopilot. There are new products in the pipeline that present some problems the plant hasn't had to figure out before—new materials, newly invented or not-yet-invented processes, that sort of thing. Yet production has to expand fast because the market is booming. There's a lot of pressure. Demand is high. Competitors, smelling opportunity, are getting into the market. Marketing has stopped grumbling and started howling.

Every day counts. A lot of communication is needed with the people in authority, the honchos at HQ who can give the go-ahead for solutions the plant guys want to try, but the intervening time zones make that difficult. There's no way the frontline people and their bosses can have quick, efficient hands-on meetings; it takes hours on a plane just to get together. Morale is terrible, which only contributes to the production woes. Efficiency is in the tank. And now the marketing people are getting *really* strident. Big orders are in jeopardy. Market share is at stake. Sales goals are starting to look as unscalable as El Capitan. Nerves are frayed, tempers short, the tribal lines clearly drawn: sales and marketing here, manufacturing and logistics here. The same bitter refrain can, however, be heard rising from around the watch fires of both camps: "Those guys are trying to *kill* us."

So HQ tries a radical solution. They take themselves out of it. They throw these two opposing tribes together, telling the plant to start dealing directly with the regional office just up the road. In other words, they knock down the wall and put manufacturing and marketing together in one fell swoop, saying, in effect, "You guys can best work this out among yourselves." Production and sales, dogs and cats, living together just as predicted. Marketers making helpful suggestions to engineers. Logistics people putting in their two cents with sales. No "proper channels" to filter and buffer. You might think pitched battle is inevitable.

But a funny thing happens. It works. Instantly. Seemingly insoluble production problems are suddenly solved. Efficiency soars. On-time deliveries become the norm. Sales projections move from the fantasy shelves back to the nonfiction section. And morale, sick as a dog one day, gets well overnight. In the space of one fiscal year, the manufacturing operation becomes one of the financial performance darlings of the whole corporation. And it happens because two tribes get a chance to work together without the dividing wall of tribalism. Credit belongs not only to them for their creativity, but also to the people back at HQ, who were more concerned about solving business problems than about building their personal fiefdoms of direct reports.

That was Lars's story. It included, of course, some butting of heads worthy of Marlin Perkins's show, *Wild Kingdom* ("I'll wait in the jeep while Jim attempts to separate them"). Each tribe's task was, in fact, complicated by the other's task. But the thing about such conflict is that, with the invisible tribal barriers down, it ends up being filed under the benign heading of "creative tension." The marketer laughs about her ignorant suggestion that ticked off the engineer. The engineer admits that the ignorant suggestion sparked a workable idea.

By thumbing their noses at tribalism instead of at each other, Pergo put a lot of dollars (and kronor) on their bottom line. And they created more esprit de corps in the workforce, with a sense that the corps is a lot bigger than just one's own tribe. They did it with one act of erasing a neat org-chart line in favor of the messy process of letting people hash out their challenges together.

It works. It's true. And it's good.

BOUNDARIES, NOT BARRIERS

Since tribes exist as part of the natural order, it doesn't take a lot of effort to demarcate them within your organization. People gravitate to others who share their job function. Which raises the question, what's the benefit in formally fencing them in when they hang together pretty well on their own?

In my company, for instance, the account management types are quite happy *not* to be doing the creative staff's job, and vice versa. In fact, the less we build a hard wall of separation between them—refusing, for example, to segregate the functions into separate departments on different floors—the more they respect one another's challenges and contributions. As one 20-year veteran copywriter told me, "If I had to do the job of the average junior AE, I don't think I'd last two weeks around here." He's able to say that because he can see and hear, every day, what some of the junior AEs in his neighborhood of the office are doing, and from his perspective it's an impossibly tough job. But then they probably feel the same about *his* job.

When you split people off into a department, you fall prey to a corollary to the Law of Unintended Consequences known as the Doctrine of Unlimited Missions. It states: *When an organization's mission is accomplished it will try to perpetuate itself by creating another mission.*

It works like this. When your company sets up a department, you establish a power structure. The mission of this power structure, at first, is simply to mark off part of the workforce as a clearly defined suborganization and then maintain the defining boundaries—create a discrete unit and keep it that way.

All right, so now the job is done. You've got yourself a department. Mission accomplished. But according to the Doctrine of Unlimited Missions, that power structure you established and gave a mission to is not at all inclined just to let things be. Having begun to consolidate part of the workforce, it will try to further consolidate, to further wall off its realm as an entity apart from the rest of the company.

Of course, hardly anybody ever *says* that's what they're trying to do, but that's what happens in practice. The group begins to define itself more and more in terms of its distinctions from other groups, other departments. It develops what I've heard called a "bounded-set mentality," thinking always in terms of what's inside the boundaries versus what's outside, focusing on the dividing lines themselves. We're in here; they're out there. Now seemingly simple boundaries have become serious barriers.

We'll talk more about this in Chapter 2. For now, let's just leave it at this: The more loosely you can organize work groups—the blurrier you make the boundaries between the already distinct functional tribes in the company—the better off you'll be.

Partitioning a company into hard-edged departments is so deleterious to the organization that in my company we don't even use the word *department*. (I'll discuss this, too, in the next chapter.) Media, accounting, production, account management, creative, account planning, and so forth—the natural distinctions that exist between these job functions are boundary enough. Let's not make it harder than it has to be.

WHY SAVE THE CONCLUSION FOR THE END OF THE BOOK?

I'm going to give away my ending—or maybe you've guessed it by now: The real point of all this is communication.

Don't put up barriers that would stifle it. Take down barriers that are stifling it now. You want a more open, more creative, more productive, more stable company? Communicate better.

There. There's your big take-away. (And now we'll take a short break so you can cover your mouth and yawn.)

A CONCLUSION LESS BOGUS THAN IT FIRST APPEARS

All right, we're back, and we're talking about communication, which I contend is the ingredient that will transform your company into a peaceable kingdom.

You're skeptical. I understand. Far weightier tomes than this have been written about how to promote communication in business. And companies obviously are listening. We're all wired. We're all reachable 24/7. We've all got killer systems to promote communication and productivity.

All well and good. And by most accounts, *very* well and good. There's more communication in business than ever. Productivity has gone through the roof. You know all the good news as well as I do.

But this isn't a *completely* new generation. Tribalism yet lives in our brave new interconnected world. Talk to people at the gym, the bar, the AA meeting, wherever you go after work, and you'll hear pretty much the same office war stories that were going around when Gregory Peck first pulled on that natty gray flannel number.

We've got more communication, but we've still got just as much tribalism. And so we've got what appears to be a flawed conclusion. How can the cure for tribalism be in communication?

Well, I think that, amid all this communicating, we've been overlooking something. We've put huge effort, invested vast sums, implemented systems out the wazoo to make sure everybody gets the communications they need. But we've done very little to make sure everybody gets the communications they *don't* need.

That is where tribalism begins to loosen its hold. That's where your company will find the extra productivity and creativity that wireless phones and cross-functional "ideation sessions" can't buy. At the place where communication isn't just the controlled act of moving information from here to there. At the place where people are getting the communications that you don't *think* they need for their job.

I'm talking about extraneous stuff—the debate about the media strategy for Client A overheard in its entirety by the art director working on Account B.

I'm talking about personal stuff—the phone message slip you see on the counter by my coordinator's desk reminding me of an errand to run for Betty, my wife.

I'm talking about dumb stuff—the jokey photocopied fliers stacked near your desk, announcing the winners of a company golf tournament you didn't attend.

I'm talking about dangerous stuff—the agency's year-to-date profitability data on one of its big accounts, freely shared with the junior creative team.

You'd think people don't need to know all that. And you'd be wrong. Because if your company culture isn't open enough for them to get all of *that* stuff, then it isn't open enough, period. Information of no apparent importance is vitally important.

For one thing, being something less than omniscient, you can't really, truly know what information will prove useful to a person and what won't. It's a lead-pipe cinch that you'll guess wrong. Would you have ever guessed, for example, that the physicists assigned the task of inventing the atomic bomb during World War II would need to know about the latest developments in foofy housewares? Me either. Yet that's exactly where they found a new kind of metal mesh to use in their atomic experiments.

For another thing, it's the information we supposedly don't need to know about one another that helps us see each other as fully dimensional human beings. You may be a nervous new hire, I may be the guy who owns the agency, but that message slip about my honey-do list hints that I have a life a lot like your own. And I know many a jaded writer and art director who stopped making snide remarks about account executives as soon as they had the opportunity to see and hear how bloody hard the suits work for the cause.

But maybe most germane to our discussion of tribalism is this: The moment you begin to mete out information based on your perception of who needs to know what, you erect what may be the most divisive tribal barrier of all—the wall of separation between those in the know and those in the dark. "I know something you don't know" is more than a school-yard taunt. It's an almost irresistible temptation to play power games.

If I had to sum up *the* distinguishing mark of tribalized companies, that would be it. A tribalized company has too much control of information. Bet on it.

Tribalism lives in the dark corners of ignorance about the working lives of our colleagues. It thrives in the judgments about who needs to know what. It breeds in the chasm between the people in the know and the people in the dark.

But tribalism loses its grip, weakens, and retreats to a corner of the attic with a nasty consumptive cough in a company that has moved beyond the *act* of communication to a *culture* of communication, where everything happens in the plain view and full hearing of everyone. Yes, yes, I know. Wisdom requires that certain information remain confidential. But I'd bet that wisdom draws the line a whole lot farther to the left than you do. At my company, for instance, it is verboten to discuss compensation—your own or anyone else's—with anybody except your supervisor, and we protect the confidential information shared with us by our clients. Two categories of confidential information, that's it. There's a lot more that's sensitive, of course, but we've chosen to trust each other with it. You'd be amazed at how few times we've been burned.

Barely Managing

How we operate a successful company without GUM (gratuitous use of management).

YOU'RE STEPPING ON MY WELTANSCHAUUNG

Creating a workplace without tribalism means asking people to work in ways very different from those they've learned either in previous jobs or simply from lifelong exposure to the business culture around us. They know how to survive the politics, keep a wary eye on their neighbors, look out for numero uno. We're asking them now to let down the defenses, throw off presuppositions, consider that a world-view in which backbiting and factional discord are considered inevitable just *might* not represent the irrefutable truth. We're asking them to believe in a peaceable kingdom.

It's scary to cast yourself upon an alien outlook that way and discard what you're familiar with, no matter how dysfunctional it might be.

In suggesting that you pursue this strange and different way, I feel a little like Canassatego, the eighteenth-century head of the Iroquois Confederacy, when he extended his famous invitation to the colonists: ". . . if the gentlemen of Virginia shall send us a dozen of their sons, we will take great care of their education, instruct them in all we know and make men of them." He had to figure the offer wouldn't exactly set off a stampede of takers. Most people aren't all that eager to change worlds. "Um, er . . . gee, *thanks,* Canassatego, that's real nice of you—

really—but I think all our sons are going to be pretty busy . . . uh, let's see . . . *planting tobacco.* Yeah, that's it, they're planting tobacco and couldn't *possibly* get away. Sorry! Thanks anyway, though!"

As you think about this whole cultural shift we're proposing, maybe it will help you to learn a few more details about our own little tribal confederacy at The Richards Group.

Our structure is to be as unstructured as we can be. There's no formal system or code for how to do that. To institute one would be (to borrow an analogy I heard recently) like building a museum of Dada. It would squelch the very spirit it was intended to promote. So don't look for formulas here. I'll simply tell you about some of our oddball practices as a rough model you can borrow from as you see fit. It's the principles that matter most anyway.

DOWN WITH DEPARTMENTS

One reason I called the company The Richards Group was because I didn't want it to sound all that organized. I wanted a name that implied that there were a lot of people besides just this guy Richards doing the work. "Group" did that. Yet it didn't imply any of the negative traits that I felt more conventional words like "Agency" might suggest—a company that's layered, hierarchical, political, inefficient, maybe just the slightest bit venal.

If a prospective client, say, had had that kind of prior impression of ad agencies, which seemed likely, I didn't want to have to go in explaining that, oh no, we're a different *kind* of agency; I wanted to imply from the beginning that we're a wholly different kind of *thing.* We're a *group,* that's all, just a friendly aggregation of people who have come together around a common pursuit, which in our case happens to be doing really nifty ads.

Like most other companies, an agency, as defined by common practice, has departments that organize everyone there into little boxes. We do not, and may heaven forbid that we ever do.

In the beginning, before becoming a full-service agency in 1976, our firm was a stand-alone creative department for hire. The staff was all designers and writers, plus the secretary and the bookkeeper. So segregating the different functions into departments would have been a bit grandiose anyway. But then as the business started to require more job functions—account management, media, production, account planning, information technology, and so forth—we resisted whatever urge there may have been to departmentalize. These new functions simply became more jobs within the group, a group in which everybody continued to do just exactly what we had always done: turn out terrific advertising, with each function doing its bit toward that end.

Maybe you think I'm splitting hairs by not referring to everyone who performs a certain function as a *department*. Here we are with some very distinct divisions of labor—many dozens of people specializing, for example, in planning and buying media, with people in clear positions of responsibility over them. Are they not, then, a department, with department heads? No, they are not, thank you very much. They are not a department, in part, because they are not physically segregated. We jumble up everybody's desks just as much as possible, as I have described. But, more important, they are not a department simply because we don't *call* them a department.

This is not just some semantic game. It's *critically* important in preventing the partitioning of the organization—*within the minds of its people*—into subgroups with their own perceived interests and agendas. The instant you say, "All right, you people over there constitute a department"—*bam*, you've just laid the cornerstone of tribalism. You've drawn a line around part of your workforce, emphasized that it is distinct in some way from the other parts of the workforce, and unintentionally invited these employees to start behaving as an interest group.

So we simply never did that. People here identify themselves by their function ("I'm an art director," "I'm a broadcast negotiator") or by their broad area of specialty—their trade, if you will ("I work in accounting," "I'm in IT"), like the guy you meet at a party who tells you, "I'm in plastics."

The same thinking went into the decision not to confer all the officer titles and honorifics that help cement the caste system into most companies. For the most part, our titles are the same as our functions. You can usually tell from looking at our business cards what we actually do for a living—writer, account planner, producer, what have you.

Over the years, as we've picked up bigger and bigger clients, the whole title thing has grown a little more complicated simply because the account groups are free to organize their members along whatever lines best serve the client. A large account like The Home Depot, for example, can have so many brands and lines of business to manage that the group has to develop its own particular positions and titles to shadow the client's organization.

By now our firm has a contempt for fancy honorifics pretty well ingrained in its culture, so you can call yourself Exalted Imperial

Poobah de Luxe if you want to and it's not going to make any difference. Not long ago, for example, some of us were sitting around a conference room shooting the breeze while we were waiting for our meeting to start — something to do with a new-business pitch we were working on. We were talking about the competition, and somebody mentioned the name of a guy from one of the other agencies.

"What's his role in the thing?" someone asked.

"Well his *title*," came the reply from down the table, "is vice chairman and worldwide creative director."

"Wow," said the young woman sitting a couple of chairs down from me, a writer. "That sounds pretty darned cool. I think maybe I'd like to be one of those."

"Fine. Be my guest," I replied. "You want to be vice chairman and worldwide creative director?" She grinned and nodded. I waved my fingers in a vaguely papal gesture, like Leo X granting a minor indulgence. "You're now vice chairman and worldwide creative director."

"All right! Thanks!" she said. We all had a laugh to celebrate her "promotion" and then went on with our meeting. And that is how The Richards Group came to have the youngest worldwide creative director of any major agency in the country. I believe she's around 24. (Don't know if she had Michael Hatley, our senior print production person, order her new business cards.)

Call people what you may, there's really only one distinction that matters much and that's whether you're a senior person or a junior person, seasoned or in the seasoning process. And even that isn't always a clear distinction. You can distinguish the newest rookies and the wizened veterans, but in between are a lot of people who suddenly one day will be leading in a job that yesterday they were doing with supervision. They're the ones clients start thinking of as their key people, the ones newcomers look to as mentors. At some point — and it's different for everybody — they've crossed the invisible line from juniorhood to seniordom. It's clear, of course, who's been given formal responsibility as, say, a group head, but beyond that we've never worried about formally listing who's in which phylum, junior or senior. You just kind of know.

I guess all this can seem maddeningly loosey-goosey if you're a status-sensitive corporate type. But really, what difference does it make? Carefully categorizing everybody by title wouldn't help us get the work done any more than if we assigned them each a number from the Dewey Decimal System. You'd never say, "Gosh, I think this radio assignment could use a vice president and associate creative director." You say, "Hmm, I think this assignment could use a writer who's funny like . . . let's see . . . Chris." You look for a person and a position. That's all.

For my own title I picked "principal"—same as the lady who ran your junior high. A bunch of other people are principals, too—mostly people in charge of account groups, the counterparts to the creative group heads. But Larry Spiegel, our media guru, is called a principal, too. And so are the seniormost designers at RBMM, our design group. What *principal* really means is someone with whom the buck stops.

As the company grew, one way we kept from adding layers of so-called organization was to start doing a cellular division sort of routine, spreading the company wider and wider with little semi-autonomous "profit cells." Principals and group heads are responsible for these.

As the company grows, we're creating new groups all the time, each on equal footing with all the others. So far there's no sign that you can build too wide. It helps us stay agile and provides lots of opportunities for people to move into places of meaningful leadership. The goal is to never, ever add a layer of bureaucracy. Wider, not deeper, is the way to go.

All this is sort of like having a lot of little agencies within the agency. Each group—creative group, account group, and so forth—has its own profit-and-loss statement, its own accountability for the work done on behalf of the clients assigned to that group.

Within a group, work responsibilities may be divvied up along all sorts of lines. For example, a principal with several accounts in her group may put an account director in charge of running one of the bigger accounts day to day, with account supervisors taking responsibility for various lines of business within that account, more junior AEs handling still smaller pieces, and so on. Meanwhile another account in the same group could be in the hands of one AE. The groups do what they need to do to serve their clients. But as far as our *company* structure is concerned, there's the group, there's the group head or principal, and there's me. That's as stratified as it gets. No one has to work up through four or five layers of corporate management to get in front of me with an idea or question.

Notice I said the arrangement is *sort of* like little agencies. That's because the group structure has very soft edges. In creative, for example, there's constant overlap and interchange, writers and art directors forming ad hoc partnerships in various groups as workloads shift and opportunities come up. The group matchups across functional lines aren't static, either. To cite one random example, Dave Snell's account planning group shares accounts with seven account management groups and six creative groups. That's typical.

The group network is fluid; it's adaptable; it keeps working relationships fresh. And it's efficient. There's no need to have a manager caste overseeing revenues and disbursements that the frontline people are well able to manage themselves. When there's a new account to be pursued or integrated into the agency, group heads from the various disciplines simply find one another and form new working alliances based on interest and capacity for the work. Sometimes senior people who aren't group heads yet will help spearhead an initiative. If they win the business, they can create a new group. Or if growth starts to stretch a group's capacity for doing the work well, we'll just do the cell division thing again and set up a new group to handle part of the load.

Whenever possible we push financial accountability out to the people who are actually doing the work. Our in-house audio production and video editing rooms operate as profit cells. So do the broadcast producers, the color retouchers, and the Macintosh designers who produce and package production art. All of these little groups, in effect, buy time from one another as needed. It helps us—indeed, forces us—to keep close tabs on the way we spend our clients' money, and it helps us know how we're spending our own.

We've made all this up as we've gone, just trying to be pragmatic about how to keep doing a good job without getting bogged down in a morass of corporateness. Nothing's very institutionalized. We'll try something for a while, and if somebody has a better idea, then we'll shift and try that. If we find ourselves with a new peg and no ready-made hole to fit it in, we'll simply drill a new hole in the right shape.

We just try not to drill very deep, that's all. Wide, we like. Deep isn't for us.

LIVE AND LET DIE (SOMETIMES)

If we're not careful, we can become obsessed with the internal workings of the company, getting ourselves tangled up in all the *organization* of the organization. By expanding outward through simply structured profit cells, my aim is to eliminate useless distractions from the activities we went into this business to engage in and to adapt easily to changing circumstances.

Sometimes that means letting a cell die, when it no longer has a natural reason for being. Accounts come and go, people leave the company, or maybe you just figure out a better way to do something. By staying loosely structured, you can let a work group die a natural and dignified death without having to dismantle an unwieldy administrative structure, fire bureaucrats, and look bad in the newspapers for shutting down a business entity. You can keep it to a relatively simple change of working arrangements, not a personal catastrophe for a bunch of people.

Students of the great collaborations note that most superstar groups are temporary. They form around a certain task or goal, do the job, and dissolve. To be sure, most of our functional groups within The Richards Group aren't that temporary; they remain in operation, serving clients, gaining new ones, managing their P&L like any going concern. But the thing is, they don't *have* to keep going. Like a temporary, ad hoc team, the group exists around the performance of its task, not around the fact of its own existence. The group *is* its work. It is not a work unto itself.

In an account group, for example, every single person is directly involved in the work of serving the clients and building their brands. There is no bureaucratic infrastructure, no member whose sole reason for being there is to help the group perpetuate itself. If the group's reason for being ceases to exist—if we resign their accounts, say—then the group qua group ceases to exist. No one feels a desperate need to keep the group hobbling along on artificial life support. It's just not that big a deal. The members simply find other spots within the organization where they can do what they do best.

I say "simply" because there has never really been a time when the company has not been growing and creating new slots for talented people to fill—a direct consequence of focusing on the real work of the company instead of on corporate navel gazing and bureaucracy building.

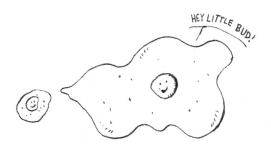

Nobody's identity is bound up in his or her work group's identity. One identifies with the company as a whole and with one's particular discipline, one's legitimate tribe, within the company—account management, media, and so forth. There's no ignominy in being part of a group that dissolves. In fact, *dissolve* is exactly the right word because of how naturally group members usually are absorbed into the rest of the agency.

Some years ago, for example, a creative group led by Ray Redding and Thomas Hripko was responsible for the Long John Silver's account. It was a demanding piece of business and, at the time, the largest in our history. The group had a couple of other, much smaller accounts they had worked with for a while, which was nice for variety's sake, but their time was dominated by the big client.

When we resigned Long John Silver's over creative differences (the client kept *trying* to make us do shoddy work), the creative team, group heads and all, simply feathered out into the agency's other creative groups, who were delighted to snap up their services. The team was too battle weary from the previous several months' struggles with a difficult client to try and hustle another major account just to keep the group together. And the group heads didn't get in a snit about some supposed loss of status. It had been their own choice to offer their services to other groups and, besides, they recognized that in this company your true status comes from your prowess, from the work you can do, and not from your titular position.

Naturally, their smaller clients didn't care how we organized ourselves on paper as long as we kept their team together in the accustomed roles, which, of course, we did. And not many months later the group re-formed in more or less its old configuration when we were named as new agency for Metromedia Long Distance, a company descended from our former client LDS, for whom Ray had done terrific work some years before.

A similar process of relatively pain-free reassignment happened with the people from all the other disciplines on the Long John Silver's account. Within a remarkably short time, a few weeks at most, every last person was settled into a new slot. You would never have known that we had just lost a major piece of business. Loosely strung as we were, the agency was easily able to absorb the blow of a major account loss. Had we been more tightly structured, it would have rattled us pretty hard.

The very act of organizing a formally structured entity within your company—a department, a division, an interest section—is dangerous.

Remember the Doctrine of Unlimited Missions? It states that when an organization's mission is accomplished it will try to perpetuate itself by creating another mission. The people you charge with the responsibility of doing the organizing are prone to just keep right on organizing till the cows come home — consolidating, reinforcing the boundaries of their department, setting in place bureaucratic mechanisms to help their creation sustain itself, whether it needs to or not.

Look at every in-house legal department you've ever seen. At some point in time, probably lost way back in the mists of history, somebody had a perfectly legitimate reason to assemble a group of legal eagles to draw up or defend or rule on something or other. But then they made the mistake of giving that group real, formal *group-ness*, establishing it as a department. And look what happens. Long after its original assignment is done, the department *always* finds something else to do. Inevitably the poor folks elsewhere in the company, who are just trying to get a job finished and shipped, end up looking like St. Sebastian in a Renaissance painting, shot through with a couple hundred arrows fired by their supposed comrades down in Legal. "Bull's-eye, counselor! That's good proactive shootin'!"

Now, don't start writing me letters. Without lawyers we're all toast — I know that. I *love* our lawyer, Stu Freidel. He's worth every penny of his princely hourly fee. But *he's not in an in-house department.* Heck, he's not even in the same city. Like the rest of us, he comes onto the team to perform a task, then rings off and goes about his other business.

As British authors Chris Seaton and Roger Ellis put it in *New Celts* (Kingsway, 1998), this is the day of "vibrant networks rather than static power bases." You see this as our various single-function groups — account management, account planning, creative, media, production, and so forth — form a full-service alliance, a macro-group if you will, around a project or account. We try to build client relationships that last for decades, so a certain degree of stability within that service group is important; rigidity, however, is not. Over time there may be changes within the alliance: the addition of disciplines like public relations or sales promotion, deletions like broadcast production in the case of a print-only client, substitutions like one creative group for another if fresh horses are needed.

Since the macro-group alliance has no formal administrative structure, no bureaucracy, it can adapt nimbly to opportunities and challenges. And when the project is finished or the account goes away (which, industrywide, happens in an average of five years), then the alliance has little or no dismantling to do. Each functional group just proceeds with its other work—clean, dignified, and with minimal disruption to the firm and the lives of the people in it.

Obviously when you're running a business you've got to be able to kill off a group that outlives its usefulness—like the dear old Buggy-whip and Razor Strop Division that used to be such a cash cow for you. Circumstances change. So be it. But it just gets so *ugly* sometimes. And that doesn't have to be.

Groups with a vested interest in existing for their own sake die desperate, spasmodic, undignified deaths—if you can get them to die at all. Like a snake that keeps biting after you lop off its head, bureaucracy does not go gentle into that good night. And like the Hydra, it can have really annoying ways of growing back the snaky severed head. It's easier in the short term just to let the blasted thing live. No wonder organizations that give their groups the bureaucratic infrastructure to sustain themselves beyond their useful life grow more and more ponderous, inefficient, and slow, creating opportunity for the rest of us, who travel lighter.

MANAGING WITHOUT MANAGERS

The way we run The Richards Group would scare some CEOs to death. There just isn't much apparent *management* happening around here. It's as if we wind the agency up every morning, give it a spin, and off it goes. Can you name another 600-person company that doesn't even have a human resources department—not even one HR person? Surely we teeter on the brink of anarchy.

Funny, but it's never been a problem. Maybe everybody's too busy getting their work done to have time for organizing anything anarchical.

Human resources typifies, I think, the problem of creating a purely managerial caste within your company. Tell someone, "Here, manage this, it's going to be your full-time job," and what are they going to do? Are they going to check in every couple of days just to make sure nothing's getting out of hand in their area of responsibility and spend the rest of their time fetching coffee for the troops? Heck, no. They're going to *manage,* friend. They're going to *find* ways to manage. It's like the old maxim that says that when the only tool you've got is a hammer, everything starts looking like a nail.

Some years ago, North Carolina adman Gene Lewis was visiting his daughter and son-in-law at the couple's farm in Ireland. Gene noticed that the farm dog, a border collie, was kept penned up for most of the time and let out only when there was work to do with the sheep. He felt a little sorry for the dog, thought it might be too confined. "He's a good dog, and you've got all this land," Gene said. "Why don't you let him out to run around some?"

"Oh, no," came the reply. "You don't understand. If we let that dog roam free, by nightfall he will have half the sheep in the county rounded up on this farm. It's all he knows to do."

That dog knew how to manage, no doubt about it. He just wasn't real good at knowing when to quit. And that's how it goes whenever administrative activity takes on a life of its own.

In my company we have never established a caste or tribe of people, HR or otherwise, whose sole purpose in life is to run our organization *as* an organization. If someone's job doesn't bear directly on the work we do for our clients—if it's not externally focused or, like payroll, at least working in direct support of the company's main vocation—I question whether we need that function around.

Obviously the problem isn't management per se. *Somebody* has to have their hand on the tiller. As James Krohe, writing in *Across the Board* magazine, says, "Good leadership doesn't make management moot, exactly, although it does make coercive management moot, which may be all that most people want anyway." Coercive, restrictive, or just superabundant, the problem as I see it is what I would call GUM—gratuitous use of management.

GUM is the usually well-intentioned but always unnecessary efforts to control what's best left alone, build procedural fences around activities better left in their free-range state, box in and label and restrict people who are well able to use their freedom responsibly.

Around here just about everything that you might call "administrative" is pushed outward to all the people who are doing the real work of the company. If, for example, you're responsible for getting a job done and you judge that you need more help to do it, then hire the help. Never mind having to follow some Code of Hiring Procedures. Run a classified ad, work your contacts around the country, call an ad-school placement office—you decide. And let's not pussyfoot around with how you're doing against some labor projection that somebody you don't even know dreamed up last year, which I guess is what some companies do. Your group has its own P&L statement. Nobody is in a better position than you to judge whether adding a new person will help do the job better or just add to overhead.

In fact, let's not even worry about where we're going to *put* this new hire of yours. If you need her, you need her. Even if we're tight on space, which we always seem to be, *not* bringing in somebody you need is a problem 10 times worse than solving where to squeeze in another desk. It's not like we're that big on personal space around here anyway.

Don't feel like you have to cover your backside with memos or keep a Starfleet Captain's Log about every little decision. We don't put a lot in writing. Our policy manual covers a few basics such as how to fill out a time sheet, how our unusual but popular FRO benefit works ("FRO" is the time sheet code for "Friday off," which I'll describe in Chapter 6), how you get vested in profit sharing, and so forth, but I rarely see anybody using the darned thing after their first couple of weeks here. There's just not that much policy to look up, I guess. And with the more complicated bits like the vesting schedule, it's easier to just call up Scot Dykema or somebody and ask a question than it is to puzzle out all the stuff about start dates and by what date you will have worked 1,000 hours that year. (Or whatever the heck the manual says. I usually just ask Scot myself.)

The level of communication we achieve by working shoulder to shoulder, undivided by artificial barriers of department and rank, renders unnecessary a complicated codex of corporate do's and don'ts. Just dive into your work and get help from your comrades along the way. You don't have to delve like a Talmudic scholar into some ever growing code of inviolable practices just to get started.

When Ross Perot was still at EDS, he described the difference between his company and General Motors, to whom EDS had been sold. At EDS, Perot said, if they saw a snake, they'd kill it. At GM, they would conduct a search for the world's foremost snake experts and commence an exhaustive study of the creature. Gratuitous use of management.

I'm with Ross. Just kill the snake.

DEMOTE YOURSELF FIRST

I've never seen any practical use for frilly corporate titles. They mean instant tribalism. The less labeling you apply to people, the better off you'll be. Simple functional titles are best, in my opinion, without all the honorifics and caste distinctions. I'm comfortable having the same title as a dozen or more of my associates. The title hardly matters anyway, except to people calling to find out how to address a letter to me. Everybody around here knows my role in the business without having special words attached to my name.

There may be hope on the title front. With the exception of the ad agency world, where grandiose honorifics still seem *very* important, more businesses, it appears, are catching on to how silly and divisive the bestowing of "important" titles can be.

For a long time one of the bellwether companies in this regard was Gore Associates, of Gore-Tex fame, where everybody's title, regardless of job function, is simply Associate. That used to be positively radical. Now it's tame, compared to what a lot of companies are doing. Some, in the egalitarian spirit of Gore, give everyone an identical title; they just take it further. At one chain of coffee shops in the Northwest everyone carries the title of Human Being.

Fast Company magazine tracks this sort of thing in their monthly "Job Titles of the Future" column. It's heartening to see a big accounting firm employ a Minister of Comedy and to learn that someone with the official title of Troublemaker is an employee in good standing of — get this — the U.S. Department of Labor. The winner for humility, though, may be the guy who's responsible for making all his company's computers work right. His title is Necessary Evil.

You get lots of groovy titles now, such as Vibe Evolver. He works for a Swedish publisher. Others manage to combine the new economy with a sense of the older ways of doing things. The title Digital Yenta comes to mind there. The list of new titles is still pretty heavy on hierarchical designations like "Director of . . ." and "Chief," but at least more people are making it clear that one shouldn't approach the hierarchy too reverently. The founder of Joe Boxer, Nicholas Graham, calls himself Chief Underpants Officer. Peter Adkison, founder of Wizards of the Coast, the company that sold your kids all those Pokémon cards, chose two very traditional titles but combined them well. His title: CEO & Janitor.

If you're a person in charge and you're brave enough to divest your organization of its fancy but divisive corporate caste labels, my advice would be this: You go first. Assume your new title of Lowly Worm, or whatever you deem fitting, but don't make anyone else change yet. After all, if you take everybody down a peg (which is how many of them will see it) all at the same time, it won't change anyone's relative position in the pecking order. Live with your new title a while. See? It's not so bad. That's what you've got to prove. A person is not his or her title; your merits — your character and skill — are what counts.

Somebody's got to take the plunge and show how it works. If you're in authority, that somebody has to be you. Destroying unnecessary hierarchy must start at the top — unless, of course, it happens through a good old-fashioned Third World–style coup, and I don't think you want that.

NEW BRANCHES ARE PRONE TO GETTING BUGS

After our billings had passed the half-billion mark, you'd think we might have been ready to consider a second office. No, thank you. One city, one office. That's it. And it would take a very, *very* convincing argument, Professor, to get me to think otherwise.

My aim is to hang on, as much as possible, to the cultural advantages, the cohesion, we had as a small company. Doing that is hard enough with one full-service office. I don't like the idea of having to do it with more.

In advertising, geographic expansion is a highly overrated concept. I can thank Leo Burnett, one of my early heroes in the business, for serving as my example on this. He disdained the arguments supposedly wiser people laid on him about the danger of becoming too provincial by staying put in Chicago. Following his example, I've always been very happy in Dallas. (Burnett did, however, expand internationally, which I don't intend to do. More on that later.)

No agency yet in existence, as far as I can see, has proved consistently excellent—or even consistently mediocre, for that matter—from office to office to office. There are always wide disparities in talent and resources. In one city, the employees are the darlings, the corporate daddy's favorites. In another city, they believe they *deserve* to be the favorites, but they're too far away from HQ to get the attention they think they deserve and so they're snippy about it. Another branch has a total inferiority complex—the hangdog country cousins quietly apologizing for their bumptious ways as they gaze through the brightly lit windows of the company's more sophisticated offices.

Now, maybe you say, "Pfff, I don't care." If the Greenwich office makes money and the Memphis office makes money and the Boise office makes money, what difference does it really make if the people in those three offices don't feel sentimentally attached to each other? They're never all in the same place anyhow, right?

Well, here's why it matters to me. It matters because your company isn't just offices. It's a brand. And it is very likely a brand that means very different things to clients and prospects in Greenwich and Memphis and Boise. Your brand may be the gold standard in one city, an also-ran in another, and the absolute dregs of the market in the third.

Inconsistency
kills brands.
Chapter 9
deals with
this in detail.

As my zil-
lionaire friend in Chapter 1 found, trying to curtail factionalism and
kingdom building and build cultural consistency across multiple
offices is a herculean job. I understand, though—in lots of industries, if
you're going to grow beyond pipsqueak size, you can't help but expand
geographically. That's not the case with my business, however. We've
never had any difficulty serving our clients from one office. And we
serve clients all the way from Portland, Oregon, to Malmö, Sweden.

If, in order to have adequate communication, a distant client *needs*
an agency person on hand, we're not going to be hardheaded about it.
We posted an account guy in Toronto for a while when The Home
Depot was getting their Canadian business cranked up. When constant face time is that important, an arrangement like that makes more
sense than having some unfortunate person spend half their life com-
muting to the client's place. But it's really necessary a whole lot less
than you might think. And those people always, always remain *ours*.
We don't consider them satellites of the agency any more than are the
people who are traveling for us on any given day.

THE SEMI-UNITED NATIONS

The clients who really need multiple full-service offices are the ones
building brands in multiple countries. When advertising successfully
crosses cultures, as some of our Travelocity and Chupa-Chups work
has done (as I write, for example, some new U.S. spots for Chupa-
Chups are in test on German TV), you can consider yourself lucky.
Most of the time, for communicating within a given culture, it definitely "takes one to know one."

Clients working across cultures naturally assume sometimes that
they'll be best served by a multinational agency. At The Richards
Group we've taken a different—and, I think, better—approach to
serving multinational clients.

As we've noted, this is the day of the fluid, adaptable alliance, as
opposed to the traditional, unwieldy, fixed power base. Rather than
trying to create a power base of international offices of our own—

which, as handy as they may sound, are always rife with inconsistency (brilliant work in Kuala Lumpur, dismal stuff in Milano, that kind of thing) — instead, we've gone off and made some friends. We've set up a much less formal but much more consistent network of like-minded agencies around the world.

We began by asking: Who is The Richards Group of Hong Kong? Of London? Of Brazil? We researched major advertising communities around the world, studied agency reels and print books from all over, dug around and asked around and conversed around to find agencies with whom we'd be simpatico in style and outlook. And we asked them, when the occasion arises, to *be us* in their culture.

Why mess with the highly iffy endeavor of starting up TRG/ Brazil? If I had a São Paulo office, I'd want it to do work just like G3, a terrific Brazilian agency. So why not do the clients a favor and just hook them up with G3 to start with? Same with Batey Ads in the Far East and Leagas Delaney in London. When our clients need them, they're warmed up and ready to do what they do best in the culture they know best.

I don't want a spotty collection of agencies — some okay, some not — with my name on them. I want great work to get done for my clients. Our agency friends around the world are the people to do it. And when a client comes along needing brand-building help in a region of the world we haven't covered yet — no problem — we'll just extend our search for an agency there whose work we'd be proud to call our own.

In short, for brand building across cultures, it's a whole lot more important to have agencies of consistent quality than agencies that are consistent only in name.

YOU WANTED YOUR OWN COMPANY, SO WHY ARE YOU SO ANXIOUS TO SELL IT?

> *Mammon: god of the world's leading religion. The chief temple is in the holy city of New York.*
> —Ambrose Bierce, *The Devil's Dictionary*

The Richards Group is not for sale.

I used to have to say that all the time, when emissaries of the ad agency holding companies prowled the earth in great numbers in search of new acquisitions. Maybe they're still out there, but I guess I said "No way, José" enough that most of them got the message and just

don't come
around much
anymore.
Now we're
known in some

circles as the last cantankerous independent, sort of the Switzerland of advertising, clinging fiercely to our autonomy.

Recently, a business reporter writing a story about yet another big advertising merger asked Mike Malone, one of our creative group heads, why The Richards Group is still operating solo when the rest of the industry has been consolidating like crazy. "We can always act in our clients' best interest," Mike answered. "When I have to ship wheelbarrows full of money each quarter to a holding company, I can't invest in either the people or infrastructure that make my agency better." Hear, hear.

I started this company because I wanted to control my own destiny, wanted to pursue my craft according to my principles and let the money follow, if it would. (It did.) And once I learned that doing good work does pay, I wanted to keep profit squarely in fourth place, out of the medals, in the list of priorities we operate by: Can we do good work, can we make a difference, can we have fun, and can we make money?

If those are your priorities, losing your independence jumbles them up. It has to. No matter how autonomously your owner supposedly lets you operate, no matter how trusting and hands-off they try to be, selling out still puts your company in the shadow of some éminence grise somewhere who's subtly looking over your shoulder ("Oh, don't mind me!") *expecting* you to deliver that wheelbarrow of money. They might not pester you about it, but they do expect that wheelbarrow. How can that not make you conduct your business differently?

As it is, we're free to *not* do the most lucrative thing when our other, more important priorities are being satisfied. And we don't have to justify it to anybody. The two times when we've resigned what was, in each case, the biggest account we'd ever had—and did so without laying off staff—it didn't take a lot of agonizing, a lot of explaining, a lot of wasted time. We didn't need some outsider's permission to do what those of us in the situation knew good and well needed to be done. We just did it and moved on. As it should be.

Doing it our way has been profitable. We do have money to invest. So, as Mike said, we invest it here. In raises and bonuses. In profit sharing. In new hires whenever we need them. In purchases and upgrades of the gadgets that help us do our jobs better. That would be an awful lot to trade away in exchange for a few fat executive bonuses and a jolly thank-you at the end of the year from our lords and masters.

But as important as that financial independence is, it may not be the *most* important reason not to sell the company. If we sell out, we instantly become part of a pecking order, a mechanism in somebody else's cultural and political machine. We become aware of our status compared to other pieces of the whole. We quickly learn always to bear in mind whom we're beholden to. We become a *subsidiary,* for goodness' sake. The very word means "subordinate." So much for our valiant struggle to maintain a flat organization with equal esteem for every function; we're in a whole different kind of system now. Tribalism, here we come.

It can happen a hundred different ways, I'm sure. If, as a subsidiary, we're under pressure to contribute profits to the parent, then our most profitable groups or accounts rise in status compared to all the others. Or maybe the ComMegaCorp conglomerate bought us to improve their creative reputation. Our status as the creative elite would, in all likelihood, make us start copping the artiste attitude, trying to live up to the rep—a culture shift that would cost us the balance we'd always fought so hard for. Whatever the details are, with a new absentee owner we'd find ourselves with a new agenda and culture to overlay or blend with or replace the one we've always had. Some people would adopt the parent company's agenda more zealously than others, generating factional conflict. It's hard enough just to pursue one agenda well. Having more is always divisive.

If you went into business because you wanted to *do* business a certain way (as opposed to just starting a business to make a killing and move on), then *any* kind of absentee owner is going to frustrate you. Selling out to a holding company would be bad enough. I can't *imagine* the complications and distractions that must come from selling shares to the public, when you get not only the shareholders but also the feds, the National Association of Securities Dealers, securities analysts, and who knows who else demanding their piece of you.

The siren song of mergers and initial public offerings can sure sound lovely, promising you the wealth to do whatever you want. But I don't care how many Cigarette boats it buys and *Fortune* covers it gets you. It's a Faustian bargain in the end. Sell your company and you cease to be your own master. And that's why I say no.

Give me liberty.

MEPHISTOPHELES RIDES A LIMO

For a while I felt like the homecoming queen, with all the finest young swains asking me out. Merger mania was sweeping through the ad biz. One by one, practically every independent agency of any size succumbed to the charms of a suitor from New York, London, or Paris. The Richards Group was one of the last holdouts. So when Jean, my coordinator, stuck her head around the corner to say that a certain agency bigwig was holding on my line, I wasn't surprised.

As always, I was happy to take the call—in this case maybe more than usual. The caller was a man whose name adorned what I considered to be one of the best agencies in New York (and, therefore, the world). Their creative product was impeccable. I had admired their work for years and was delighted to have a chance to become acquainted with one of the agency's principals. He was, of course, cordial and charming, but since this obviously wasn't a social call he came quickly to his point. They were aggressively seeking partners (read: subsidiaries) around the country and, given the caliber of The Richards Group's work, felt that we were a natural choice to come into their family of agencies.

Certainly I appreciated the compliment. But I explained to him, as I did to all the others, that I had long since decided not to give up the agency's independence. Although I didn't explicitly say so, his overture wasn't even slightly tempting. Flattering, yes. Tempting, no.

Why sell? The agency was certainly having no trouble attracting terrific clients and talented employees. We were on solid financial ground, making profit-sharing contributions at or near the legal maximum every year, while continually adding new disciplines and technology to serve our clients. Our reputation was growing; trade pubs on both sides of the Atlantic were including us in their lists of the world's best creative shops—right along with my caller's agency. In other words, what's not to like? So I said thanks anyway, but I really wouldn't consider selling out.

Maybe he thought I was playing hard to get. After all, from his perspective, he was offering me the deal of a lifetime. "I certainly understand your reasoning," he said, "but would you be willing to talk about it face to face? Why don't you let me come out to Dallas and take you to lunch?" That's a long way to come just for a friendly lunch with no hope of deal at the end, but he was willing to come anyway, so I said okay.

Not surprisingly, he was as impressive in person as he had been on the phone. We had a very nice lunch. But of course it did nothing to change my mind. No financial offer could compare with the priceless independence my company already enjoyed. Nor did the opportunity to sit on their board hold any attraction. I don't even have board meetings *here.* Going to New York for one certainly held no big attraction. Naturally, he also promised that here in Dallas we'd have "complete autonomy." His company and mine held very similar attitudes about the work; our approaches were much the same. My agency's culture wouldn't have to change a bit, he declared.

But that's what they always say. I've seen plenty of these dream-match mergers, and I've seen *Faust.* I know how these transactions work.

By the time the coffee arrived at our table, my visitor knew that, other than making a new acquaintance, his trip hadn't produced much. Now that I think about it, he probably had more than an inkling of that before we even went to the restaurant. After his flight arrived that morning, he had come to the agency for an introduction and my usual little tour. Then it was lunchtime. "I've got a car right downstairs," he said, "so let's take mine."

When we hit the lobby I realized that he wasn't talking about a Taurus he'd rented at the airport. Idling at the curb in front of our building was a limousine. Long, black, dark windows—very presidential. Other Groupers, on their way out for lunch, were checking out this big mystery machine, wondering aloud whose chariot *that* was. "You know what?" I said. "I think I'd be more comfortable if we took mine. I'll drive."

Before that moment my visitor probably couldn't have known this, but to my way of thinking this is not an organization where it's okay for the boss to be whisked off to lunch in a 30-foot-long car with a liveried driver. That's *exactly* the way things work where he's from; he wouldn't give it a second thought. But I can't claim to scoff at corporate caste systems and then go cruising off in the Brahmin-mobile. So we left the stretch curbside and headed down to the parking garage for my station wagon.

At that point, our gentleman caller could have predicted that his mission to Dallas was going to come up empty. Odd though our agency may be, we've got our soul. And we have no intention of selling it.

RUNNING THE COMPANY IN 10 MINUTES A DAY

Please don't hate me for this. My best, honest estimate of how much time I spend on purely administrative stuff pertaining to the running of the company is around 10 minutes a day on average—maybe 15 if you count time spent talking shop with Scot Dykema and whoever else comes on our early morning run.

By "administrative stuff" I mean any activities that make me, even though I'm the head of an ad agency, indistinguishable from the generic company presidents you see on commercials for things like AFLAC and large American sedans. Ninety-five percent of the time, I still get to be pure adguy.

It hasn't been that hard, really. All I've done is listen to the counsel of people like Herschel Levit, my most influential teacher back at Pratt Institute, who preached simplicity as the essence of genius. So mostly it's been a matter of not adding complications to the organization. We have one agency office, in Dallas. We have no shareholders other than myself. We have zero departmental boundaries to create energy-sucking turf wars. It's just a simple organization. Compared to people I know who run companies even half this size, I just don't have that many corporate-level plates to keep spinning.

Everything else I do outside those 10 or 15 minutes has something directly to do with the fun stuff, the real work—noodling out strategies, looking at alternative approaches, helping find and assign the people who will be the best for a certain task, presenting the work to clients—those sorts of activities.

Now and then, when some of us are standing at the table, squinting down at pieces of paper, trying, say, to figure out why a layout isn't quite working yet, I love to snap the pen out of my shirt front and fiddle with possible solutions—showing, as David Ogilvy used to say, that my hand has not lost its cunning. Most of the time, though, I'm more of what authors Warren Bennis and Patricia Ward Biederman call a curator, "whose job is not to make but to choose."

As curator in chief, it's my job to offer judgments about alternative directions in the work, to choose leaders and provide a sounding board for them when needed, to be around as the court of last resort on the rare occasions when disputes between colleagues are not resolved by the self-appointed guardians of the company culture—that is to say, by just about everybody in the joint.

One of the most important jobs of the curator is simply to squelch GUM, gratuitous use of management.

Nice people, team players like most of my colleagues, sometimes try to follow the rules to the point of seeing rules where none exist. Before you know it, some new Procedure with a capital P has appeared from nowhere and started to GUM up the works.

Recently, for instance, I heard an AE make a passing reference to the "account management employee review form." I think my face took on, for just a second, an expression a little like that of Janet Leigh in that scene from *Psycho,* where she turns around in the shower and sees Tony Perkins with the knife. Just the sound of the phrase gave me the willies. We're scrupulous about giving employees an annual progress check, but each group in the agency goes about it in whatever way works best for them. We've never even had guidelines for how to conduct a review, let alone an *official form.* That is, to borrow a line from Jeremiah (the prophet, not the bullfrog), "something I did not command or mention, nor did it enter my mind."

"Excuse me for interrupting," I said when I regained the power of speech, "but *what* official form was that you just mentioned?"

So he repeated what he had said, and it soon became apparent that this "official" form was a prime example of the casual occurrence that magically, through the alchemy of GUM, takes on the authority of holy writ.

A recently hired AE, simply being helpful, had shown his supervisor the form his ex-employer used for annual evaluations. It had some good questions on it. So the supervisor made a copy and started using it for his group members' yearly reviews. Communication being pretty good around here, other account groups heard about this handy new tool and made copies for themselves. And somewhere, somehow — presto change-o! — this piece of paper that had begun simply as a small bit of competitive intelligence data roared to life as The New Written Form That We Must Use For All Account Management Employee Reviews. It's like those urban myths — the Doberman choking on the burglar's finger, the fried mouse in the bucket of chicken — nobody knows exactly where the story starts, but people will swear that it's true.

One reason I found this written evaluation thing so absurd is that it pertained to account management. They, as a tribe, are inveterate note takers, people who *for a living* scrupulously, reflexively write down everything even remotely important. Nobody needs a prepackaged written form, least of all them. An annual review isn't a court of inquiry anyhow; it's a conversation.

So I contacted the principals and organized a little bonfire of the vanities down in the parking lot with the "official" form.

Actually I didn't do that. I simply suggested, nicely, that we desist from its use. If I had made a major issue of it, within 24 hours it probably would have morphed into another urban legend: "Stan said we're not allowed to put anything in writing anymore, not even sticky notes." We're not *that* ready for the paperless office.

Okay, so we're talking about curating. It's the very first agenda item of the week. Every Monday at 8:00 A.M. sharp, unless I'm traveling to meet with a client, every writer, art director, production manager, producer, and account planner in the agency squeezes into one of the large conference rooms for the weekly creative meeting. We go around the room, group by group and person by person, and read our individual lists of every single assignment in the agency. The meeting usually lasts till around 8:45.

It's where we get an overall picture of our workload. If one group says, "We're light right now," and another says, "We're drowning," it takes about 10 seconds to resolve the disparity. The Monday meeting is where I can ask, "What is that?," when someone is working on a project I've never heard of. There's no way I can be directly involved in every single project, of course, but I never want to be in a position of not being able to have an intelligent conversation on the spur of the moment with any client about any job we're doing for them.

Admittedly, it is not the most scintillating meeting you'll ever sit through. But it serves an important curatorial function. That single hour of communication saves us untold hours of headaches throughout the week, as we match needs with resources and move work through the agency. The right hand knows what the left hand is doing. Just as important, having a little basic knowledge of what your peers are working on does wonders for unity within the organization. You see what you have in common: some cool projects, some more prosaic ones, desperately busy times, occasional lulls. You're in this together.

By the way, in case you're wondering, the account management folks don't get off light. Their weekly meeting is Tuesday at eight o'clock.

But back to Monday. Here is how a recent Monday, and a pretty typical day in the life of *moi,* went.

8:00–8:45	Meeting with the very busy creative staff; no one's complaining this week about not having enough work to do.
8:45–9:00	Pour a second cup of coffee, take a phone call, talk to a couple of drop-in visitors about assorted work in progress.

9:00–9:30	Cally Shea and Kristie Guilmette, an up-and-coming writer/art director team, have booked a half hour to talk career direction and the change of groups they're about to make; we chat about future responsibilities they want to aim for, the kind of work they could use in their book and on their reel at this stage in their careers, and, in general, how to keep a couple of rising stars happy.
9:30–10:00	Producer David Rucker and creative directors Kevin Paetzel and Lee Coleman have the reels of three directors they've bid for an upcoming Home Depot Expo shoot; we talk over the relative merits, eliminating one director from consideration, and the guys will submit the other two to the client, one as their recommendation and the other as backup.
10:00–10:30	Account guy Dirk Van Slyke, who handles our Jiffy Lube account, and I go over the speech I'll be giving at Jiffy Lube's national convention in a few weeks, and he fills me in on a couple of new business opportunities he's working on.
10:30–11:00	Two creative teams—group heads Mark McKenzie and Jed Schroeder and writer/AD team Brian Pierce and Matt Dalin—get my opinion on three rough cuts, half of a six-spot TV package for SuperValu grocery stores; the cuts look great, so it's a fast meeting, leaving a few minutes to go over the next few days' calendar with Jean Howe, my coordinator.
11:00–11:15	A typically short yet wide-ranging talk with Mike Malone about clients, his creative group, anything he feels a need to discuss; whenever Mike calls to get on my calendar, Jean simply lists it as "Malone—misc."
11:15–11:30	Return phone calls.
11:30–12:00	Terence Reynolds comes by to talk about marshaling people to tackle the work at hand; Terence, an art director, is responsible for Shift, our growing urban-marketing group.

12:00–1:30	Orientation lunch in the agency with 11 new employees who have started lately; I'll have the same discussion with 11 more at the same time tomorrow—a little history, a little philosophy, hopefully a generous dose of encouragement, and Q&A as needed.
1:30–2:00	Finally some time to "cruise," as Jean calls it, and be the guy who stops at *other* people's desks for a change.
2:00–3:00	Into a conference room with members of Pete Lempert's account group and the Coleman/Paetzel creative group for a look at the latest round of TV concepts for Nokia wireless phones.
3:00–3:30	Back to my desk, where account people Pete Lempert and Margaret Ostarch and creative guys Jim Baldwin and Mike Renfro show me the latest version of new print work that I'll be helping present to the president of Galaxy Aerospace, the business jet manufacturer; we spend the rest of our half hour brainstorming strategy ideas for reaching new customer segments for Galaxy.
3:30–5:00	Dennis Walker and Doug Rucker's creative group and assorted members of the account management and account planning team gather for our second internal review of a new branding campaign for the Alliance Parts portion of our Freightliner account; it's turning out to be a surprisingly tough assignment, so instead of reviewing much print and radio we spend most of the session reexamining the creative strategy.
5:00–6:00	Another big multidisciplinary team, this time featuring Malone's creative group, circles up for the first of three internals leading up to the presentation of a new year's worth of TV concepts to the Florida Department of Citrus.
6:05	In the car, heading home; with four more days pretty much like this one coming up this week, I've got to go have a life.

You see why I've never had time to take up golf.

What else you see, or so I hope, is that I'm still doing, every single day, the work I went into this business to do. I'm not ashamed to say it: I'm having a ton of fun. We've designed our company so that everybody here is free to do the same, to pursue whatever their chosen discipline may be and to enjoy it, without the factionalism, fear, and other vexations that are too often what businesspeople mean by "just another day at the office."

Learning to Function without Dysfunction

Building an open workplace requires rethinking a lot of the usual ways of business. But believe me, you won't miss them.

A NORMAL DAY AT WORK? NO, THANKS

Daniel Patrick Moynihan, the former senator, has eloquently decried the normalization of social decay—our acceptance of levels of violence and other ills that we would have considered outrageous a generation ago. It's the sort of thing you're referring to when you lament being unable to let your children play outside in your neighborhood without a vigilant adult on the scene. It wasn't like that when you were a kid, but now it's "normal."

Well, we've normalized a lot of social ills in the office, too. Nothing nearly as menacing as what the senator warns about, granted. But still. In most workplaces today people live with a degree of political ferment and ambient fear that, at one time, would have been implausible outside the plot of a soap opera. Now it's a normal day at work, a real live soap opera, only without the organ music you really need for proper dramatic effect. Lots of things about working life have gotten better, sure. You're a lot less likely to be maimed by a runaway machine than Grandpa was. But Grandpa would probably shake his head in disbelief at the soul-maiming dangers *you* have to dodge every day.

I thought about this recently as Dick Murray, one of our agency principals, recounted his first visit to The Richards Group. Dick was president of the DDB Dallas office when he came over to pay a friendly call and see this unusual agency he had heard about. I walked him around the office, introduced him to a few of my colleagues—the usual get-acquainted tour of our company. Dick said that when he got home that evening, he told his wife, "You know something, I saw an agency today that was just like when I was getting started in the business."

Dick, I should point out, is a veteran adguy, but he's hardly the Ancient Mariner. The span of time he was talking about was scarcely more than two decades. It struck me as he told his story: The ad agency business is thought of as one of the most diabolically political industries on the planet—nature of the business, right? But we forget that it really wasn't always so bad. Not everywhere, at least, and not even very long ago. When he was a young AE in New York, Dick experienced a business fueled by the energy of pursuing great work. He was part of a team, and it was exciting. When he came for our tour, he realized that a wholly different atmosphere had become "normal."

Whatever business you're in, it's time to question your "normal" business practices. We operate, many of us, on the basis of unchallenged customs and ingrained presuppositions about the way organizations need to be structured and run. We haven't actually paused to ask, "Wait a minute—*why* does it have to be this way? Why do people have to be sorted and segregated by size, function, and shape of their head like bulk screws in bins at the hardware store? What are we really gaining from all this so-called organization? Why must factionalism be accepted as an inevitable feature of corporate life? When, exactly, did SOP *become* SOP?"

It's easy, of course, to take the position that things are good enough, so why fix what's not all *that* broken. Working life may not be paradise, you could say, but for the last dozen years or so the economy hasn't exactly been limping along, has it? We've achieved some spectacular results. Why mess with success?

Why? For the simple reason that the ends—growing companies, growing employment, all that—don't justify the inefficient and often ignoble means used to get there.

In the city of Leipzig, in Germany, is the largest railway station in all of Europe. It's a splendid structure, and when you look at it today, that's all you see — the magnificent achievement. You don't see the difficulty that went into achieving it. Writes Uwe Siemon-Netto in *Civilization* magazine: "Two rival kingdoms, Prussia and Saxony, built the station together at the beginning of [the twentieth] century, each installing its own staff, complete with mutually hostile cleaning men who pushed rubbish back and forth between their respective territories."

A lot of us, I believe, are like those cleaning men, wasting time and energy pushing garbage off on one another as if it's a duty of our position. That's inefficient and costly for our companies, obviously. And just as important, it's demeaning to the people doing the work. They may not *feel* demeaned, since, after all, this garbage-pushing is "normal." But the truth is, we're made for better than this.

HIERARCHY RHYMES WITH MALARKEY

Being a manager means never having to be less condescending just because you're wrong.
— Catbert, evil HR director in *Dilbert*

Whose bright idea was it to set up distinctions between the people who *run* things and the people who *do* things, to establish corporate command structures with carefully guarded levels and ranks and rigid lines of communication, and then expect the system to make us more productive? And why is it considered such a bold act of iconoclasm when a company refuses to erect such barriers within its workforce?

Think of the martial concepts that have found their way into business. Senior officers. Frontline workers. Chain of command. Badges of rank. The tradition of structuring companies as if they were the Eighth Army is so well established that it almost seems wrong to suggest that business is not really *supposed* to be that way. Rigid control structures with their buttressing traditions and conventions work fine, I guess, if you're invading France. But if you're trying to serve clients or bring products to market, hierarchy produces exactly the opposite of its intended result.

In her book *Systems of Survival: A Dialogue on the Moral Foundations of Commerce and Politics* (Vintage, 1994), Jane Jacobs describes the dysfunction and, at its worst, the "monstrous hybridization" that can result when the structures and practices of inherently regimented "guardian" entities like the police and the military are taken up by commercial organizations, which work best when there's free exchange of ideas and disdain for the status quo.

Jacobs writes that "every improvement in efficiency or production or distribution requires dissent from the way things were previously done. So does every new kind of material used in production. So does every innovative product." Progress in commercial life, she says, hinges upon "[i]nnumerable practical acts of dissent . . . subversive of things as they are."

The guardian ethic, by contrast, values tradition, loyalty, and "the chief principle of organization for guardians," respect for hierarchy. In certain contexts, those values are vital. If you're a general, for example, you definitely want to discourage entrepreneurs from starting up their own armies in competition with the old one. But in a commercial enterprise, adherence to tradition, demands of loyalty, and respect for hierarchy are stifling. Yet plenty of business leaders *love* them.

Control structures are inherently conservative, self-preserving. They bolster themselves by adhering to the ways of the past. They have to. They were created in reaction to certain circumstances. If the circumstances change, they're toast. And so they wall themselves off from discovery and creativity, the sworn enemies of the status quo.

All right, you say, so we ought to cast off restraint and cast down our entrenched power structures. How, then, do we maintain a clear direction, maintain any vision for action? In other words, how do we keep up a disciplined approach to the company's business without management perched solidly in the driver's seat with a firm hand on the reins (and a whip stashed discreetly within reach) to keep the workforce from kicking over the traces?

You do it through *this* discipline: the business discipline of branding strategy carried through to every aspect of your business. (I'll discuss this in Chapter 9.) A true branding strategy applied from the mailroom to the boardroom removes much of the need for a caste of People in the Know who make judgments and issue directives for the People in the Dark who actually do most of the work. Done well, it can provide a welcome sense of purpose and a highly adaptable plan of action for every function and person in the company. The only thing it's bad for is those entrenched, self-seeking power structures.

B.S. IN MANAGEMENT

Naturally, imposing arbitrary rules and needless bureaucracy is a bad idea. Every good manager knows this. So they implement only

You ARE A HUMAN RESOURCE!!!

well-reasoned, carefully de-signed management struc-tures, which more often than not is *also* a bad idea.

It's GUM, gratuitous use of management, accentuating the divide between the people who are in charge and the people who aren't. When it comes to administration, anything beyond the bare minimum is more likely to shore up walls of tribalism and create new inefficiencies than it is to help people do a better, more fulfilling job.

My pet example is human resources. If you ever find an HR depart-ment at The Richards Group, you'll know that you can go ahead and paint over my name. HR, the most purely internal of all bureaucracies, could in most cases be accurately renamed Department of Tribalism Maintenance. It perpetuates itself (remember the Doctrine of Unlim-ited Missions?) by finding new ways to keep people in organizational boxes where they get to do lots of little tasks expressly for—you guessed it—the HR department.

Look at the name itself, "human resources." Doesn't that sound kind of, well, *creepy* to you? It's like people—living, breathing, feeling people—are objectified and viewed as mere assets, as if they were lathes or dump trucks or chromium deposits. It reminds me of that movie *The Matrix,* where evil machines kept all the humans alive just to use their bodies as an energy source. So don't call me a human resource. Them's fighting words.

In companies that have been around a while, HR used to be called the "personnel department," which in my opinion was a better name since it at least implied that the department had to deal with living persons. But that turned out to be a problem of its own since persons, by nature, don't like being meddled with and treated suspiciously, which is pretty much what the personnel department was there to do. As a result, the depart-ment got a bad reputation and had to change its name for PR reasons, kind of like when Russia's NKVD changed its name to the KGB. "Oh, you're right, comrade, that makes it something *completely* different."

Did I mention that I feel strongly about this?

I THOUGHT I WAS A COPYWRITER!!

So here you have a de-partment that was originally created, I suppose, to deal with some particular inefficiency or aggravation and yet in our nation's business culture has come to *personify* inefficiency and aggravation. The Germans (speaking of efficiency) have a special word for this sort of thing: *verschlimmbessern*—to make something worse by trying to make it better. More literally translated it means "to fix something more broken."

Once they're institutionalized, factions within the company always have the trappings of legitimacy. HR, with its body of codes and conventions and accepted practices, has the appearance of being the true and right way of keeping all the little worker-chicks gathered safely under the corporate mother hen's protective wing, as it were. Yet the overwhelming experience of people who actually have to deal with HR is that *it doesn't work.* Most management structures are like that. A managerial caste, because it is essentially divorced from the functions that define the organization's true reason for being, will not produce what it ostensibly was put there to produce: a better, more efficient company. It will feed itself.

People keep trying to find the elixir that will transform the sow's ear of self-perpetuating corporate management into the silk purse of some quality-and-efficiency-producing dynamo. Just look at the management fads of the past few years. Attila the Hun was big a while back. These days the Dalai Lama seems to be in vogue, although Machiavelli has continued to hold his own, too. Sharks have had their day in the sun, as have SEALs (the U.S. Navy commando kind). I heard a lot about reengineering for a while but wonder now if it has been, itself, reengineered. Charismatic leadership is a current craze, which is great if you've got a personality like Herb Kelleher at Southwest Airlines, but it makes me wonder if the less dynamic of us must somehow undergo a personality transplant if we want to be great leaders and, if so, who will be the donor.

Joanne Ciulla, a former Fellow at Wharton and Harvard, has written a book, *The Working Life* (Times Books, 2000), that deals with, among other things, these sorts of theories for pumping up your managerial muscles. Their common goal, Ciulla suggests, is to help the powers that be squeeze more work out of their employees without the inconvenience of having to actually pay them more money. The reason all the tricks come up short is—surprise!—people are too smart to buy the BS that management tries to sell them.

The wall between the Managers and the Others justifies every other factional barrier in the organization. If you're not all in this together—producing ads or marketing widgets or healing the sick or whatever your organization was put there to do—then you simply won't get what you want out of your people, no matter what you call the department in charge.

"You Know, George, This Is Nothing That a Good Bloodletting Won't Cure"

I'm not impressed by elaborately articulated management methods. Just because it's got a lot of cool terminology, impressive charts, and enthusiastic adherents behind it, that doesn't necessarily mean it isn't a complete crock. Don't waste your time on any approach to leadership that doesn't actively address the factional barriers that disrupt the flow of communication, your company's lifeblood.

Next time you reach for a new method that's the "obvious" answer to your company's organizational ills, consider the example of a therapy that centuries of top medical professionals considered to be just the ticket for everything from fevers to hernias: bloodletting. An intricate "science" backed up the practice, and any physician worth his salt knew just when to reach for his handy flume, lancet, and scarificator (or, if he wanted to go organic, his jar of leeches) and open the patient up for a good healthy bleeding. One to four pints was typical. And you didn't get a little cup of OJ afterwards, either.

Bloodletting was considered a marvelous gift to the healing arts. One Henry Clutterbuck, M.D., in his definitive 1840 work, *On the Proper Administration of Blood-Letting, for the Prevention and Cure of Disease,* effused that "its good effects, when properly administered, are, in most cases, so immediate and striking as not to be mistaken. . . . In short, blood-letting is a remedy which, when judiciously employed, it is hardly possible to estimate too highly." Nobody seemed particularly bothered that patients had a funny habit of, well, dying. Our own George Washington, suffering from a sore throat, died after being drained of nine pints in 24 hours.

Of course, this ignorant practice fell from favor long ago, right? Well, not really. A noted doctor and medical textbook author named Sir William Osler was still recommending it well into the twentieth century. It just goes to show yet again that once enough people have invested enough money, ego, and reputation in a particular point of view, it can take more than just a huge weight of contrary evidence to kill it off. In fact, bloodletting persists to this very day. If you fall ill while visiting New Delhi, a street phlebotomist will be happy to drain off the impure blood for you. No matter how long ago a practice was proved manifestly bogus, there's always some sucker still willing to give it another whirl: Maybe it'll work *this* time.

Traditionally, a bleeding session ceased as soon as the patient started feeling faint. In this regard, bloodletting was superior to a lot of our current management setups, which continue sapping the energy out of the organization indefinitely. Naturally, though, scrupulous leaders have no intention of doing such a thing. That's why they'll be careful to implement only the most reputable and scientifically justified practices. Just like Dr. Clutterbuck.

PASS ME THE OCCAM'S RAZOR, PLEASE

> *Pluralitas non est ponenda sine necessitate.*
> —William of Occam (fourteenth century)

> *Keep it simple, stupid.*
> —Late-twentieth-century translation

Back in college, my advertising design teacher, Herschel Levit, used to symbolically thump extraneous elements in the designs his students turned in (a story I'll tell you in Chapter 5). As I watched him do that I didn't know that I was learning one of the great principles of medieval philosophy. It's called Occam's razor, but for me it could just as well be named Levit's finger: "Plurality should not be posited without necessity."

Einstein, typically, summed up the idea with a much breezier sound bite: "Everything should be made as simple as possible, but not simpler."

Would that we stropped that old razor and aggressively took it to our companies. As business leaders, we should be figuring out ways to get rid of hierarchy and division, not ways to do them differently. We need only enough administrative involvement to provide an orderly framework within which the tribes in our companies can do what they're gifted to do and then be properly compensated for it.

Our products and markets and technologies are so complicated, it's natural to think we need complicated ways of dealing with them. Often, however, the opposite is true. *People* are so good at handling complexity that the systems and procedures we strap them with just get in their way. Xerox learned this when they found that all their efforts to systematically outline repair processes for their copiers were less effective than letting their technical people swap repair tips over lunch.

Departmental lines, ladders of command, "proper channels," chapter-and-verse procedural rules, backside-covering documentation—these are largely a waste of good energy. Design your company the way Herschel Levit taught me to design ads. Start with a goal and a blank sheet of paper. Add elements in number and proportion as needed to further the goal. And then, when adding one more element

DILBERT®
by Scott Adams

Needless plurality in action.
DILBERT REPRINTED BY PERMISSION OF UNITED FEATURE SYN-DICATE, INC.

would diminish and not enhance the purpose of the design, *quit adding more stuff.*

Running an organization is one activity in which "What's the *least* I can do?" is a perfectly proper question.

Some Policies Need Term Limits

Every hour, in a tower overlooking the old town square of Krakow, Poland, a trumpeter dressed in medieval garb opens a window and plays a stirring fanfare. The bright, clear notes ringing off the roofs of the old town are like echoes from the sixteenth century. Tourists on the square stop and listen, transported. Then abruptly, right in the middle of the piece — right in the middle of a *note* — the trumpeter suddenly just quits, choking off the music with an inelegant honk. Performance over, window closed, just like that.

It's so startling, first-time listeners on the plaza blink for a moment or two and look at one another with mystified expressions. "It sounded like the guy got *shot,*" someone will say. Which, as a matter of fact, is precisely what happened one day over 400 years ago. A trumpeter playing the very same fanfare was shot — *hissss, THUNK.* An arrow, right through the throat in midnote. (Tough audience, apparently.) And so every day since, his successors have been playing it exactly as he did as a memorial gesture.

It's a peculiar tradition, but charming. And at least the Krakow trumpeters know *why* they play the tune that way. Companies, on the other hand, often have practices that are every bit as odd, almost as old, and a lot less quaint, and which they continue without really seeming to know why — vestiges of some long-ago event but without the commemorative purpose. Policies that have long since outlived their usefulness (if they had any usefulness in the first place) continue to be venerated simply because they issued from Important Personages, usually people so high in the tower that not even a well-aimed arrow could reach them.

An acquaintance who works in sales and travels a lot for his employer told me this story. Once, during a period of corporate belt-tightening, a company kahuna voiced some concern about travel expenses, leading a certain high-level bureaucrat, with typical overreactive zeal, to issue a directive: Henceforth all travelers on company business would be required to take the cheapest available flight. On many routes, the cheapest flight was, of course, the red-eye, but that was just fine with the company since flying in overnight for an early sales call had the added benefit of eliminating the need for a hotel room and dinner the night before.

My friend and his traveling colleagues appealed (through proper channels, of course), pointing out that arriving for a meeting rumpled and exhausted was hardly an effective selling strategy. Plus, on the other end of the day, they often had to kill hours waiting for their cheap flight home instead of taking a more convenient one — not the most efficient use of a salesperson's time, and costly in terms of time away from the family, besides. Didn't matter. "The policy clearly states," came the reply, "that you must take the cheapest flight." No mitigating factors were stated in the policy, nor were any seriously considered since the bureaucrats enforcing it didn't travel.

"Fly cheap." In the company's culture of tribalism and constricted communication, rescinding that edict would be about as simple as trying to repeal the Bill of Rights. And so, long after the corporate bigwigs (who, by the way, never saw the travel policy as applying to *them*) eased up on the austerity program, the poor salespeople were still schlepping around the country with bags under their eyes the size of sample cases.

Tribalized companies are marked by uncritical, unbending acceptance of every policy and procedure, even when new information becomes available or new circumstances arise to render a previous management decision invalid or out of date. They think in terms of regulations. They're scrupulous about writing them down. And, as a Benedictine monk told author Kathleen Norris, the problem with written rules is that somebody is going to want to enforce them.

It's one thing if a rule ended up on the books as some manager's knee-jerk reaction to an obscure event, like the law in San Antonio that made it illegal to urinate on the Alamo (meaning, presumably, that it would be okay to let 'er rip on the Gunter Hotel next door). You can live with those regulatory oddities. But most company policies are more sweeping. Like the travel policy my friend was stuck with, they affect you day in and day out, either abetting you in your work or, more often, slowing you down.

The more open your organization is, the more plainly you can view your procedures through the lens of common sense and get rid of the ones that aren't working. For years at The Richards Group we had a dress code. Dress *guideline* might be the better term. The more-or-less-official statement said, "Dress like you're going to the bank for an eighty-thousand-dollar loan," so it left quite a bit of room for personal interpretation. But the fact that we had an apparel policy of any sort made us, in some people's minds, likely candidates for the title of America's Spookiest Ad Agency. "Their creatives wear ties? What's next, '666' tattoos?"

We all knew our dress code was unusual, but that was okay because we had a good reason for starting it. Our largest client was MBank, the account that had launched us into the agency business in the first place, and in our best nontribalized fashion we and our clients felt free to make ourselves right at home in each other's offices. Bankers were always in the agency. Our folks were at the bank daily. One of our copywriters, John Stone, actually kept an office there.

So we, the agency people, chose to adapt ourselves to our client's culture. The most conservative bank president from a West Texas branch could walk into the agency for the first time and feel that he was among right-thinking businesspeople not *all* that different from himself, even if some of our fashion choices might get you some slightly sideways looks in San Angelo. Besides, so many of us were running to the bank all the time, it didn't make sense to keep an extra set of bank-meeting clothes at the office. We'd be changing costumes constantly. So the dress code was definitely a "when in Rome" sort of decision. It *removed* little hurdles and distractions.

But then circumstances changed. MBank went away. The whole casual Friday thing was getting started, to be followed by casual Monday through Thursday. There was no reason for our "eighty-thousand-dollar loan" guideline anymore. We were known for it, sure, but it certainly wasn't central to who we are. So we just quit. And now I get kind of grumpy on those rare occasions when I have to wear a suit someplace.

And that's the end. We had a dress code, and then we didn't. Which is a really boring ending to the story, I know, but isn't that really how little procedural matters should be—simple, undemanding of much time and attention, and just kind of *over* when they're over? I think so, too. And that's one reason that I'm comfortable, regardless of the day's attire, without bureaucrats keeping a bunch of out-of-date policies on artificial life support.

POISONOUS TOADS AND POLICY MANUALS

"The longest-lasting effect of a thing is usually not the announced or intended effect." Thus reads the Law of Unintended Consequences. It is more binding on business than anything even OSHA or the EPA has dreamed up. And it applies especially well to control measures insti-tuted by management and institutionalized through written policy.

A certain company, on a campaign to eliminate fruitless spending, mandated the use of cheaper toilet paper. Because the cheap paper was less reliable than the good stuff, people used twice as much—wiping out, as it were, the intended savings. Plus there were more plumbing clogs and, therefore, higher maintenance costs.

It probably took no more than a day or two for the consequences of the cheap-TP policy to become apparent. But the fact that cheap toilet paper was already a matter of official policy meant that the consequences couldn't be dealt with in a simple, commonsense way: Just change back to the other paper. Management, having invested ego and reputation by committing the policy to writing, required iron-clad documentation that the policy had failed. The crummy paper remained in use for months, with higher overall costs the entire time, so sufficient data could be gathered for a proper toilet-paper report. Good grief.

When you write rules, draw departmental lines, try to shape the organism of the company through force of law, you never know what you're *really* doing. Splitting an ad agency, for example, into separate departments for account management, creative, print production, and so on, is *supposed* to produce efficiency, a more manageable structure. It turns out to be the death of efficiency.

Why gamble with imposing a bunch of control measures on your organization, activities that have nothing directly to do with the company's vocation? You're not going to like a lot of the results. And who needs the distraction anyway? It's hard enough to think through the possible consequences of our legitimate projects.

Take the civic-minded Nashville radio station that joined forces with the city police department to give away tickets to see the Tennessee Titans in Super Bowl XXXIV. Huge local interest, nice PR for the PD—sounds good. So here was the promotion. The station announced that somewhere in Nashville, a uniformed officer had two Super Bowl tickets, free for the asking. The idea, obviously, was to initiate lots of friendly contact between the gendarmes and the citizenry.

But what a miscalculation. The city went bonkers. Fans' cars were chasing police cruisers through the streets. Pedestrians were dashing through traffic to chase cops, some of whom hadn't even been told about the promotion. The station immediately called off the giveaway, but it took a while to quell the mayhem. The promotion, said a police spokesman, looked good on paper. That's always the problem. *Everything* looks good on paper.

Such was the case with one of the more famous contemporary examples of the Law of Unintended Consequences in action. It's a fitting parable, I believe, for the trouble we can cause with our attempts at hard-and-fast management controls.

Much of eastern Australia today is infested with thousands of grotesque, four-pound monsters called cane toads. Roughly the size and around double the weight of a can of Foster's Lager, you see them along roadways by the hundreds. They are equally at home in towns and cities and in the bush. People sometimes find them raiding catfood dishes on porches and patios. They're a scourge. The toads' bumpy skin secretes a powerful toxin that makes them unpalatable to any would-be predators. Their only natural enemy in the area is the motorcar.

Cane toads are a living, breathing, poison-oozing management initiative. In the 1930s the government brought them to Australia from their native Central America to control the cane grubs that were endangering the sugar crop. The authorities were unaware that while cane toads would eat birds, bugs, small mammals, and other amphibians, they wouldn't eat the cane grubs. In other words, the toads did nothing for the problem they were introduced to solve and, thanks to their talent for reproduction, have become a problem far worse than the grubs ever were. But it sure looked good on paper.

Dealing with the consequences of this attempt at management has been a seven-decade job, with no end in sight. So severe is the cane toad plague that the government recently considered importing a *deadly toad virus* from Venezuela. Doesn't *that* sound like a great idea. Fortunately, they did a little checking this time and found that the virus was also likely to make certain native frogs croak, so to speak. That was enough to dissuade them.

And that much, at least, is encouraging. Apparently those particular managers have learned that sometimes what you think is a problem isn't half as bad as how you try to solve it.

SHAKESPEARE WOULD BE FLATTERED (TILL HE HAD TO WASH THE POOP OFF HIS CAR)

> *The past can scarcely tell us what we ought to do, but it can tell us what we ought to avoid.*
>
> —José Ortega y Gasset

As a final caution on the subject of management actions that create a need for further management, let us recall the late-winter morning in 1890 when a New Yorker named Eugene Schieffelin walked joyfully into Central Park and, with noble intent and deep sentiment, performed an act of altruism that plagues us all to this day.

Mr. Schieffelin was an eccentric manufacturer of pharmaceuticals (his company was the predecessor of today's Schieffelin and Somerset, the liquor importer), and in the ample leisure hours his means afforded him, he indulged a special penchant for Shakespeare. Specifically, he was fond of the birds that are so often mentioned in the Bard's works—43 species by one count—so fond, in fact, that he purposed to bless the American continent with every single one of them. His earlier importations of bullfinches, nightingales, and skylarks had failed to establish breeding populations. But on March 6, 1890, he released into the chilly Manhattan air a species that would succeed beyond his wildest nightmares.

That day, Eugene Schieffelin gave us the starling.

Shakespeare mentions the starling just once, in a line spoken by Hotspur in *Henry IV* ("Nay, I'll have a starling shall be taught to speak nothing but 'Mortimer' . . ."). Accounts differ as to how many birds Schieffelin had shipped from England to release in the park that day— 100 seems to be about right—but nobody disputes the number of their descendants. There are at least 200 million starlings in North America today.

It didn't take long for Schieffelin's modest initiative to take wing. The first pairs of his birds nested in Manhattan that spring. A year later they had found Staten Island. By the eighth year starlings had gone suburban and were living in Connecticut. And by the late 1930s their offspring were pooping on cars all the way to Vancouver. Starlings compete with bluebirds for nesting sites, and usually win. They've driven out nice birdies like northern flickers, redheaded woodpeckers, and great crested flycatchers. And if you happen to live in a neighborhood they fancy as a roosting spot, they make you feel like you're living in a Hitchcock movie. I know of hotels and office parks that fire cannons (blanks, of course) at sunset to shoo off the nasty, noisy hordes of starlings.

Poor, dumb Eugene Schieffelin had no inkling that he was unleashing a pestilence upon us that March morning. He wasn't even trying to exercise some sort of control, as the cane toad people had been. He was just trying to be *nice,* trying to extend to our country a little bit of European civilization in the form of a harmless bird (and, judging by what Hotspur said, a bird that can *talk,* to boot!). His motives, one has to think, were pure and good. He simply wasn't able to project all the consequences.

And neither can we as business leaders when we institute new policies in our companies. Less is always best. It pays to take a very good, very hard look at any new initiative, however well intended it may be, and judge whether it just might be superfluous, lest we one day find it dropping little surprises all over us.

Who Is Stan Richards, and Where Did He Get This Stuff?

A brief history of The Richards Group and how its open workplace got to be that way.

EVERYTHING I NEEDED FOR BUSINESS I LEARNED IN ARTSY-FARTSY DESIGN SCHOOL

At this point you might want to know a little of my personal history and that of my company. If not, fine. By all means, jump right ahead to the next chapter. I should warn you, though, that if you do skip ahead you'll miss some important principles of doing business without tribalism and fear (and doors), and some insight into how you might put the principles into practice. So here is some historical perspective.

One fact may explain as well as anything why my company has developed along unconventional lines. I'm still working my first job out of college.

Well, first and third. There was one brief and exceedingly miserable period at another agency. (It was the kind of experience I'd like to forget, except that the hard-earned lessons were too valuable. It taught me exactly what I wouldn't want my own company to be like, ever. I'll get to that.) At the end of my short sojourn on the Dark Side, I went back to doing exactly what I had been doing before: working on my own at what would eventually become The Richards Group.

It had started as almost a whim, an impulsive decision to settle in Dallas and hang out my designer's shingle (exquisitely lettered, of course) instead of continuing west to L.A., where I had been sure destiny was calling me. I was 20 years old, fresh out of Pratt Institute in Brooklyn, when I landed at Dallas Love Field with a suitcase full of clothes and a portfolio bulging with my student work. *I* was bulging, too—bulging with confidence. Okay, maybe it was cockiness I was bulging with, but at 20 aren't you supposed to be a little cocky?

A fair amount of confidence was, I suppose, justified. I had just graduated near the top of my class from one of the country's premier design schools, and the samples in my portfolio represented the best work I had done there under the tutelage of some of the top professionals in their fields, in New York or anywhere else. Surely, I thought, that black leather portfolio case represented my ticket to the top of the graphic design business.

Looking back, I always approached art with a lot of confidence. For that I can thank my mother, Ruth. She was my first great career influence. Early in life, every kid is an artist, an artesian well of creativity, but most of the flow gets stanched by the time the kid is seven or so. Most of the time grown-ups seem all too happy to throw stones down the well—always for the kid's own good, of course—subtly letting you know how it *should* be done, praising the times when you color inside the lines. Kids do what they get rewarded for. It doesn't take long to turn a little artist into a little conformist. My mother wasn't like that. To her, every drawing I did was precious.

We lived in Philadelphia, where my dad was a bartender. For all I know, there might have been 100,000 other little kids in that city with more talent than I had. But that didn't matter. Fed by my mother's praise, I drew more and more until—what do you know—I actually started to get pretty good. By age 10 I was eagerly attending painting classes every Saturday near our home. By the time I got to high school, I already had my eye turned toward a career in art.

My exposure to the art world up to now had been in the fine arts. Fortunately, in high school I discovered that there was such a thing as *commercial* art, and for the first time I realized that I didn't have to be a gallery artist to have a career in art. And to me *that* was fine. The image of the noble, starving artist shivering in his drafty garret had never held much romance for me. Now I knew how to be an artist and still— at least theoretically—pay the heating bills.

As college time drew near, I looked at all the best art and design schools in the Northeast: Cooper Union, Rhode Island School of Design, the Philadelphia Museum School, Pratt. They all had a lot to offer, but in the end I chose Pratt because they offered one thing that none of the others could match. They had a basketball team. And basketball was my other passion, second only to art.

I arrived in New York in the late summer of 1950 and plunged into a creative hotbed like I had never seen. Pratt attracted a lot of good kids— *really* good kids—many of whom were graduates of New York's legendary High School of Music and Art, the school of *Fame* fame. Flakes, bohemians, scrappy kids off the streets of the Bronx and Staten Island—they didn't make for the most conventional-looking student body in the world. Nobody would be mistaken for Donald O'Connor in those movies with Francis the Talking Mule. But that didn't matter, just like it doesn't matter in my company today. This crowd had talent in spades; that was clear. If I had been the star art student in high school on the strength of my mother's early encouragement and a certain amount of native ability, well, here, I quickly learned, I was going to have to add something else to those qualifications if I was going to stand out. I was going to have to work my tail off.

Mine was the last class ever in Pratt's three-year program at the end of which you'd get, not a bachelor's degree, but a certificate. The following year Pratt began its four-year bachelor's program. My fellow freshmen and I enrolled in exactly two general education courses: freshman English and art history. That was it. Everything else we studied for the next three years was direct preparation for our profession as art directors, graphic designers, interior designers, illustrators, what have you.

People are always surprised when they find out that the head of one of the largest independent ad agencies in the country has no degree. But the fact is, artsy-fartsy design school ended up teaching me everything I've needed as an entrepreneur and agency owner. The same principles that apply to the craft of advertising work equally as well for managing a company—if you know how to apply them.

When I went to design school, the old (and, in my opinion, well-reasoned) tradition of master and apprentice had more influence in the advertising business than it does today. You didn't have to have a university degree on your resume to qualify for an agency job. Your portfolio contained your credentials. In fact, ours is one of the few industries left where the work in your book far outweighs the GPA on your transcript—or should. A broad and in-depth education is important, of course, and these days a university is often the best place to get it. But it's not the only place. To this day I would have no qualms about hiring a young writer or art director who doesn't have a degree—if the person could show me a killer book.

Pratt, like most of the best advertising and design schools today, had very much a workshop mentality. You didn't just sit listening to the masters, then go off and finish assignments on your own. Interaction with your fellow apprentices was a vital part of the process—and a part of my company's culture today that we work very hard to maintain. If the caliber of my fellow students was slightly intimidating, it was more than slightly exhilarating. I was surrounded by incredible talent. For example, I soon hit it off with a couple of other new guys, who became my best friends throughout school.

One was a kid from New York who, like me, was aiming for an advertising career. His name was Lenny Sirowitz. The other was a lanky New Yorker who came to Pratt to study design, emigrated into photography, and later traded his still cameras for the motion-picture kind. His name was Steve Horn, and he was to become my roommate for our last two years of school. So there we were, three 17- or 18-year-old guys starting college together, and today all three of us are in the Art Directors' Hall of Fame. That's how good that freshman class was.

Pratt was extremely competitive, but it was also extremely supportive. You could count on other students to help you push your work and make it better—again, that workshop atmosphere we strive for at The Richards Group. Working with my peers, showing them my work, and putting in my two cents' worth on theirs, I learned the inestimable value of freely offering up your babies to constructive criticism.

And then there were the teachers. James Brooks, the great abstract expressionist, was one. Through what the art history textbooks call his "dynamic interaction" with artists like Pollock and de Kooning, as well as through his own painting, Brooks had a profound effect on twentieth-century art. You can see his work in museums all over the world—big, energetic canvases with flowing figures that exude spontaneity and freedom from convention. Yet, surprisingly, at Pratt Brooks taught the most tedious and, in ways, tradition-bound subject in the whole school: lettering. Brooks had, in fact, worked as a commercial letterer back in the 1920s. So the real surprise may be that he found his way to abstract painting. Of course, after studying lettering with him, I can see why he needed the outlet.

The disciplines he taught have all but disappeared from advertising education today. I once heard a young art director lament, "My life would be great if I didn't have to deal with type." It can be fatiguing, sure, but as I told that young AD, I've worked on thousands of ads over the years and have yet to do a single one that didn't involve typography. Maybe it was just the copyright line, but it was typography. When we hire new ADs at The Richards Group, we have to teach them letterspacing, word spacing, the whole theory of lettering. Even with the best computers and graphics software money can buy, good typography still isn't something you can get from a pulldown menu.

Brooks was a master. While his friend Jackson Pollock was punching holes in paint cans and swinging them from ropes, the reticent, studious Brooks was teaching us things like how to create a letter form, starting with pencil, and eventually, after an excruciatingly detailed process, finishing it with a crow quill pen. Everything was done by hand, and everything had to be perfect. We learned how to draw, say, a Bodoni letter and learned why it looked the way it did. We learned how to enhance the form but stay in the character of the font. And we learned, most of all, sheer nose-to-the-grindstone discipline. There was no other way to do this stuff. Imagine a sample of Spencerian script—all curves, not a straight line in sight. It might take 30 hours to draw. And if it's not perfect, it will take 30 hours to fix. The result may look free-flowing and spontaneous, like Brooks's canvases, but make no mistake, the real fluid in every fluid stroke is sweat.

It's little wonder that I remember James Brooks as the man who taught me true respect for craft. In an environment like his class, you learn very quickly that talent alone can't do the job. It takes tremendous discipline to excel in this business. You learn that discipline can often overcome a shortage of talent but that talent can never, for very long, overcome a shortage of discipline.

At the start of my second year at Pratt, when I declared my major emphasis, advertising design, I met the man who was to become the most influential figure in my life from that point forward, right up till today.

I think that most of us with successful careers, whatever our field may be, can trace our success back to one person who had a deep, abiding influence. We all stand on somebody's shoulders. I stand on Herschel Levit's. Levit taught advertising design. At least the syllabus *said* it was advertising design. Sometimes it seemed he was teaching anything *but* that. My first day in his class was completely mystifying, totally disorienting. And utterly life-changing.

I knew going in that he was going to be, in all likelihood, the toughest instructor I would have at Pratt. That was his reputation. But nothing I had heard prepared me for that first session. He began by calling roll. So far, so good. Then, motioning for us to follow, he walked out of the studio classroom and down to the institute's auditorium. There, he sat down at the piano and for the next two hours delivered a detailed exegesis of Arnold Schoenberg's 12-tone system of musical composition. No scene-setting, no context, just this out-of-left-field seminar accompanied by the most bizarre, atonal, cacophonous music (if you could call it music) that I had ever heard.

When you've had a little high school music appreciation, a brief introduction to Bach and Mozart and Beethoven and Mahler—*maybe* Mahler—that first exposure to Schoenberg is like sonic assault and battery. There's no way to relate to it. Our ears were brutalized as Levit dissected the 12-tone system as if he were speaking to a class of graduate students in music. Then, after two hours, he turned from the piano and casually said, "All right, see you next week." We were, to say the least, baffled. Thank goodness nobody said, "Uh, Mr. Levit, aren't you going to give homework?"

That session in the auditorium and the two years of Herschel Levit's classes that followed changed me. He was the teacher who opened my mind. While teaching us advertising design (yes, he did get around to that), he would allude to literature, music, dance. He taught us—*showed* us—not to narrowly pursue our craft without serious respect for the other arts. From him I learned the importance of listening to jazz, attending the ballet, debating the motivation of Rothko and Barnett Newman. Eventually it dawned on me that even the Schoenberg seminar had a point: that even the most universally familiar elements, like the notes we've heard since our mommas' first lullaby, can be rethought and presented in startling new ways. You may never directly apply all of these influences to advertising, he led us to understand, but let it all seep into your head where, somehow, it will shape you and your work.

Levit was, indeed, one tough instructor. Class time often centered around a critique of our rough layouts. We'd pin our pencil sketches up on the walls of the studio and he would stroll around, offering praise and criticism. Bad work would be forgiven, if you had really tried. But if you hadn't, watch out. If he spotted a halfhearted effort, Levit would unpin it from the wall, turn, and tear it in half without a word.

Tough. But he was also funny. He used humor to wrap velvet around the big iron hammer that would demolish your work when it was weak, and your ego, if you had it coming. One of his favorite mannerisms was aimed at silly ornamentation and other extraneous elements in layouts. Levit, a modernist, hated anything superfluous. He wanted simplicity, and he'd make the point abundantly clear by leaning up close to the layout, briskly thumping the offending, nonessential element with his middle finger and pretending to brush it right off the paper. Squint, thump, brush. No words spoken. And none needed. You might have pinned up your layout feeling like one of the giants of design, but after the Levit Thump you'd feel about as tall as Toulouse-Lautrec. When critiquing work at The Richards Group, I sometimes borrow the thump technique as my silent tribute to my greatest teacher.

I owe Herschel Levit a tremendous debt. He kept me from becoming a technician and made me a designer. And he did something else at least as important. He taught me an abiding distaste for anything extraneous—and not just in graphic design, either. In all my practices, business and personal, I try to identify what is nonessential, give it a good solid thump, and brush it away.

I can scarcely imagine a better rehearsal for a life in advertising than the rich and intensely demanding three years Pratt gave me. Here, in brief, is what I learned there—not conventional B-school skill sets but principles that nevertheless prepared me well to be not only a designer but a business builder.

1. How people look doesn't count for much. How they perform does.
2. Competition and cooperation can mix just fine. Talented people can help push each other's work even while they're competing for the top honors. There can be honor in rivalry. You do your best work in formidable company.

3. Discipline matters more than talent. Time and again, at Pratt and in my own agency, I've seen a strongly ingrained work ethic out-perform pure inborn talent. A lot of the people who get credit as being most creative are really just the most disciplined workers.
4. Craft counts. Time you invest up front is time you'll save on the back end.
5. Extraneous stuff must go. To me, this is the cardinal principle of management. Simplify, simplify, simplify.
6. To the creative mind, nothing is irrelevant. Nursery rhymes, Bach cantatas, rap, rockabillly, Chilean folk music, Korn, the hum of fluorescent lights—dump 'em all in the hopper. It's all grist for your creative mill.

Landing in Dallas

After graduation from Pratt, I packed my belongings, said goodbye to my parents and friends and teachers, stepped into a New York taxi, and headed off on the first leg of my big move to California, where destiny awaited. While the cab made its way through Brooklyn and Queens, I thought about how exciting it was going to be to start my new job, working for Saul Bass. The groundbreaking designer/filmmaker had set up shop in Los Angeles a few years earlier and by now, the spring of 1953, was about to become famous for single-handedly reinventing the art of the motion picture title sequence. His first great title, for Otto Preminger's *Carmen Jones,* wouldn't come out till the next year, but I had known his graphic design work for a long time. He was a fixture in the award annuals and trade magazines, producing the most exciting graphic design in the country—at least the most exciting outside New York, where three years had been enough for me. Working for Bass was any 20-year-old designer's dream job. There *was* one minor detail, though. Saul Bass had no idea I was coming.

This didn't bother me in the least. There really had been no need to write, introduce myself, and inquire about the availability of a position. I had been one of the top students at Pratt Institute, for heaven's sake. My portfolio was stuffed with leading-edge work. Why, I had even been selected by the faculty and my fellow students to design the latest Pratt yearbook, the highest honor in the whole school. (It also gave my portfolio a most impressive weight!)

So naturally Saul—as I knew he would want me to call him—would hire me. All I had to do was show up and go through the, I suppose, necessary formality of an interview. Simple! Looking out the car window at the grimy, gray building fronts, I smiled, thinking about how living near the Pacific would certainly be a welcome change.

Of course, it wouldn't hurt to have a few practice interviews beforehand, just to stay sharp. I wanted to make the best possible impression on my would-be new employer. That's why I had decided that instead of flying directly to L.A., I'd stop over in Dallas. I had never visited Texas, wanted to see some of the sights, and figured Dallas would be as good a place as any to spend a few days showing my book around before flying off into the sunset and a shining future in the Promised Land of the West Coast. And so, I boarded a plane at LaGuardia and a few minutes later was climbing out over the gleaming towers of Manhattan, across the Hudson River, and off to Dallas, Texas, population 432,927. After arriving at Love Field I found my way downtown, checked into the Y, and started looking for places to interview.

I knew only one name in Dallas, but it was a good one: Neiman Marcus. Their in-house creative department turned out some pretty tasty retail work. I was familiar with some of it because they often hired top illustrators and photographers, whose work I followed.

Now, in retrospect, I wonder if I would have even bothered stopping in Dallas if Neiman's hadn't been there. I had never, to my knowledge, seen any other advertising or design from Texas (not counting the King Ranch brand on the rumps of steers in Western movies). But the presence of Neiman Marcus was enough to suggest that there must be a design *community* in Dallas—other good practitioners I could meet. There wasn't, as it turned out. Not yet. But the work produced by that one in-house department was enough to legitimize the whole city in my eyes.

Have you noticed how many times a city has gained a reputation as a creative center simply because one brave, lonely, determined individual or firm finds a way, against all odds, to do national-caliber work there? All it takes is one person, one place, doing good work to change everything in a town. Chick McKinney put Raleigh on the map. Richmond had Dave Martin. Ron Anderson and Tom McElligott birthed the incredible advertising renaissance of Minneapolis. I've gotten a lot of credit for Dallas and the Southwest. But I might not have ever landed here if it weren't for Stanley Marcus and the standard he established. There might not have been a design community here, but if there was Neiman's, there was hope.

So I called them and was put in touch with a creative director named Art Shipman. Sure, he said, he'd be happy to see me. I headed over to their retail palace on Commerce Street. Art leafed through my samples, which were mostly posters with a definite Euro/minimalist flavor, as was the style of the day in New York. He liked what he saw. Didn't have a job to offer, but he was quite positive about my prospects and urged me to keep interviewing around town.

Encouraged by the reception at Neiman's, I started making the rounds of the local ad agencies. It didn't take long to realize that where the level of work being done in Dallas was concerned, Neiman's sat up on a mesa all by itself and everybody else in town was way down on the valley floor. In 1953, "Big D" definitely did not stand for Design. This became clear at my very next interview. It was with the creative director of an agency that was pretty successful at the time, but went on before long to prove the dictum of cowboy poet and voice-over talent Baxter Black that ad agencies generally have the life span of a tanning salon.

As I walked into the CD's office, an ad displayed on the wall caught my attention. At the top it had two black-and-white illustrations. On the left was an eye. On the right was a human foot. They were a little spooky-looking, like something from a medieval anatomy text or an ancient book about freemasonry. The ad, though, wasn't about secret rites. It was about corn pads. Below the illustrations was a headline: "Their Eyes Are on Your Feet." If this was the work he displayed on his wall, I didn't even want to see the stuff they weren't so proud of.

As you might expect, my interview with the corn pad creative direc-tor did not go swimmingly. Dallas was a bustling but still very provincial city, and this guy was of the old Yankee-go-home, we-don't-need-your-carpetbaggin'-kind-around-here school of thought. The mere fact that I had just arrived from Sodom-on-the-Hudson was two strikes against me. But I gave it the old college try. I outlined my background and my plans for going on to California and told him I was making the rounds of Dallas agencies to get some input from professionals (I said this with a straight face) about my book. "All righty," he said, stubbing out his Lucky Strike and reaching for a fresh one, "let's see what you've got." I passed the portfolio across the desk.

He didn't say much as he paged through my work. He squinted at the samples, taking occasional drags on his cigarette and now and then ask-ing encouraging questions like, "Now, what were you trying to do *here?*" I answered as earnestly as I could. Even as an idealistic 20-year-old I could see that there was no selling this guy on the aesthetic behind my work. Hopefully, he just wouldn't burn any holes in my layouts with that cigarette.

He closed the portfolio on the desk and folded his hands on top of it. "Young man," he said—and I just *loved* this because an older person calling you "young man" is like when the state trooper who just pulled you over calls you "Hoss"; you're about to get taken down a peg. "Young man," he said, "you told me you wanted some professional input." That was true, and I couldn't wait to go get some. "Well, my input to you is that this work here"—he patted the portfolio without unfolding his hands—"is junk. We don't need, uh, *design* like this in Dallas, nor anywhere else, for that matter." If I believed this pontiff of the prairie, my education, if you could call it that, had been a waste of time and money. And apparently his keen eye found me to be an incorrigible case because he suggested, not that I stick around and learn from the master, but that I learn an entirely new trade. Maybe the military. And whatever I did, Dallas was not really the place for me.

It's a good thing I was used to having people—*good* people—offer brutally honest appraisals of my work. I knew the difference between tough criticism offered in good faith to help make the work better and bitter criticism intended to strip the recipient of his dignity. So, fuming, but with dignity and layouts unscathed, I thanked Mr. Cornpad for his time and hit the streets again.

My first impulse was to phone the airline and find out when the next flight to L.A. was leaving. But, I thought, why let one jerk spoil an otherwise pleasant stopover? I liked what I had been seeing of the city and, with the one exception, everyone I had encountered, from the CD at Neiman Marcus to strangers in the corner coffee shop, had been wonderfully welcoming and helpful. Mr. Cornpad may have said, "Yankee go home," but everybody else seemed to say, "Make yourself at home." So I got directions (from another friendly stranger) and headed to my next interview.

To my everlasting gratitude, the interview was with Marvin Krieger. Marvin was creative director of Rogers & Smith, the biggest agency in town at the time. He was happy to meet with me, delighted that I had decided to stop over in his town. I told him my story about going to work for Saul Bass and showed him through the work in my portfolio, school yearbook and all. He was clearly pleased with what he saw and offered the highest level of encouragement as I presented the work. "Very, very nice . . . beautifully done . . . great idea."

"Stan," he said when we had gone through all the samples, "it's obvious I believe you're a gifted designer and this is top-notch work. It's fresh and different. To be honest, it's *too* different. Not for New York or for your Mr. Bass out in California, but it's just too different from what we do here. I'm sure you understand that." I did.

He continued. "Even if we had a slot for you, which we don't, but even if we did, I don't believe you'd be anything but frustrated at the kind of opportunities we could offer you." I agreed and started to thank him for being so generous with his time and encouragement, collect my samples, and go. But Marvin wasn't finished.

"Stan, we may not be ready for this kind of work yet, but I'll tell you something. This city is changing. We're not the little backwater we used to be. Dallas is going to come a long way. And I believe you could find a tremendous opportunity to grow with it if you'll set up shop here." Slightly startled, I sat up straighter in my chair. This was a completely new idea, opening my own graphic design practice. Marvin saw that he had gotten my attention.

"I won't lie to you, you'll probably have to struggle to stay here, till the market catches on to what you do. But you're a young guy, and you probably travel pretty light, don't you?" One suitcase back at the Y. That's pretty light, all right. "You won't be risking much to give it a whirl." And then he gave me the best closing line of any pitch I have ever heard in my life.

"If you stick it out," he said, "I believe you can do what Saul Bass has done—right here in Dallas."

Well, now. *This* was certainly an interesting concept. And in that moment, right there in Marvin Krieger's office, my dream began to change. Work for Saul Bass? Heck, I could *be* Saul Bass!

"You think about it," Marvin said, clapping a hand on my shoulder as he walked me to the elevator. "And let me know how I can help you."

Thinking about it didn't take long. To be honest, I think by the time the elevator doors closed between me and Marvin's smiling face, the deal was probably sealed. "Going down, sir?" the elevator operator asked. "Yes, please," I said. In fact, though, things for me have been headed up pretty much ever since. Within a few days, I had found a garage apartment, rented a one-room office in a crummy old building downtown, and become the (hopefully) up-and-coming new designer in, of all places, Dallas, Texas.

Marvin was right: The days ahead weren't the easiest. But that rather rash decision I made as a 20-year-old to settle here is, to this day, one of the best I've ever made.

Epilogue: The Day I Got to Be Saul Bass
Flash forward 15 years. It's now 1968. The graphic design practice that I started with Marvin Krieger's encouragement has grown into the prospering little firm of Stan Richards & Associates.

Saul Bass, meanwhile, survived the blow of not getting me on his staff and became the world's greatest designer of title sequences for movies, including *The Man with the Golden Arm, North by Northwest, Vertigo,* and *West Side Story.* Hitchcock fans still debate the extent of his involvement, but Bass also designed—and, depending on whom you talk to, maybe even shot—the shower sequence in *Psycho.*

Dallas being Dallas and not Hollywood, I haven't by 1968 gotten into the movie title business. However, as Marvin predicted, I have ridden a long wave of growth in the city and region and have built the elite creative outfit in town. We are a creative outsourcing firm, although in 1968 nobody is using that term yet. Agencies use us as an extension to, and in some cases as a replacement for, their own creative departments. It's a good deal for us. They handle most of the mundane assignments and use us when they really need to call in the Marines. We're having a great time, even without Janet Leigh in the shower.

Then, out of the blue, I get my first, and so far only, title-sequence job. And it's a doozy.

Our little studio's biggest client is Glenn Advertising. (The Glenn name is long gone, but the agency remains, having become the Dallas office of Bozell & Jacobs, then BJK&E, and eventually Temerlin McClain.) One of the guys there, Bob Berry (who will go on to become one of the principals of the Berry-Brown agency), has a buddy in the film business in L.A. He must be a pretty good buddy, too, because he calls Bob one day and offers him a juicy-sounding assignment. Would Glenn Advertising do the ads for a new picture that's scheduled for release in a few months? It's a film by George Roy Hill from a script by William Goldman—a Western and kind of unconventional, but should be pretty good. It's called *Butch Cassidy and the Sundance Kid.*

Not a bad entrée to the movie biz. Bob thinks about it for probably a millisecond and says yes, he thinks they could probably work that in. Then he calls me.

We dive enthusiastically into the project and within a few weeks have a bunch of ad comps ready to show. Bob flies to L.A. and presents them to the producers, who love the work. He calls us with the good news, and we get to work right away on the final artwork, grateful for our brush, however brief and however peripheral, with Hollywood glamour. We're working, remember, for Glenn, so it's an unbilled performance for Stan Richards & Associates. But we're not complaining. Even if the picture's a flop, we've got some nice work to show and a great story to tell.

A couple of days after Bob's presentation in California, I get a phone call. "Hello, Stan? This is Bill Goldman. I saw your ads for the

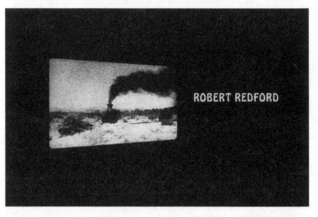

How many people can truly say that every movie they've ever worked on has been an Oscar winner? The title sequence for *Butch Cassidy and the Sundance Kid,* designed (in an unbilled performance) by Stan Richards & Associates.

film and really loved what you guys did." Wow. What a mensch (we talk this way in the film business) he is to take the time to call up the ad people and compliment us for our work on his movie. I'm impressed. But it's not just a social call.

"I've got a question for you," he says. "We're having a helluva time coming up with an opening title sequence." Hopefully he doesn't hear my chin hitting the desk. "Would you guys be interested in working on it?"

"Yes, sure, absolutely," I stammer, amazed that I'm being asked to bail the great William Goldman out of a creative problem.

Maybe you remember our solution: a flickering, sepia-toned film within a film, an early newsreel-style reenactment of the Hole in the Wall Gang holding up a train. Apparently the sequence works. At any rate, it doesn't keep the movie from winning four Academy Awards in 1970.

Despite the film's status as a bona fide classic, it is to this day the only title sequence I've done, my one big day in the Hollywood sun. But at least I can say that every movie I've ever worked on has been an Oscar winner. And not even Saul Bass can match that.

Setting Up Shop

My arrival on the Dallas business scene played like it was straight out of the chapter in *The Fountainhead* when Howard Roark, the idealistic young architect, rents a little office in a doggy old building, sets up a drawing board, and sets out to transform the state of his craft. There were a couple of key differences, though. Gary Cooper never portrayed me in a movie version. And unlike the Howard Roark character, I didn't have to take a job in a quarry but managed to drum up enough business to keep from starving.

My one-room office was downtown in an old commercial building called—how's this for originality?—the Commercial Building. The surroundings were as dull as the name. It had been built some decades earlier more for function than for its contribution to the city's skyline, and by the time I set up shop it was gimping along just ahead of the wrecking ball, smelling vaguely of dust, old floor sweep, and mimeograph fluid.

The Commercial Building did have one great virtue, however. It was cheap. As long as the elevator and men's room worked and I wasn't being brained by chunks of falling plaster, the ambience didn't matter that much anyway. I spent my hours there hunkered over the drawing board.

To this day I'm not big on fancy office space. The Richards Group offices today are nice, certainly. We're in a good building, and we tried to do something architecturally interesting with the space and furnish it well. But the emphasis is definitely on function and comfort. We're not into bird's-eye maple paneling or themed conference rooms or corporate sculpture collections.

Warren Bennis and Patricia Ward Biederman have noted the high incidence of ratty-looking offices among highly creative companies. "Someday," they write, "someone will write a book explaining why so many pioneering enterprises, including the Walt Disney Company, Hewlett-Packard, and Apple, were born in garages. . . . We can speculate on why great things are often accomplished in dull or tacky surroundings. Perhaps a bland or unattractive environment spurs creativity, functioning as an aesthetic blank slate that frees the mind to dream about what might be. Maybe a great view and chic décor are distractions and thus counterproductive when important work is being done. But the truth is that most people in Great Groups spend very little time thinking about their surroundings. They have wonderful tunnel vision."

I thought I was just being thrifty when I rented that first dumpy office. Turns out I was being brilliant.

In any case, I soon found sufficient freelance work to pay for the office, my garage apartment, and all the potato soup I could eat. Several of the small agencies in town sent regular projects my way, and I also worked directly with a few clients, mostly banks.

Texas must have had more banks per capita than any place on the planet. All the way up until the 1980s, state law forbade branch banking, a prohibition born of Texans' fierce independent streak and historic distrust of centralized power. As a result, every single banking office in the state was a separately chartered institution. Dallas had a handful of big banks downtown, where the old cotton, oil, and commercial money resided, and then dozens of smaller institutions all over town. The vast number of little banks were the lifeblood for a vast number of little advertising enterprises, including mine.

There hasn't been a time since when my company hasn't had a bank client. In fact, it was one of the large Dallas banks, Mercantile, that gave us their account in 1976, transforming The Richards Group from an outsourcing firm to a full-service agency.

But I'll come to all that. In 1953 and 1954, I was a hungry kid in my early 20s just starting to get a name around town for design like they hadn't seen around here before. My work started to catch on. I met another freelancer who was looking for office space, and I subleased half of mine to him. Some months I even had enough work to pass along some overflow to him.

It was too soon to think about actually hiring employees, and I didn't especially want to be a business owner yet anyway. I was having too much fun as a real, working designer; it was paying the bills. Still, as my name got out, people would call asking about jobs, and if, knowing there was no position available, they were still willing to come by, I was always happy to see them. After all, it was just that sort of interview that had led to my settling in Dallas. (We'll talk more about interviews, even with people whose work is dismal, in Chapter 5.)

Slowly my little freelance practice gathered steam. After two years I had produced some fairly prominent local work, won quite a few awards, gained a nice reputation. What looked like the big payoff came one morning in 1955 when the phone rang at my palatial world head-quarters in the Commercial Building.

It was Sam Bloom, whose 40-person Bloom Agency (now Publicis Dallas) was already one of the largest in town after just a couple of years in business. He had a proposition for me. Sam wanted to improve his agency's creative product, and he thought I was just the man to make it happen. If I would come to work for him as creative director, he would put me in charge of the agency's three-person art department and three-person copy department (the notion of creative teams hadn't found its way to Dallas yet), and he would compensate me in the amount of $12,000 a year.

Twelve . . . thousand . . . dollars. My eyes lost focus for a second, and all the strength drained out of my limbs. In 1955, $12,000 was a princely sum. The average per capita income in those days was a couple of thousand dollars a year.

"So, what do you think?" Sam asked. My mind went back to the previous evening's three-course meal—a bowl of potato soup and two glasses of soda.

"I think," I said, "you just got yourself a creative director." I was 22 years old.

And with that it was bye-bye, Commercial Building. And hello to one of the worst, and most valuable, lessons of my life.

CONFESSIONS OF A DYSFUNCTIONAL ADVERTISING MAN

The honeymoon was short.

I started in my big new position as creative director of the Bloom Agency on a Monday. By Wednesday I was in my first pitched battle with account service. By Friday I was sorry I had ever taken the job.

I have to blame my own youthful inexperience as well as judgment clouded by the blinding green fog of the huge salary offer I had snapped up so hastily. If I had been a little wiser and done my homework a little more thoroughly I would have realized what the new CD would be getting into: an agency totally, completely dominated by account people.

In my naïveté, I failed to understand how the ad world works. Some agencies are run by account people. If you're in creative, don't try doing anything daring (meaning, not seen a hundred times before) while you're there unless you happen to like the feeling of what someone called being bitten to death by ducks. Other agencies have creative people in charge. If you're a person with much sense of order and decorum—if, for example, you ever use the word "budget" in a serious context—then you had best hang on because your ride is going to be rough.

Silly me, I thought there might be some sort of balance to be had, maybe even a productive tension between two points of view. Turns out that was a fantasy. I could have just as plausibly decided to go off and live with hobbits. But whether I knew it at the time or not, I was gaining a resolve that I would use later as I tried to create an agency that *did* have balance, where the staff wouldn't be divided against each other, where nobody would be a second-class citizen, and where the product, great advertising, would depend on the contributions of every discipline in the company. Most of the time The Richards Group works pretty close to that ideal; we work together here. And, folks, it really ain't that hard.

But all that, as they used to say, would have to wait till after the war—tomorrow, when the world would be free. And right now, in the battle I had just gotten into, I wasn't free to pursue my utopian vision.

Even though I regretted the move to Bloom, I decided to stick it out. My feeling is that even if you really screw up and take a job you hate, unless your employer somehow reneges on his or her end of the deal, you ought to stay a while. Sam held up his end. He had promised me the CD position and a fat salary. Beyond that, he hadn't made any promises, and I hadn't asked for any. So I stayed for one year. To the day. I wouldn't take anything for the experience now, but at the time it was miserable— my first and worst lesson in the dynamics of dysfunctional companies.

During that year, I was crosswise with account management every single day, Monday through Friday, and sometimes on weekends. We were so crosswise you could have used us as a T square. My nemesis was one particular account guy. He and I epitomized the classic agency dysfunction. We had *completely* different agendas. His was: Do whatever you have to do to keep the client. Mine was: Do whatever you have to do to do good work. And never, ever did the twain meet. Somehow it never occurred to him that presenting good work just might be, in itself, good account service. And I never saw how shameless toadying and brown-nosing ever did anybody any good. This AE guy hated me — truly, deeply *hated* me. When we butted heads, we looked like wild yaks on one of those nature shows on PBS. Big running start, and . . . *bam!*

Here's how it went. I, along with the creative staff I now directed, would come up with solid ideas and strong layouts (we almost never did broadcast). *He* would bring them back from the client and drop them on my desk. "Client didn't like it." Every time, "Client didn't like it." No further explanation, as if none was needed.

"O . . . kay" (about two seconds between syllables). "What . . . exactly . . . did they not like?" I would ask, trying to resist the reflex of clenching my teeth.

His reply was usually some version of the infamous "they-couldn't-really-say-what-they-want-but-they'll-know-it-when-they-see-it" response. Which, translated, means they want just exactly what they've always seen before: complete goat tripe.

I could see an impasse developing in the first week. After two weeks it was getting real old. The guy could not or, I suspected, would not sell good work. "Their eyes are on your feet" — he could probably get four-square behind that.

After a few of these episodes, I started wondering if the clients were even seeing the work. Which may have been a little paranoid of me, but paranoia breeds like prairie dogs in companies partitioned, as this one was, by factionalism.

An obvious solution would have been to let the creatives present their own work to the clients. Let them explain their motivations and reasoning and, if necessary, defend their choices. I don't know one good agency where the creatives hand off their work, wave worried good-byes like mothers sending their sons to the front, and wait nervously to learn whether their ideas survive and, if so, in what disfigured condition. Even at The Richards Group, where some of our most discerning and articulate advocates of creative work are account people, we have our best success selling the work when the writers and art directors themselves, even the stammering newcomers, can go eye to eye, *mano a mano*, with the people who manage the brands and write the checks.

Unfortunately, in the agency where I now found myself, that simple, sensible solution would not even be considered. That's how strong account management's hegemony was. They controlled all contact with the clients. In fact, AEs in those days were often known as the "contact men," the implication being that contact was their bailiwick alone and anybody else could just forget about it. We creative people might have been doing the producing, like the Holsteins in a dairy, but we were considered no more capable of selling our product than the Holsteins are.

The other problem, I realized a few weeks into the job, was that I scrupulously met my deadlines. Ordinarily, of course, meeting deadlines is a virtue. But who *set* the deadlines? My nemesis. All he had to do was sandbag us a little, set the deadline a couple of days earlier than it really needed to be. That way he could get our best work summarily executed while there was still time to pump out some dreck before the real deadline. So I launched my own tactic.

Now, I am not proud of what I'm about to tell you. Hopefully, if I were in the same situation today I would formulate a more, shall we say, mature response to the problem. But at the time it was the only thing my frustrated 22-year-old brain could come up with to try to fulfill what I saw as my mission: to do good work at all costs.

So here's what I did. I got passive-aggressive on the guy. Every time he brought back a layout, nicely rendered, looking deceptively alive . . . lovely, serene, like it was only sleeping . . . yet, in fact, stone dead, thanks to him—every time he did that I would *somehow* miss my deadline for the next project. "Oops! We're late? Why, goodness me, imagine that."

Actually, "passive-aggressive" may not be quite the right term, because I was actively holding ads hostage. If he wouldn't sell the work, well then, he couldn't *have* the work. Understand, I don't recommend this tactic. Even if I won a round now and then, it was impossible to produce good advertising in a place that probably should have had UN peacekeepers on patrol to keep us from shooting each other.

Inadvertently, through all this I was learning another valuable lesson: When people in the office can keep secrets from each other, such as what's really going on in the meetings with clients or what the creatives are really doing with the ads, then no good will come of it. Even if there's nothing untoward going on, it *feels* like there is. Witness my paranoia about the ads never even being presented. And thus was planted the seed of my unusual, open-concept office. But this likewise would not come until long after the cessation of hostilities.

We went on like this for a year. It felt like five. I guess he won our little contest because I left. At the end, I had almost nothing to show for my tenure as the hotshot creative director. Well, actually, I did have

At the wheel of my '56 Porsche, the consolation prize for my miserable year on the Dark Side of the ad business.

one thing. During the year, I had bought a new 1956 Porsche Speedster. I paid $3,150 for it—no problem on my big-bucks salary. It was my consolation prize for a miserable 12 months of tribal warfare.

And so, 365 days after I started, I loaded up a few things in the passenger seat, drove away from Bloom, and headed home to my apartment-*cum*-office for a new life as Stan Richards, freelance creative guy and the poorest Porsche owner in Dallas.

VALUABLE LESSONS—AND MORE POTATO SOUP

Even though I was now a battle-scarred agency veteran, older and wiser than before, getting reestablished was to prove harder than getting established in the first place had been.

Leaving Bloom and going freelance again meant starting my career over from scratch. A year had been plenty of time for my old clients—all the agencies in town who most needed and appreciated my services—to forget I existed. All of them had found ways to live quite nicely without me. Turning up new clients would be much harder plowing. The difficulty was compounded by the fact that I had grown accustomed to having plenty of money in my pocket. It wasn't easy going back to lean times.

In retrospect, though, it was all more than worth it. That one miserable year of dysfunctional agency life taught me lessons that I've applied ever since.

I learned, for example, that money is lousy compensation for the soul decay that comes from going home night after night knowing you've been a party to crappy work that day and you'll be a party to more crappy work tomorrow. There's a story repeated with boring regularity in the advertising trade press: Rising creative star leaves hot shop for megabucks offer to become CD of an agency with a sworn commitment to turn their schlocky creative product around. Of course, what almost always ends up turning around is the direction of the star's career. After that first article or two, he or she is never heard of again. I'm glad that wasn't my story. I had never really been heard of to begin with and still had a whole career ahead of me to redeem my mistake. True, I wouldn't be buying any more new sports cars for a while, but at least I could sleep the sleep of the righteous again.

Most of all, I came away from that job with an abiding hatred for the chasm that exists between the disciplines within companies. And I recognized that you can't solve the problem with parties at the office and picnics in somebody's backyard on Saturday.

I read something once about cocktail parties for American and Soviet embassy staffs in a foreign capital during the cold war years. Civility, even conviviality, appeared to reign. But the real tensions relaxed not one bit. The two naval attachés, say, chatting away over in the corner would each have a pencil stub and notecard in his trouser pocket for jotting surreptitious notes about his counterpart, his rival. His enemy. Nice surface appearances, but underneath, war. It's the same at the office. Social functions cannot overcome company dysfunction.

You have to figure out something to do in the office itself, something to affect the conduct of the daily work. I didn't really know *what* yet, but the challenge was clear. And, as somebody once said, "A problem well-stated is half-solved." If I didn't know exactly what to do, I certainly knew what *not* to do. For that, I am grateful for the Year of Living Miserably.

Still, lessons, however valuable, don't buy groceries. And soon I was going to be poor for two. At the same time I was trying to get my freelance practice back on its feet, I was getting to know a pretty nurse named Betty Pugh. Before long we were making wedding plans.

It was my good fortune that, in addition to nursing skill (which I thought might come in handy with the way I was constantly beating my head against the wall trying to get work), Betty also has a marvelous head for numbers. After we got married, with her managing the books we were able, on her meager nurse's salary and my pitiful freelance earnings, to rent a decent little house, pay our bills, and put plenty of potato soup on the table.

We really did eat a lot of potato soup. And we had a great time. Besides spuds, one thing that was dirt-cheap was gasoline, and I did have that sexy little Porsche that was paid for. So on weekends our recreational indulgence was to drive in sports car rallies. I did the driving. Betty, stopwatch in hand, navigated. We had a blast. Our first son, Grant, who now is a partner in Grant, Scott & Hurley agency in San Francisco, was born at around that time. Second son Brad, now a clinical psychologist in New York, was born not long after.

Later on, whenever I took a substantial risk with a client—say, producing some risky advertising that, if it failed, would cost me a bread-and-butter account—I always remembered how much fun we had during those first couple of years when we were living on soup. If going back to that life was the worst thing that could happen, well, then taking a risk didn't seem all that scary. Some people turn to Wild Turkey for courage. I turn to potato soup.

For quite a long time, until the business was established enough to hire a staff bookkeeper, Betty did the billing. It wasn't always a big job. One month early in our marriage I billed a grand total of $135. That was my all-time record for bad months.

The thing is, I had projects. I was working. But I was learning, and our bank account was reflecting, the cost penalty of craftsmanship. If I had been willing to crank out shoddy work, I could have done three or four little ads, or whatever it was I was doing, in the time it took me to do one the right way. It would have been easy to get away with that. Clients certainly weren't demanding the level of attention I was putting into their work. I couldn't charge a premium for my work because as a designer I was a commodity. If I wouldn't do the job for the money available, well, they'd go to somebody who would—never mind the difference in quality.

So I did the work, did it with all the fussy, obsessive attention to detail I darned well wanted, and gladly bore the cost penalty—because I could sleep well at night, satisfied that I was doing the best work I possibly could. And because I was nice and full of potato soup.

GATHERING DISCIPLES

> *They're not the best at what they do, they're the only ones that do what they do.*
> —Music impresario Bill Graham on one of rock's most
> enduring bands (and brands), the Grateful Dead

In those early years the majority of agency executives and client ad managers still found my approach to design baffling—"too different" was the usual verdict. But others—the ones who appreciated how a higher level of originality and craftsmanship could help them stand out—started taking notice of my work, tracking me down, and throwing projects my way.

Marvin Krieger's prediction that Dallas was going to come a long way as a communications center was starting to come to pass. As the city grew as a commercial and financial center and as jet travel and the ubiquity of the national media connected Dallas more closely with the rest of the country, local agencies and advertisers gradually were becoming less insular. Increasingly, they wanted their work to be more like the advertising and design they saw coming out of New York and Chicago. And I had the good fortune of being the first person in Texas doing the sort of new, more sophisticated stuff that they were beginning to aspire to.

Liener Temerlin, who ran Glenn Advertising, started using me on a few projects. They went well, and more projects followed. Glenn was in the process of becoming the biggest agency in the area (and they still are, under the name Temerlin McClain), and my business grew along with theirs. Soon they were my biggest client, and they would remain so for over 15 years, until my company made the leap from creative resource to full-service agency. Liener and I have been competitors now for a long time, but I'm still grateful for the start he and his agency helped give me.

I worked with other agencies as well. As a consequence I had lots of opportunity to observe daily life in the traditionally structured agency. Most of them, thankfully, weren't in the state of open warfare that I had experienced in my own brief agency career; however, there was some dysfunction in every agency I observed. Account people and their agendas stood opposed to creative people and theirs. Higher-ups and people with plum accounts lorded it over juniors and those working on less desirable business. Some clients received lavish attention from the best people. Other, less visible accounts got stuck with second-stringers. Power plays and backbiting were commonplace. The degree of dysfunction varied, but the basic structure of tribes and castes—and the resulting inefficiency—did not.

The biggest problem I saw was how convoluted and constricted communication became. Account people might be the only permitted channel of communication between the client and the creatives, media people and whoever else worked on the account. Everything was done via memo. An AE would send a CD a memo, and if the CD didn't understand something in the memo he'd send his own memo back.

Sometimes creative directors would filter all information from the account people before passing it along to the writers and art directors. It's like the Gossip game you played as a kid, where a message is whispered down a long line of people, morphing as it goes. A simple directive from the client, such as "Mention at the bottom that we're open late on Thursday," might have to proceed through three or four channels before reaching the art director, who probably would receive the message in some heavily altered form like "List the hours every day of the week for each store location individually."

I saw that as agencies grew, the layers of management piled up like strata on a prehistoric floodplain. Before her work reached the client, a lowly writer might have to run a gauntlet of approvals by the associate creative director, the creative director, the senior creative director, the executive creative director, as well as de facto approvals by the several layers of account management, who could keep the idea from ever getting before the client if they didn't like it for some reason.

The employee roster of one medium-sized agency could have more titles than *Burke's Peerage*. Some years ago, for example, of the 300-some employees at one Dallas agency, 95 of them—nearly a third of the staff—held the title of vice president or higher.

As a freelancer, since I was working from the outside I was pretty well immune to the political foofaraw. I could do what seemed best for the client without feeling like I had to juggle all the competing personal agendas. So I worked, I watched, and I mentally filed away all my observations about agency life for the day when I could try a different way.

Eventually I had more work than I could handle alone and hired my first employee, a designer named Martin Donald. Betty and I had turned a spare room downstairs at our house into an office. Martin moved his drawing board in next to mine and, with that, Stan Richards, freelancer, became Stan Richards & Associates. (Betty was still handling the accounting, which justified the plural, "Associates.")

Beginning with Martin, who worked with me for a couple of years, my little company became a home for talented people, like-minded seekers, with a passion for the craft and an idealistic notion that it's possible to create a thriving, creative business without knuckling under to layers, cliques, and politically motivated compromises in the quality of your work.

The feeling then, and one I still try mightily to preserve, was the atmosphere of a workshop, an atelier. In a workshop, somebody (in this case, me) is in charge, you've got masters and apprentices and levels of experience in between, but you don't have the feeling of an all-powerful boss with subservient employees who work there because, well, they have to work *somewhere.*

The atmosphere I want is one of colleagues pursuing a mission, disciples of a common vision. Our vision in those early years was to show that craftsmanship and intelligence count, that you can enhance the visual environment and still sell effectively. We believed that consumers are intelligent, sentient beings who can, at some level, appreciate the difference that wit and careful crafting make in commercial communications, even if they can't say, "Golly, Margaret, that Helvetica Medium sure is kerned nice, ain't it?"

We broke a lot of new ground. As the 1960s began, ours was still the only design studio in the whole Southwest region turning out national-caliber work. Or if there was another one, they weren't as fortunate to break out of obscurity. Stan Richards & Associates became something of a bellwether and a natural destination for bright young designers and writers. We remained a small company for many years, so it's not like we were hiring them by the dozens. But the men and women we did hire were the cream, and we usually found them, not at the famous design schools, but at places like East Texas State. We proved that Texas didn't have to be a backwater, that homegrown talent could find expression and prosper without having to migrate to one coast or the other.

Our little monopoly as the elite creative outfit in the area didn't last, of course, thanks largely to our own people. Simply by pursuing our craft and pouring energy into helping other talented young people pursue theirs, we ended up spawning much of the Southwestern graphic design community. Over the years, a lot of brilliantly gifted designers started with us, then went on to run their own firms. Woody Pirtle, Jack Summerford, Rex Peteet, Don Sibley, and many other A-list designers worked here.

They didn't, however, work in my spare bedroom. Two was pretty much the limit there. So as the business grew (we even hired a book-keeper so Betty could resign as unpaid CFO) we soon had to move into real office space. And when we did, that's when I opened up my mental files, reviewed my notes about the kind of office I *didn't* want to have, and commenced my Great Experiment.

STEP ONE: COMING UNHINGED

Real staff, real office—time to start figuring out how to promote a culture inimical to the spread of paranoia and politics, if such a thing were possible.

I thought back over my unhappy year at Bloom, analyzed the atmosphere at my clients' offices, and concluded that one essential element creates fertile ground for office politics. That element is secrecy.

Information is a powerful political weapon. If you're in the know— privy, say, to a client's long-term strategy—while others around you are in the dark, you can wield information as a display of superiority. And you can hobble subordinates who, if they had the same information as you, might apply a little initiative, outwork you, and win your job. By controlling important business information, the lazy and incompetent can avoid exposure.

That's bad, but maybe even worse is what happens when you control *unimportant* information. You promote paranoia.

There's a whiff of the nefarious about anything taking place behind closed doors, no matter how innocent it may actually be. We're all a little insecure. A closed door is a suggestion that they could be talking about us in there. Or, if they're not talking about us, why do they feel like we need to be excluded? What's going on that they don't want us to know? We'd better find out before we get blindsided by whatever it is they're plotting in there. Of course, chances are that whatever is going on is utterly unimportant as far as we're concerned. But it doesn't feel safe to assume that.

I saw that kind of paranoia, and felt my share of it, plenty of times around ad agencies. And then there's the fact that when there *is* treachery going on, slander being spread, a plot being plotted, it's happening in secret.

Recognizing all that, I did two things. I committed, as the owner of the company, to be a reckless sharer of information with my coworkers. Some things, like salaries, do deserve complete confidentiality. But the kind of business information that could be wielded as a weapon of power—with that, let anybody who wants to know, know.

Say we're in danger of losing the Widgetcorp.com account over a conflict about the agency's compensation. A lot of companies would confine that knowledge within the upper account-management ranks.

But why? A lot of other people work on the account. What's to be gained by letting them imagine a reason for the trouble? They'll probably imagine something a lot worse than the truth.

So first I committed to share information widely myself, encouraging others to do the same.

The second thing I did was to bring a hammer and screwdriver to work and remove every office door in the place, starting with my own. That was well over 30 years ago. Since then we've moved several times, each time removing more and more physical barriers. Walk through our offices now and it's hard to tell whether you're looking at the desk of an account director or the new AE she just hired or the coordinator who takes their phone messages.

We do have doors on the conference rooms, but even there we've struck a blow against paranoia. All the small conference rooms have a square, unshuttered window in the door, right at eye level so every passerby can check out who's in there and what they're doing. The bigger, more formal conference rooms don't have windows in the doors. They have peepholes, like you probably have at home. Except the peepholes don't look out; they look inward—a wide-angle view of the meeting for anyone to see. It makes for dull viewing. But that's just the point. Everybody's just working, minding their own business. So you can go off and mind yours, unworried about being outside the door.

It seems like such a small thing, pulling pins out of the hinges and schlepping the doors into the storage room. A lot of people over the years have thought it was kind of nutty, like maybe *I* was the one unhinged. But that one act did more to defeat paranoia and politics than any other single thing we've ever done. Removing doors had symbolic power, sure, but it was also practical, making it difficult for any of us to keep secrets and making mine the most *un*private private company I know.

A Big, Hairy Leap of Faith

Throughout the 1960s and the first half of the 1970s, our merry little band of creatives at Stan Richards & Associates produced advertising, collateral, logo designs, corporate identity work, annual reports, the occasional package design and, in the one case I told you about, the opening title for an Oscar-winning movie.

By the mid-1970s the staff consisted of maybe two dozen people— mostly designers plus a couple of writers, a secretary, and a bookkeeper. A lot of the designers happened to be pretty fair copywriters as well.

That's why we needed only a couple of writer-writers on staff.

As for the lone secretary and book-keeper, that may seem a bit lean on the staffing, but I've always operated on the belief that when you're focusing on your craft, you don't need to carry the support staff of a transatlantic luxury liner. At The Richards Group today, we have coordinators who support the various groups within the agency much as our one secretary supported the whole studio years ago. One creative coordinator, for instance, may be responsible for a group of 8 or 10 writers and ADs, plus perhaps a print producer or two. A coordinator will book travel, handle portfolios of job candidates, issue purchase orders, help get presentations done and out the door, and—the most important thing for the agency—nudge, cajole, hector, and hassle the group to make sure they get their daily time sheets in. With smart go-getters in the job, we do just fine with a low ratio of coordinator*s* to coordinat*ed*.

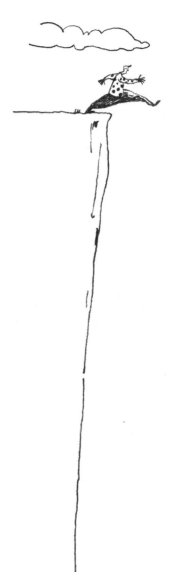

As for other support staff, we have no traffic managers as go-betweens for creative and account service. Instead, we expect the creatives and account folks to talk to each other, set and meet deadlines like grownups, and get materials where they need to be, when they need to be there without hand-holding from a traffic person.

No personnel or HR department, either, for reasons I talked about in Chapter 3. As I said, if you ever see an HR department at The Richards Group, you will know that I have departed this earth and that my dying wishes have been utterly disregarded. We haven't needed a personnel department yet, not even slightly, and I can't imagine that we ever will.

But let's return to the 1970s. We had a great team. My biggest problem, in fact, was people outside the shop giving me credit I didn't deserve. In part because I spent most of my time on creative matters—which I find fun—instead of administrative stuff—which is boring and oftentimes not all that necessary anyway—and in part because of the name of the firm, our clients tended to focus too much on Stan Richards and not enough on the Associates. There was a presumption that I did everything myself. Yes, I saw it all. Yes, I influenced most of it, helped present a lot of it, and did actually write and design some. But no way could I be the Man on every project.

We had a whole studio full of great people who weren't getting due credit for their creativity and hard work. It was time for me to stop getting top billing. So, to recognize in a public way that this is not a solo act, we changed our name to The Richards Group. My name stayed up there for accountability's sake, but we let my name be an adjective. The Group is the thing.

Life as a creative outsourcing firm was sweet. Agencies brought us in on a lot of their best and most challenging assignments. We got to make a real difference for them and their clients, made some good friends, got nice press, and won plenty of awards. Every day held something new and intellectually stimulating. It was fun coming to work.

Then I went and messed it all up.

Or at least I *could* have messed it all up. As it turned out, leaving the freelance world, where we were doing great, and taking The Richards Group into uncharted and shark-infested waters as a full-service agency could be viewed as a bold and brilliant leap of faith. In any event, it has paid off bountifully for me and many hundreds of others. As it turned out.

At the time, though, it could just as easily have turned out to be a leap of abject boneheadedness. We worked for ad agencies. If we *became* an ad agency, we would be waving bye-bye to virtually every client we had. Thus, it was not something I had ever given serious consideration to.

Then, one day in 1976, the phone rang. It was Gene Bishop, chairman of Mercantile Bank, one of the larger Dallas banks and a classy operation any way you looked at it.

"Stan," he said, "we're about to put our advertising account up for review." At this point I was thinking he wanted to ask my opinion about some of the agencies in town. "I would like," he continued, "to invite The Richards Group to pitch our business—if you want to be invited."

I tried to swallow, but my mouth had suddenly turned as dry as a month-old rice cake.

"I realize," Gene went on, "that by pitching you would, in effect, be going into competition with your agency clients. I can't make you any guarantees; we're going to go about this as thoroughly and objectively as we can. But I do have a high regard for the work you and your group have been doing, and I think you would stand a good chance. You think it over and let me know what you decide."

Oh, I thought it over, all right. All night long for several nights I thought it over. Mercantile, one of the biggest advertisers in the area and a top-notch organization, was exactly the kind of brand I would want to launch an agency with. *Would* want—if I were ready to give 100 percent of my current accounts a big old kiss adios.

Gene Bishop and Mercantile were handing me what could be the opportunity of a lifetime, a shot at a trophy account for a new agency. So it was great opportunity versus sure thing (and a pretty nice sure thing at that). I tried to weigh our chances. On creative credentials we probably would have it sewn up from the start. But in terms of every-thing else that makes a full-service agency a full-service agency—account service staff, media, pretty much anything beyond that one secretary and bookkeeper—The Richards Group had nothing to show.

Ultimately it was the potato soup that decided it for me. I had wor-ried quite a bit about my staff. If we went for the Mercantile business and lost, what would happen to them? But then I realized they were constantly being recruited anyway; they'd probably all have jobs within a week, if it came to that. And they were young. At 43, I was the graybeard of the office. The staff, I decided, would be just fine. And as for me, the worst thing that could happen would be starting over as a lone freelancer and living on the cheap. The last time that happened, Betty and I had the time of our life, potato soup and all.

It was decided. Betty was on board. The Groupers, while perhaps a little pale looking and feeling fluttery in the midsection, were excited and ready to go for it. So I called Gene and said yes, we'll pitch. He was delighted.

The story has a happy ending, of course. After a careful review of the capabilities of several Dallas agencies, the bankers, in the best tra-dition of their profession, made a most judicious and provident deci-sion. They hired The Richards Group for creative and KCBN (which, despite the appearance of its name, was an ad agency and not a radio station) for media and coordination. Eventually, once we got account service and media up to speed, the whole account moved over to us.

Dual-agency arrangements like that are almost always miserable disasters. In fact, I would go so far as to say, if you're a client, don't even try it. Your chances of success are roughly equal to your chances of landing a quadruple lutz — on thin ice. Either both agencies feel constantly threatened, which is a lousy way to promote good relations and solid work, or one gets treated as the sweetheart and the other as the ugly sister, which is also guaranteed to yield bitter feelings along with crummy and inconsistent work.

When Taco Bell tried it back in the mid-1990s, with us supposedly doing the brand advertising and Bozell supposedly handling field work, the whole deal collapsed into a tangled, frustrating mess within months. Roles started getting mixed up, with agency pitted against agency practically on a project-by-project basis, until it felt like we were in a nonstop pitch for an account that was supposed to be ours already. It wasn't pretty for the brand management at Taco Bell, either. At the end, PepsiCo sent them all packing. I don't know how *they* felt, but we were relieved when it was over.

For the time it lasted, though, Mercantile's two-agency setup worked out pretty well — the rare exception. Jim McGhee, one of our principals and now one of the longest-tenured Groupers, was an AE at KCBN until we hired him about a year into the Mercantile relationship. "When we saw the first work The Richards Group did for the bank," he recalls, "we all just said, 'Wow, there's no way we could have done that.' We were actually quite happy to be in on the arrangement."

If he thinks *they* were happy, he should have seen us the day we won the business. It's hard to know which emotion ran stronger, jubilation or relief.

Authors of business books are fond of that line by Theodore Roosevelt about how it's better to dare mighty things, even though you fall on your face now and then, than to be one of the poor schlubs in the gray twilight where there's neither victory nor defeat. I'm paraphrasing, but you get the drift: an early-twentieth-century "Just Do It." I agree with Teddy. I've never heard of anybody who, on their deathbed, said, "Darn it, I wish I had done less." But I would add this: Before you go charging up San Juan Hill, just make sure you've got plenty of ammo.

We did have plenty of ammo when we charged the Mercantile hill. We had the best creative staff for 1,000 miles. Our first campaign proved spectacularly successful, for the bank and for us. It ran for more than a decade, until the Texas economic meltdown of the 1980s took the bank down with it. But the funny thing about the campaign — a campaign so successful it made a bank *interesting,* so successful the institution actually ended up changing its name to better reflect the message of the advertising — the funny thing about that campaign was, it wasn't really our idea. The agency didn't come up with the concept. The client did.

I suppose if there were ever a time when you'd want to reject an idea because it's NIH (not invented here) it's when you've just started your agency, you're supposed to be the creative hotshots in town, and you're working on your very first advertising out of the chute. A lot of eyes were on us. We had everything to prove. A precedent to set. And a client who came up with a great idea while shaving. The whole thing started with one word: *momentum*. Gene Bishop thought of it as he watched the razor mow down his whiskers one morning.

Well, so be it. To me, a good idea is a good idea, and it matters not one fraction of an iota who on the team comes up with it. The voice talent came up with "We'll leave the light on for you" for Motel 6. Jim McGhee, the account guy, wrote a line — "What does the *Post* say?" — that became a highly successful campaign for one of the newspapers in Denver. A young account planner recently contributed a key line of copy for some Home Depot advertising. We've got a lot of these stories. One of the dumbest, most prideful things you can do as an agency creative person is reject out of hand any idea that doesn't originate with the so-called creative people. Yet creatives do that all the time. And agencies summarily reject any idea that's proposed by a client or tossed on the table during a focus group — anything NIH.

That's dumb. Truly good ideas are so rare, so hard to produce, so fragile, that we ought to first genuflect before anybody who comes up with one and then count ourselves heroes and worth our keep if we simply manage not to screw it up in the execution. Take 'em however you can get 'em. And be thankful.

So the new, improved, full-service Richards Group got its first idea from the client. It was no puny idea, either; we created advertising with it for more than a decade. During our 11-year tenure, the bank grew from $800 million in assets and one location to $23 billion in assets and 125 banking organizations. Momentum and the animated "M" device that each commercial ended with took on a life of their own. Bishop and company dropped the old-fashioned name Mercantile in favor of a streamlined, snappy, *nuevo* naming system. The holding company became MCorp, the bank MBank, their ATMs MPact machines, and so on.

They were a smart client. When we presented new corporate identity work featuring logos in bright, exciting red, it would have sent most bankers into instant apoplexy: "Red ink?! Are you guys *crazy?*" Not these bankers. They were marketers; they knew branding. They liked the red logo.

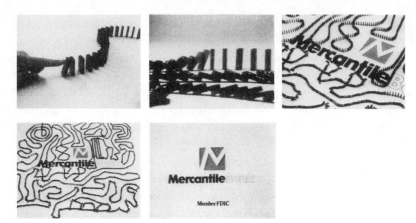

The commercial that introduced "Momentum." It featured the handiwork of Bob Specca, "the Domino King." Writer and art director: Stan Richards.

Alas, in the late 1980s and early 1990s Texas received its economic recompense for all the "Drive fast, freeze a Yankee" bumper stickers people put on their Suburbans back during the energy crisis. MBank was hit hard, taken over by the FDIC, and liquidated. They weren't alone. The other big Texas banks either cratered or were bought out, too. But in a way our MBank relationship continued. Their head of marketing and our main contact through most of our years together was a natty young executive named David Gravelle. Today he's one of our principals, the head of Richards/Gravelle, our public relations and financial and health care marketing group. And practically the entire

Our first campaign as a full-service agency had serious momentum of its own, running for more than 10 years. Glenn Dady and Melinda Marcus were the creative team behind this billboard.

group that Gravelle called his agency dream team is still here: AD Glenn Dady, designer Dick Mitchell, writer Mike Malone, Linda Fenner in accounting, and production manager Michael Hatley.

Tragically, the only dream team member absent today is writer John Stone. He was killed in a car crash while on his way to the bank one morning. John and I were the only two agency people in the room the day we pitched the Mercantile business. He was a brilliant financial writer, maybe the best I have ever known.

Thanks to "Momentum," The Richards Group gathered some momentum of our own as our work attracted the attention of advertisers around Texas and beyond. We've had double-digit growth, sometimes almost triple-digit growth, in our billings nearly every year since. "Momentum" put The Richards Group on the map. It was our first big idea as an agency. And yet in its seed form it wasn't even *our* idea.

Sometimes being smart means simply being smart enough to take what's handed to you.

Putting More Force in Your Workforce

What I've learned about hiring, training, and retaining terrific people. And, now and then, saying so long (at least for a while).

WHAT THIS BUSINESS NEEDS IS MORE AMATEURS

Not long ago I read a line that I liked. It was on a fourth- or fifth-generation photocopy pinned up on the wall in, of all places, an old sundries store, right next to the soda fountain. "Choose a vocation you love," it read, "and you will never have to work." "Chinese proverb," it said at the bottom.

Now, personally I'm a little skeptical about the "Chinese proverb" part. You see an awful lot of little aphorisms billed that way, most of which I suspect are actually written by a guy named Maury who works out of the Brill Building in New York City. In any event, regardless of its provenance, I like the adage about loving your vocation. I like the fact that it was photocopied and pushpinned to the wall by the soda jerk in a sundries store. It makes him and me brothers in a family that I wish were a whole lot bigger: people who love showing up at work every day.

We get so caught up in our careers, in trying to be *professionals*, that we forget what it means to be an *amateur*: somebody who does it out of love, *pour l'amour*. I got into the advertising business because it gave me a way to make a living doing what I would gladly do for free: expressing ideas through art; figuring out extraordinary ways to say ordinary things; meeting and hashing out ideas with bright, interesting, funny people. If this is work, then I feel like I've pulled a fast one on society all these years, because this is fun.

One reason my organization has worked so well for so long is that I've always tried to hire people who, like the soda jerk and me, have the old fire in the belly, the lover's zeal of the true amateur.

For a good example, look at Ed Brock. He's the "B" in our design group RBMM. Ed (who, by the way, once cycled through China and never once encountered that proverb about choosing your vocation, which I think proves my earlier point) is a filmmaker, an animator, who joined me as a designer in the early days of the agency and was part of the cadre that spun off the design group as a separate operating unit in 1979. He was the first person at either RBMM or The Richards Group, other than me, to celebrate a twentieth anniversary as an employee.

Ed's reel of work is a wonder—elegant and wacky and inventive and, in terms of media and technique, impossible to categorize. The guy could empty the grass bag off your lawn mower and animate something spectacular out of the clippings. He is, by and large, a soloist. He looks at your storyboard or conceives the film himself, assembles the materials, works out the technicalities, and shoots it, typically, with a fine old camera that I think he bought at Sergey Eisenstein's last garage sale. Click, shoot a frame. Then move the little pile of grass clippings and click, shoot another frame. Then rearrange the clippings again, and so on. He works like a medieval stonemason dressing columns for a cathedral. You can feel the artisanship.

Ed, you can tell when you're around him, does it for the love. More so than most people, I'd wager. You'd never be able to assemble a staff composed entirely of Ed Brocks, but you don't need to. A few people like Ed, strategically placed, can leaven the whole organization. All you have to do is find people with apparent potential and evident zeal to do something with the potential, put them around an Ed Brock, and watch the inspiration happen.

Benjamin Zander, the Boston Philharmonic conductor, said in *Fast Company* magazine, "As leaders we must never forget that one of our main jobs is to remind people why they went into music, or into art, or into business." Ed, quiet soloist that he is, is a leader for us simply by demonstrating that the heart of this business is to exercise the talents and interests that started us leaning toward the business in the first place instead of toward, say, poultry farming or titanium mining.

So why *did* you go into the business? There's another line I like that was spoken by everyone's favorite philosopher: Elle MacPherson, the supermodel. "I wanted so badly to study ballet," she said, "but it was really all about wearing the tutu." You see people like that in this business, people who seem to like the trappings of *being in* advertising more than the substance of *doing* advertising. "Sure, the commercial sucks, but we got to stay at Shutters during the shoot!" They look swell in the tutu, but please don't ask them to dance.

Most of the people I've had the good fortune to work with over the years, certainly the ones that I've gone out of my way to work with, have been the dancers, the people who are just as happy showing up in sweats and doing a workout at the barre as they are decked out on stage doing the dying swan. So to speak.

What I'm about to say next, I've said often. I think a lot of other creative directors who really care about the craft say it a lot, too. But it's still true, so forgive me for saying it for the bazillionth time: The work we do designing a matchbook matters just as much as the work we do producing a spot for the Super Bowl. The stakes are lower, sure, and we all get jazzed a whole lot more by the glam jobs. But I'm talking about the work itself, when you're hunched over your keyboard honing the Single Most Persuasive Idea to put on the creative brief or fussing with the mechanical.

My agency still does an awful lot of tiny, little jobs that we could either farm out or just ignore and let the client's print shop figure it out. Those little jobs are important; we need them. They're as much a litmus test of what we're about as the seven-figure extravaganza. I truly believe that if we give the little job, the "unimportant" job, short shrift—if we ever start phoning it in—we infect ourselves with a subtle carelessness that will, somehow, manifest itself in the big jobs.

I read once about a manufacturer whose factory produced an excellent, high-quality product. It was lawn mowers, as a matter of fact. Then, in the same factory, they started producing cheaper, store-brand mowers for a retailer. Different parts, different production runs. Seemed like it should work just fine. But sure enough, the flagship brand started suffering quality problems. They couldn't accept run-of-the-mill work on Monday and expect to produce exceptional work on Tuesday. So for the sake of their own brand, they had to stop making the el cheapo machines. Our business is the same way. Slapdash work in one area pollutes the work that we deem more important. And our lukewarmness toward the less sexy side of the craft betrays our preference for the tutu over the dance.

Now, advertising is, I'll have to admit, pretty cool. It's got cachet. If you're in this business you are at least one degree of separation closer to Kevin Bacon than your Uncle Hal in the engineered-surface-coatings-and-paints business. There's nothing wrong with wowing the relatives with your story about working with—I don't know—the same hairdresser who did Jennifer Love Hewitt's last movie. So, okay, enjoy it. It's cool. I will say this, though: A lot of the people who year after year do the best work in our company—coming through with the most or best concepts, hitting on the most insightful strategies, negotiating the best deals, whatever it may be—are some of the *least* cool people, in the *Rolling Stone* or *In Style* magazine senses of the word, in the whole place. It's as if they don't have the desire or the time to affect some ad-person persona. They're maniacs for what they do. Ad wonks.

Look, if you've got real style and Donatella Versace calls you at home for pointers, more power to you. That's cool in its way, too. But when it comes to work, I don't care about the tutu. Just show me your moves.

When I talk about being an ad wonk, here is a caveat: You really can't eat, sleep, and breathe this stuff, this *advertising* stuff, and expect to be all that good at it. The office can't be your life. Advertising, as an industry and as an activity to occupy our days, properly exists to take in, process, and redisseminate influences from without—from our clients, from consumers, from the culture—and not to *be* all that much in and of itself. We show up every day in a big building full of phones and computers, and we sell things. Nothing is more boring than a bunch of ad people sitting around talking about The Business like it's somehow more important, *per se*, than any other random person's business. Insular is insular, no matter how hip you look. It's the outside stuff and how we bake it up and serve it that makes this business interesting.

That's why I've learned to be hitting that elevator between 5:58 and 6:02 P.M. If I'm still in the office at 6:10, you know something big is going down. I've got to go out and get some more influences to use in the office tomorrow. I've got to participate in family life, read a book on opera, watch *The Simpsons*, follow the Dallas Mavericks (because, as every Mavs fan knows, suffering purifies us), wash and wax the car, work off last night's bowl of ice cream—have a life.

I'll tell you shortly about some of my coworkers over the years. The best of them, I've noticed, are like human vacuum cleaners of ideas and influences. Carl Ally, one of the architects of modern advertising, said, "The creative person wants to be a know-it-all. He wants to know about all kinds of things: ancient history, 19th-century mathematics, current manufacturing techniques, flower arranging and hog futures. Because he never knows when these ideas might come together to form a new idea. It may happen six minutes later or six months, or six years down the road. But he has faith that it will happen."

That is what an *amateur*, in the best sense, is like. You can be like a kid playing out in a field, collecting whatever interests you, bringing it all home, and saying, "Hey, let's figure out how to make something out of this!" A professional relies on method: *We shall do certain things and achieve certain results.* Confident, but bloodless. The true amateur brings that measure of faith. When you're in this business because you love it, you can be like the McGyver character from the old TV series, emptying your pockets and fashioning solutions to thorny creative problems out of whatever fragments and scraps and half-remembered notions you showed up with that day. You don't know for certain *how* you're going to get it done, but you've got faith.

The disciplines of the craft—letterspacing a headline, communicating a strategy cogently, vetting an AICP form—we can teach you all that. You can have half a brain, you can have zero experience. What you *don't* have really doesn't matter that much. Not as long as you have a whole heart.

TRYING ON THE OTHER GUY'S HAT

All the incidental contact that comes from working without physical barriers helps tremendously to keep functions from devolving into factions. But it's where the tribal boundaries come together and even merge a bit around a common task that you deal tribalism a death blow. Here at The Richards Group, for instance, because we don't go out of our way to emphasize the differences between tribes, we don't get bent out of shape when someone makes a friendly foray into another tribe's territory. In fact, the positive ripple effect of a little act of intertribal exchange can go on for years.

Small case in point: Some years ago, when we were the agency for T.G.I. Friday's, we found ourselves with a crash assignment for Friday's at one of those times when the agency seemed to be half-buried in crash assignments for all our *other* clients, too. It was a routine crisis. Every agency has them now and then. Friday's had a new product, buffalo wings, that they had decided to rush into the market, and they wanted new TV on the air fast. In fact, the air date was set, and it was already looming. When they got the assignment on a Monday, the account team backed out a schedule and realized that we needed to be presenting concepts to the client within—good heavens!—about four days.

The creative group that handled Friday's was stretched close to the limit already, and it was unreasonable to expect them to come through on the wings job without dropping the ball somewhere else. So we turned to our time-honored solution: the process indelicately referred to throughout the ad business as a gang bang. We put out an APB to every creative team in the place, from interns on up: If you can make time in the next few days to work on this, you've got a crack at a national TV campaign. A large conference room was booked for everybody to come and present their ideas on Friday. Time was so short that we invited the client to attend that meeting to see the first-round ideas. A fast briefing was held for anyone who could attend, and a creative brief and deck of background information went out to everybody who wanted it.

As it turned out, two of the takers were account guys, Doug Martin and John Lee. Neither of them worked on the Friday's account, but since they worked in the middle of the hubbub with everybody else, they heard about the assignment and saw how swamped the creative staff was. That's one important point. The guys were in a position, physically, to know what was going on outside the confines of their daily responsibilities. The second important point is this: They weren't walled off mentally from considering how they might help out.

"You know what," John told Doug, "the creatives are so busy, I can imagine *nobody* showing up at that meeting on Friday. Do you think maybe the agency could . . . ?" And they agreed: Yep, the agency could very well come up empty on this one. They, John and Doug themselves, might be our last line of defense. It was a long shot. They might get laughed at. But what the heck, it was worth a try. So they cancelled their evening plans for the week, put on their creative hats, and stayed late, concepting TV spots after they got their regular work done.

Now, you're probably anticipating the ending. Friday comes, the overextended creatives have been unable to solve the assignment, and the two account guys save the day with a terrific idea that they present with charmingly primitive storyboards.

Well, it didn't turn out that way.

The account guys had been wrong about the turnout. When they arrived at the meeting on Friday, scripts and stick-figure key frames in hand, the conference room was full, jammed with bleary-eyed creative teams ready to present. New kids, creative directors from other groups—

nearly half the creative staff was there. Feeling slightly sheepish and more than a little relieved that they wouldn't have to present, John and Doug took seats in a corner of the room. They made themselves inconspicuous and quietly enjoyed their cohorts' presentations, as we went around the group listening to campaign after campaign.

They kept their mouths shut through the whole meeting and wouldn't have said anything at all, but one of the creatives outted them. When I said, "Okay, I guess that's everything," an art director chimed in. "Wait, Stan. I think *these* guys have something."

They protested, tried to get out of it, but we ganged up on them and made them show. They went at it like troupers, and it was fun. The ideas, while perhaps not ready for the One Show, weren't the worst we heard that day by a long shot, and we had a great time watching them present. But still, what good did it do for these two AEs to make their well-meaning but ultimately unnecessary gesture?

Well, it's true they didn't get to be the heroes, but at the time you would hardly have known that. They got more claps on the back and generated more buzz around the office than the team that actually came up with the campaign. Art directors and writers were genuinely impressed that those guys would invest the effort for the team. Nobody felt threatened. The client appreciated the demonstration of a commitment to do whatever it took. Other account people were encouraged to contribute to the creative process. And John and Doug, having walked a mile in the other guys' moccasins, came away with new respect for their counterparts in creative. Their quixotic little sojourn in another tribe's customary territory was good for the whole organization.

As for the beneficial ripple effect, so far it's reached at least two other agencies. Doug went on to work on Nike at Wieden & Kennedy and, emboldened by his pleasant experience on the T.G.I. Friday's project, did the same thing there—chipped in with a TV idea for Nike. And this time it actually got produced. No wonder those guys at Wieden have such a great creative tradition; they're not narrow about where they'll get their ideas. Then, after a few years at Wieden, Doug moved on to Leagas Delaney in San Francisco. I called him there to refresh my memory about this little story.

"It's weird you called about this," he said. "I was just thinking about it myself." Only an hour or so before, he had given a young AE who works for him a gentle push to present some of her themeline ideas to a creative director whose team had hit the wall on a project. How'd it turn out? "Great. The CD really appreciated it, and she felt terrific."

Will they produce one of her ideas? Who knows? But her willingness to cross a boundary and chip in has already produced an effect that could pay off for years down the road.

Not bad for a couple of evenings of drawing stick figures.

"Your Work Stinks — Can We Hire You?"

I have, at least on paper, a lousy background for running a 600-person company. Graduate of a three-year art school, freelance designer, failed ad agency department head, freelancer again—you know the story. In practice, of course, I've done just fine, and when it comes to talking the talk I can throw down the boardroom rebop with the best of them (although I never, ever use the words "synergistic" or "at the end of the day . . ." and wish to be slapped sharply if I ever do).

My point is, you can't always tell from reading the *Racing Form* how well the pony's going to run.

I haven't got a single management course to my name. Being a reader helps a lot. But beyond that, practically everything I know about managing an organization I've either extrapolated from principles of the creative disciplines (e.g., the cleanest, simplest arrangement of elements is almost always the best) or learned from observing how other businesspeople do things, both well and badly. For example, you'll recall that I noticed in clients' offices how letting people keep secrets promoted tribalism, so in our office we simply started promoting lack of privacy.

I have never felt particularly handicapped by my lack of formal "professional formation." So as a consequence, I've never been a stickler for impressive credentials as a prerequisite for anybody's gainful employment with my company. Earlier I mentioned, for instance, that we built a killer studio with talent hired straight out of schools like East Texas State (now called Texas A&M-Commerce). Even if you're not in high tech, where everybody knows that a dropout can become the richest person on the planet, ability and not credentials is what should count.

In the ad business, at least where art directors and writers are concerned, your resume doesn't matter all that much. Creative people know this.

One writer in town who grew up in southern Louisiana devotes as much space on his resume to his first job as a rice shoveler as he does to some of his school and agency background. Which I appreciate. *Everybody* had college and agency stuff on their curriculum vitae. He's my one link to the exotic world of rice shoveling.

So, fine, you have to do a resume; have some fun with it if you dare. Your portfolio tells your story anyway, shows what you can really do. Or it's supposed to. I've found, however, that a lot of the time even that doesn't tell the story fairly. Some of the best hires we've ever made at The Richards Group have been based on the slimmest evidence of ability.

My colleague Mike Renfro, writer and sometime NPR commentator, was not long out of UT-Austin, working in print production at a tiny agency. He didn't even have a portfolio of work when he saw a classified in the back of *Adweek*. Two of our creative group heads, Glenn Dady and Melinda Marcus, were looking for junior writers and ADs. Send in five samples, the ad said. Sneaking around after hours, Mike managed to cobble together four, not five, sample ads that he had written in his spare time. He typed up a cover letter and sent them in. Amazingly, a couple of days later he got a call for an interview. He rummaged around at home, found a necktie to wear (we had a dress code at the time), and came up to the office, wondering which of his samples most attracted Melinda and Glenn's attention.

It was odd, though, in the interview with Melinda, who was the writer on the team. She didn't *seem* all that excited as Mike went through the obligatory Presentation of the Work. Probably just not very demonstrative, he thought. When he finished presenting, Melinda set the ads aside and looked at him across the desk. "Mike," she said, "I'm going to be honest with you." Hmm, this did not sound like a prelude to high praise. "To be honest, we're not real fond of your work." And Mike was thinking, "For this I put on a tie?" But she wasn't finished.

"We weren't crazy about any of the ads," she went on, "but we loved your cover letter." *Cover letter?* "We thought it was just terrific."

As far as I know, Mike didn't save his four samples—and that's probably just as well—but he did save the letter, a self-deprecating explanation of why he was short of the requisite five samples.

"Dear Ms. Marcus," it began, "I know you said five. It's not that I'm an idiot and can't count . . . it's worse. I'm a production manager and don't get to write as much as I'd like. I do have more than five samples, but part of being production manager here is the ability to hide important materials from AE types. [Tribalism turned into a copy point! Now that's resourcefulness!] I've done such a great job, I don't know where the hell anything is myself. You know, just the other day I was telling my brother-in-law, Luther . . . sorry, I digress.

"Anyway, that's why there are four and not five. I *can* count. I can count at least as good as I can spel. Tank Yu. Michael Renfro."

In those two paragraphs, Melinda and Glenn saw what they needed to see: real wit and originality in writing about a product, which in this case was Mike himself and his pathetic little portfolio. So on that skimpy basis, they hired him, a rank novice who ended up becoming one of the best copywriters in the country, especially in radio. He's been here ever since, except for a brief, parenthetical stint with Chiat/Day. You can read Mike's account of his experience as a homesick Texan in Venice, California, in his book, *Under the X in Texas* (Texas Tech, 1995).

Mike wasn't the only future star we discovered in spite of the double whammy of unimpressive credentials and crummy samples. David Fowler, who at this writing bears the title Creative Director, North America, at Ogilvy & Mather, also was hired on the strength of the cover letter, which had the sound of a guy who could actually *write.* Which, of course, he was. All the press David has gotten as creator of the Motel 6 campaign that's still running more than 13 years and hundreds of spots later somewhat eclipses the fact that he also wrote a ton of other great ads and campaigns for our clients before moving on to Goodby, Ammirati, the Fox network, and now O&M.

So I imagine you'll be paying a little extra attention to your next cover letter.

This is a great business for people whose backgrounds are unconventional and who aren't easy to pigeonhole. David Ogilvy always gloried in his erratic history as a chef, stove salesman, failed tobacco farmer, and researcher before turning to copywriting. People with broad interests thrive. When he was a Fellow at Oxford in the 1920s, C.S. Lewis wrote in his journal a description of Arthur Lee Dixon, a math professor: "His knowledge is very great and yet no one would think of him as a learned man. He talks to all of us so readily on our own subjects that one forgets he has a subject of his own: or rather, mathematics seem to lie so easily side by side with Ovid, Tasso, golf, Kant, Gilbert & Sullivan, Trollope, and French inns, that it appears as one of the normal human interests. It is a mere accident whether a man happens to include mathematics among his hobbies—as it is an accident whether he includes draughts." This Dixon would have made a terrific adguy. And he probably would keep scrupulously accurate time sheets, too.

It's tremendously satisfying to discover a diamond in the rough. But not all our great hiring discoveries would come under that category. Some have gone through quite a bit of polishing already but just happen to be stuck in bad settings. This happens a lot. Experienced people from less-than-stellar agencies come in with their samples, and with too cursory a look you might conclude that they just don't have the talent we're looking for. But just because some people have been in the business a few years, that doesn't mean their work is necessarily a measure of them, any more than the neophytes' work portrays them fairly. You still have to look with a very discerning eye. These judgment calls aren't easy. Even Melinda, who sponsored Fowler and Renfro into the agency, missed some. One of our longtime creative group heads keeps a rejection letter from Melinda in a file with the acceptance letter he got from me just a few months later. It's a subjective business. You have to try not to let it drive you schizo.

With people like Renfro and Fowler we had to say, "Never mind their inexperience, I think there's talent there." With some of the people who have been around a while we have to say, "Never mind their *experience*, I think there's frustrated potential there." It would be sheer arrogance on our part to conclude that nothing good could come out of a bad agency. A bad agency can beat bad work out of the best people.

A couple of years ago, one of our CDs took a chance on a midlevel writer from an agency of ill creative fame, one of those balkanized shops where creative people live under the heel of fear-driven account management and good ideas die terrible deaths. This writer's book was, on the whole, mediocre at best for someone with her experience. It was a bit thin and had lots of unproduced work. However, the unproduced work was significantly better than the produced work, and that's a pretty clear sign of good talent wasting away in a bad environment. Sure enough, she was another star just waiting to rise. All she needed was a supportive setting and some good strategies to work from. *Voilà!* The kind of smart, versatile writer you wish you had a hundred more of.

As that writer's story demonstrates, all the time and energy agencies waste on factional conflict costs them a lot of good people. Either they're rendered creatively impotent right where they are, or they quit. Sometimes that's our gain, as I've just described. But sometimes the whole advertising industry loses good people just because they don't see anyplace else to go in the business where they won't be wearing themselves and others out with all the headbutting. At a gallery opening recently I met a former agency artist who now makes her living as a massage therapist. I asked her why she made the career change. "Because," she said, "I decided I'd rather help relieve stress than help cause it." Apparently she believed that her creative standards doomed her to a life of battling the Philistines. Now, maybe she would have been ready to get out of the business anyway, but I know there are a lot of agency people out there who don't realize that they can have a better career without actually changing careers.

If you're only recruiting people from good companies, you've got a problem. People don't like to *leave* good companies. Why should they? They're in a *good place.* You can get them to do it sometimes, but it often takes a lot of enticing. *Bad* companies are your happy hunting ground, if you've got the discerning eye and you don't mind counseling some shell-shocked veterans through the initial adjustment to your culture. "No, no, it's okay, you and your ideas really are safe here."

In the case of the writer I just told you about, when we saw what a keeper she was, we simply asked her, "Hey, got any friends back at your old agency who might like to talk to us?" Yes indeedy. And in keeping with the birds-of-a-feather principle, she hadn't been hanging out with slouches, either. We've ended up hiring several terrific people, thanks to that one relationship. Now, we'll take worthwhile resumes and portfolios from anywhere, headhunters included. But I sure do like the efficiency that comes from all of us simply working our channels of personal contacts.

To be honest, The Richards Group has been a little late coming to this hire-your-neighbor program. Recently an out-of-town headhunter presented us with a candidate who piqued our interest. Nice book, someone we'd definitely like to talk to. Look through the samples again, check the address tag on the portfolio—good grief, the guy lives five blocks from our office. I think he probably had several classmates working here. We're not going to get all huffy and try to cut the headhunter out of the deal just because the guy is local. But I just wish the candidate had known that, in one sense, we're just like the Fantastic Sam's in the strip mall down the street. Walk-ins are welcome. Maybe we should put that on our door.

GROWING YOUR OWN

For a long time The Richards Group rarely hired senior people. We were almost always able to promote homegrown talent into senior positions as creative group heads, account-service principals, media directors, and so on.

The agency was around a dozen years old before I ever hired a creative director from the outside — Doug Rucker, who's still here leading one of our creative groups. That was also around the time that Larry Spiegel, a heavy hitter who had come up through the BBDO organization, moved across town from Tracy-Locke to head our media operation and Rod Underhill came out from L.A. as a principal, running the account-service group for Motel 6 and several other accounts. At the time, the late 1980s, our billings were passing the $100-million-a-year mark, and we were picking up new accounts too fast to fill all the necessary senior slots from within. Dozens of senior-level people have come to the agency since then. Many have stayed for years and years, just like the three guys I mentioned.

For some people our company culture is a blessed relief after years of trying to work while constantly watching their back for sharp implements. It was like that for Dick Murray, another one of our principals. (I told part of his story in Chapter 3.) In two years as head of DDB's Dallas office he grew it into a sizable operation, a success which, unfortunately, attracted the attention of certain opportunists in the parent company. They had cast scarcely a glance toward Dallas when the office was puny and insignificant, but now it looked like a nice jewel for their personal tiaras. "Suddenly," Dick recalls, "I was taking shots from all sides."

For some reason the home office decided to transfer him out of the branch he had led so successfully. It's as if the muck-a-mucks back East were saying, "Hey, Dick, here's a reward for your contribution: ka-*pow!*" So the two of us got together. He came to The Richards Group bringing no accounts, just a ton of experience and a major-league contact file. We put the resources of the agency behind him, and he proceeded to build a terrific account group from scratch. Ten years later Dick says, "I've been able to accomplish more here, and do it on my own terms, far better than I was ever able to do anywhere else."

Not every senior person brought from the outside has had such a happy experience, however. We've got a weird culture: no officers, no departments, no perks or special badges of rank, no doors. There have been times when people who signed on from more traditional employers just could not get used to it. We always try to be up front about our flat, collegial organization — check your ego at the door and all that — but not everyone really understands the change of life it can entail.

One woman arrived from New York bringing 18 or 20 years of experience, a fine portfolio of work . . . and her own antique wood office furniture. Our offices at the time were of the minimalist, rubber-and-matte-metal contemporary style, but, as I've said, we try to make room for idiosyncrasies. I can't work very well with speed-metal music in the room; maybe she can't work with metal cabinets. So we gave it a chance.

She set up her salon arrangement and set out to try to work in the manner to which she had become accustomed, which is to say maneuvering for her political advantage against people who are doing the same for theirs. The thing was, here nobody else was maneuvering; they were minding their own business. Her hard-edged, competitive style didn't fit in any better than the furniture. All perfectly understandable, considering how long she had worked in politically charged offices. But she just couldn't seem to make the adjustment to our culture. It completely fried her circuits. She grew extremely frustrated and left within a few months. No hard feelings. I respect her talent, but I'm glad she moved on. It definitely was not working for any of us.

Even the people who like the culture and thrive here will tell you that it can take a lot of getting used to. It's just so, well, *foreign*. When Doug Rucker, for example, signed on from another major agency in town in 1987, we were delighted to have him and he started contributing terrific work from day one. Even so, he says he didn't really feel at home here for two full years. It's kind of like moving to a different country. The people may be wonderful, the way of life pleasant, but no matter what you do it's just going to be strange to you for a while. And that's okay. Do try to make yourself at home. Keep the folk songs and cuisine of the Old Country, and your native dress if you like; we all benefit from the influences. But please, just don't try to import the old political system.

So you can see why we still like to recruit gifted kids fresh out of school and help them develop into homegrown leaders within the firm. We, like Seymour Cray, the supercomputer designer, view inexperience as an asset. Talented novices, he said, "do not usually know what's supposed to be impossible." What's "supposed to be impossible," in our case, includes free exchange and cooperation between creative and account management, the freedom of juniors to work on major assignments, and the opportunity for everyone, no matter how inexperienced, to present and defend their own work.

Rob Van Gorden, our account director on Chick-fil-A, started out at a major Chicago agency. "There," he says, "if you're a new AE, for your first six months you'll have five layers of management above you looking at every memo you write. Here when you start as an AE, you're doing something important the very first day."

Not that we throw novices in the deep water without so much as a swimming test. New AEs go through a training program, something like a residency, in which they work hands-on with senior people in print production, account planning, media, and so forth. With 40 years ahead of them to serve as a liaison between clients and all the disciplines in the agency, the least we can do is give them a solid working knowledge of those disciplines.

We also have a mentor program. Every new employee gets to pick someone who's been around a while to be their mentor. Job functions don't really matter in the pairings. Your mentor can be anyone other than your immediate supervisor. The mentor may be in media and the protégé in creative, for instance. It's not a training arrangement, at least not in the sense of job training. It's more like cultural training, a chance to learn the ropes of the organization, ask dumb questions (as if there were any such thing) in a safe environment, and, in general, simply feel like you've got an advocate, that you're not all alone in the big, wide world of work. Supervisors are there to help train you in the functional parts of your job. Your mentor helps with the squishier aspects of how we approach life, work, and problem solving around here.

Where training for job functions is concerned, immediate supervisors do a lot of teaching. Among the creative directors, for example, the ones with an art direction background have to spend a fair amount of time teaching newly minted ADs to draw. Most young ADs go all the way through school and never learn how. They're terrific at art direction, many of them, but lousy at drawing. They have to spend hours going through magazines finding photos to scan into their layouts. Anything that can be done with a Macintosh, they can do, but don't ask them to dash off a quick sketch for a pencil rough or marker comp. And that's a tremendous handicap.

Often, when you're presenting concepts, it's best to show rough layouts instead of a bunch of comps that *look* like finished ads but haven't had the *thought* that should go into finished ads. With roughs it's clear that the discussion is to be about the fundamental ideas. Details, you can fuss over later. But I've seen young art directors who, in order to create an artfully rough sketch, have to build what is essentially a finished comp on the computer and then trace it. That's part of the handicap. The other part is that lots of times you need some rudimentary drawing skill even to communicate an idea to your creative partner.

So that's why the senior ADs end up teaching basic illustration skills, along the lines of how to draw Spunky the deer on a matchbook. We use a kind of cartoony style, a few quick lines to get the basic idea across, and just about anybody can learn it. You don't have to be like Glenn Dady, who's been a group head forever but could just as easily have had a nice career as a caricaturist. Gary Gibson, another longtime group head, would starve if he had to make a living as an illustrator. But he's a master at the three-curves-and-a-squiggle style of rough illustration. It gets the idea across, it's got charm, and he's good at teaching it to his charges.

Not surprisingly, a lot of the old-timers (meaning, in advertising, anybody over the age of about 27) end up teaching college classes on the side. Texas A&M and Southern Methodist University have tapped our staff for advertising classes many times. UT-Austin brings people in to critique student work. So does Portfolio Center in Atlanta. A woman from account management is teaching English comp a couple of nights a week at a local junior college. But it's Dave Snell, one of the senior account planners, who has the glam assignment at the moment: teaching seminars at the Miami Ad School.

We really can't afford to have senior people who have no interest or skill in mentoring and training. The agency expands outward, not upward. New groups are forming all the time as we gain new business. Our organization is so flat and our business moves so fast, we need a constant supply of men and women ready to step into new leadership positions without years of moving up through the ranks—because, well, we don't have much in the way of ranks to move up through. Here if you're not a junior, you're a senior; there's nothing in the middle. In that setup, supervisors are the linchpin. They're huge.

A couple of years ago a Virginia-based group called MasteryWorks surveyed 500 people about their jobs and found that more than 475 of them, over 95 percent, had quit a job because of a negative relationship with their boss. Now, in the face of that statistic, tell me you don't want to bust your behind to create a supportive, mentoring organization.

Good and bad experiences are made at the level of your immediate supervisor. "She defines and pervades your work environment," write Marcus Buckingham and Curt Coffman, of the Gallup Organization. "If she sets clear expectations, knows you, trusts you, and invests in you, then you can forgive the company its [shortcomings]. But if your relationship with your manager is fractured, then no amount of in-chair massaging or company-sponsored dog walking will persuade you to stay and perform."

"Stay and perform" is what people tend to do here. Assuming you can be happy without being named second-associate-vice-something-or-other, you don't have to leave to find the career advancement you're after. At last count we had a dozen group heads and principals who started here either directly out of school or within the first two or three years after. Ad people are some of the gypsies of the business world, job-hopping constantly, but over the past 20 years or so The Richards Group has averaged only about 7 percent annual turnover. And even that low number is a little deceptive. More than a few of the people who leave us end up coming back later. Once a Grouper, always a Grouper. Or so I would hope, anyway.

Thinking of Quitting? Let Me Help You

After much investigation and objective deliberation, I have concluded that The Richards Group is *the* best employer in the country today. Maybe ever. Any right-thinking American would, I think, agree. It's certainly the only company that *I* would like to work for. Even so, we have unaccountably been overlooked by the business mags when they compile their annual "Best Companies to Work For" issues. Somehow we always slip under their radar. It must be because we're impeccably modest and would never stoop to self-promotion. Oh, well. Each of us must bear a measure of injustice in this life.

In any event, despite our rightful station as best employer in the galaxy, people do, from time to time, bail. I've mentioned a few of our distinguished alumni who have scattered to the four winds—people like Woody Pirtle, Jack Summerford, David Fowler, and Grant Richards.

Here are a few more you might know. Account guy Mark McGarrah and art director Brian Jessee have a thriving agency down in Austin. Producer Lisa Dee has Beaucoup Chapeaux, the production outsourcing firm. Greg Lane, who was Lisa's partner for a while, landed in Chicago as head of broadcast at DDB-Needham. Creative director turned commercial director James Dalthorp started out here long ago, fresh out of UT-Austin. Writer Thomas Hripko got so good at presenting the scripts he wrote for Tom Bodett and others that he ended up as a much-in-demand voice talent himself, with his own production company, The Radio Spot.

This could go on for pages: Groupers who have become clients, Groupers who hold senior positions in agencies around the world,

Groupers who have started dot-coms, Groupers with thriving free-lance careers, Groupers who've become educators.

As I hope you can tell, I still claim these people. It's a kick to see my old colleagues doing well in other far-flung pursuits, and I take it as a compliment that people like that chose to stop through here for a while.

I have never—not once—felt betrayed when somebody quit. Disappointed? Sure. Ever so slightly dissed? Maybe once or twice. But never betrayed. Skeptical eyebrows always go up when I make that statement, but it's true and here's why. Nobody owes the organization anything except a good, hard day's work. Only once in the history of this company have I worked with anyone with whom I took a vow of lifelong commitment—my wife, Betty. And even *she* quit as soon as we could afford a paid bookkeeper. You and I work together in good faith, sure, but it's not some heavy, holy *institution* we've gotten into. If you see something that looks like an opportunity, explore it.

And talk to me about it. To me, to your supervisor, to your mentor—wing it on out there. I'm dead serious about this.

You can't really explore an opportunity if you're trying to do it in on the sly. You need to be in a position to compare apples with apples, and if you're sneaking around job-hunting in secret, you're not in that position. Your would-be new employer is talking to you about your salary prospects, your expected career path, and so forth, so we need to talk about all that stuff, too. Lay it all out. See where you get the best deal. Hopefully, you'll think it's with us. But if not, we certainly can't fault you for leaving.

I realize it doesn't work like this in a politically charged company, where there's hell to pay if they catch you checking out new jobs. But my feeling is, if your bosses see your little exploration as disloyalty, then they've got some kind of insecure codependency thing going on and you should get out of there to keep from being stuck in a sick relationship. "You were a squalid little guttersnipe when we hired you. Your career was a *joke*, a sad, pathetic joke. We taught you everything you know, gave you your first *gold card*. And after all we've done for you, what thanks do we get? You send out . . . your *resume*." Get any whiff of that attitude from upstairs? They've got a problem. Move on.

A number of times I've talked to employees about moves they were considering and had to agree, like it or not, that they'd be missing a big opportunity not to leave us. In a recent instance, I dearly hated to lose Jan Deatherage, who left to get her Ph.D. She was a principal of the agency—not exactly somebody you could replace overnight by running an ad in the *Thrifty Nickel*—but given what she wants to do with her life I would've been a lousy friend to try and weasel her into stay-ing. Besides, I believe in ultimate justice enough to know that if I talk somebody into sticking around out of my own interest and without regard for theirs, it will end up hurting me down the road. The worm always turns. So if you're ready to launch out of here, then Godspeed, John Glenn.

Sometimes people use me as a sounding board but don't really ask my opinion about whether to take another job. That's okay, too. A num-ber of years ago, one of our senior writers was being courted by Chiat/Day, who were setting up a Dallas office for their regional Nissan-dealer account, which was new at the time. The writer had been stuck with a run of bad luck for several months, presenting a lot of good work to clients but always seeming to come in with the runner-up campaign. Along with a nice raise and the considerable prestige of the Chiat/Day name, they were promising lots of TV. And with only one creative team in the new office, there was no danger of coming in second.

So he dropped by my desk one afternoon and we talked it over. It was a short conversation, as it turned out. He outlined their offer and why he was considering it, and I started to ask a few questions — whether they have profit sharing, what their plans are for the new branch — questions I would consider if I were in his shoes. Then I asked, "Do you think you'll be okay in the second and third year when you get an assignment for, say, another year's Labor Day Sell-a-Thon spot?" Some people would be fine with that. He might have been one. I was just asking.

But as soon as I said it, he sat up. "You know, that's a good point," he said, even though, technically, I hadn't made a point — just asked a question. "I hadn't really looked at it from that angle. Thanks, I appre-ciate the chat!" And with that, off he went to turn down the offer. Ten years later we're still working together.

Of course, if he had left and the new gig hadn't worked out, he would have been welcome to return. That happens all the time. Mike Renfro did it when he went to Chiat/Day in California for a few months. Production guru Michael Hatley did it, too. He worked in the lucrative world of printing sales for 12 whole weeks before returning and picking up where he had left off.

Robin Ayres left RBMM for five years of full-time mommyhood before deciding that having three boys wasn't keeping her busy enough; now she's a principal of the firm. Kevin Swisher, today a cre-ative group head, went off to grad school and became a freelance mag-azine writer for a while, returning with a newfound appreciation for regular, twice-monthly paychecks. Account planning director Karen Dougherty moved with her family to Florida for a couple of years, but they somehow managed to miss North Texas and returned, much to our delight.

Even as I write these lines, yet another returnee is just settling in for his first week as a new/old Grouper. Writer David Longfield left us and became the creative director of another agency in town. Seven years later it's a pleasure to welcome him back.

Being able to say so long but not good-bye is simply good business. Employers who burn every bridge with departing employees only hurt themselves in the long run. People come back from their extended adventures with a treasure trove of experience that benefits everyone. Dirk Van Slyke, now a senior account guy, left and spent several years as the client of another agency. Another longtime account person, Vince Bove, did exactly the same thing; he became head of marketing for another client of the same agency Dirk's company worked with. We've learned lots of juicy stuff from these guys since their return.

For those with an entrepreneurial bent, we can often find creative ways to help you achieve your personal goals without actually having to lose you and your brains and talent. Ed Brock, Steve Miller, Dick Mitchell, and friends, with their designers' sensibilities, saw their future not with the ad agency we had become but rather in a true design firm. So we spun off RBMM in 1979, with very happy results. (The studio and its principals became well known around the world, although there has occasionally been minor confusion about what the initials RBMM stand for. A Japanese magazine once ran an article about Dick with the caption under his picture identifying him as "Richard Brock Miller Mitchell.")

Several years ago, writer Todd Tilford and account guy John Beitter got together as ringleaders of a pickup team going after funky and edgy pieces of business such as Hummer and the Doom video game. A hybrid sort of team—not quite a normal creative group, not quite an agency start-up—they didn't exactly fit any of our precedents or pre-existing categories. But so what? If it works, why worry about fitting it into some hypothetical org chart? So they built their own box, so to speak. It's called Pyro Brand Development and operates more or less autonomously out of a space downstairs from the rest of the agency.

Anybody else in the company is equally free to pursue something nontraditional and maybe hard to explain. For that matter, you're free to pursue something totally traditional if you like. Our policy is that you are welcome to quit your job without leaving the company. The greener pastures you're looking for may be right here.

It's not an insult to our exalted profession if you're not 103 percent happy in your current career track. So try something different. A creative coordinator recently switched to media. A very capable production manager thought account management might suit him better, so he went through the training program and now is a very capable account guy. Probably half of the broadcast producers started out in a completely different function, including, in one case, the mail room. Changing careers like that is a long, arduous process that takes great commitment and persistence. Why complicate it by changing to a strange new company? We're happy to help if we can.

Another thing: Around here you're not penalized for asking off an account. You can do that any time you see fit. Individuals can; groups can.

Somebody asked me once if this wasn't a recipe for anarchy. Aren't people—especially those volatile creative types—playing a constant game of musical accounts whenever they get their feelings hurt? In a word, no. I can't think of a single time when I have seen someone make what I thought was an immature, rash decision to move off an account without giving the relationship a chance to smooth out. People, I have found, are stalwart enough to endure a certain level of frustration, as long as the agency isn't compounding the frustration. And how would an agency compound the frustration? With the implied threat of a political backlash if you ask out of the situation. In a politically charged environment, there's always a penalty for not pressing on, however foolishly, through an assignment you're not well suited for. Your supposed weakness in quitting becomes someone else's political advantage.

We don't play that way. So you've got lousy chemistry with your creative partner? Change partners. There's no shame if a relationship just doesn't work. Same with your group assignment. Find a group you think you'll be happier in, and let them know you're available when they've got an opening. Be open about it; you don't need to sneak around. Collaborations often need fine-tuning. There is, I repeat, no shame in that. It's a whole lot easier to let people change groups if they feel the need than it is to replace good people who quit because they feel stuck in a frustrating situation.

You and I are not impersonal gears in a machine. We're complex personalities in a complex system. At the risk of sounding like a guy from California, we've got to let this thing be organic, let it have some, like, flow. Which, paradoxically, can make the company — this hodgepodge of fallible, emotional beings — run, on its best days, like the CAD-CAM'd, graphite-composite, perpetual-motion machine it isn't.

HOW TO LOSE PEOPLE PROFITABLY

Success has ruined my nifty turnover statistics. Ad people in general are infamous job-hoppers. Groupers, though, have always been inclined to stay put. In times past I loved being able to quote figures about the average tenure of our staff, which was extremely high for our industry. But for a number of years the company has been growing so fast, hiring at such a furious pace, that we now have a high percentage of relatively new arrivals. I'm still able to brag about how people tend to stay here for a long time. It's just harder now to prove it statistically.

As always, I still conduct our new-employee orientation meetings myself and find, more often than not, that the fresh new faces in these sessions end up becoming familiar faces I'll be working with for years to come. As an employer, I'm very proud of that.

There is, however, a definite downside to low turnover. Hair-trigger firings and draconian layoffs have never been part of our company culture, thankfully. That's one reason people like to settle down in this company. Plus, during our frequent growth spurts we're working at full blast, just happy to have enough people to get all the work done.

Reluctant to fire. Contented workforce. Need the workers. These factors together could, if we're not careful, cause us to keep marginal performers around forever, giving them annual raises we'd rather pile on the stars. As a consequence, I've had to work out a philosophy of turnover management. It involves viewing slowdowns and account losses as special opportunities.

In a traditionally managed agency, the loss of a big account almost inevitably triggers a layoff. A handful of superstars and/or skillful political apparatchiks may survive, but otherwise it's carnage time. Practically the whole group that handled the account can hit the street with one big sickening thud. That never made sense to me, ethically or practically. It's a lousy way to treat people, and you inevitably lose good ones you should be trying to keep.

Here's what we do when a big account goes away. We use it as an opportunity for *all* the groups, whether they worked on the departing business or not, to take stock of their staffing and, like mutual-fund investors, rebalance our "portfolio."

Your group's understaffed right now? Great. Some very good people just got freed up to help you. Chances are you already know them and their work, so grab 'em for a chat before somebody beats you to it. If you want to see people's self-esteem (not to mention their regard for the company) go through the roof, just watch what happens when two or three group heads are dropping by with invitations to join their teams.

Got some people in your group who haven't gotten their act together since their last not-so-hot review? Now's probably the time to cut them loose, while good replacements are available. And consider that there's usually a pretty lengthy transition period—30 to 90 days—when an account goes away. You don't have to settle all this before sundown.

The upshot is that we're able to keep our best people; we even out disparities in groups' workloads; we fire the very minimum number— the chronically poor performers who, face it, really need to move on and find something they're good at.

Obviously, our open workplace greatly aids the efficiency of this process. Cross-group moves and intergroup cooperation are normal. There's already a general awareness of the supply-and-demand situation—who needs help and who's got time to give it. So we get our rebalancing done with a minimum of upheaval. But even a more traditionally compartmentalized company can accomplish the same thing if you're willing to take a little time for group leaders to huddle and assess their staffing situations together.

You can actually turn a seemingly negative situation—the loss of an account or a general slowdown in the business—into a tremendous morale booster. It's in the lean times when you can most powerfully demonstrate to your employees that they and their talents are highly prized by the organization. That's one way you build a workforce that's proud to stick together through thick and thin.

THE TOODLEBIRD WILL GET YOU IF YOU DON'T WATCH OUT

Cultures all over the world have legends of strange and furtive creatures dwelling among them. There's Nessie in Scotland, Ogopogo in Canada, Bigfoot in the U.S. Northwest. Nepal has the Yeti; Mexico, the Chupacabra.

The Richards Group has the Toodlebird.

According to the legend, the Toodlebird is a great, black feathered creature — said to be like a raven but much, much bigger — that swoops in suddenly and silently to carry Groupers away, clutched in its terrible talons, never to be seen again.

Such occurrences do, of course, take place in every company, it being one of the less pleasant facts of business life that sometimes, for some reason, someone has to be "toodled." It usually happens quickly and away from plain sight. Thus, anthropologists say, every corporate culture has some sort of Toodlebird myth. Or so I'm told.

Different company cultures do, however, regard the Toodlebird with widely differing degrees of fear. In some workplaces the T-bird is an ever looming specter, a dark threat seldom far from employees' minds. Some bosses even like to carry the Toodlebird around on their shoulder like a parrot. *That* keeps the crew stepping lively — and usually jumping ship in droves, I might add. Here we've been pretty successful at keeping the big bird well out on the fringes of consciousness. He's not a major worry for most. Some people — mostly on the creative staff — even consider him to be a useful presence, a motivator almost like a mascot.

For creative teams, there's a point in nearly every project when you feel stuck — addle-brained and stupid, as though you'll never have a good idea again. One writer and art director team, having hit that point in their project du jour and with a deadline looming, were sitting silently with their feet up, drinking coffee, minds drifting. Suddenly the AD sat bolt upright, eyes wide. "What was that?!"

"Huh?" said his partner.

"Didn't you see it?" the AD asked, trembling melodramatically. His eyes scanned the ceiling in mock terror. "It was a shadow . . . the shadow of a giant bird. It flashed right across my sketch pad."

"Yeah," yawned the writer, stretching and reaching for his pencil. "We'd better get back to work." They did, pushed through their infertile spell, and came up with an ad.

I don't think we'd joke about the Toodlebird in our company if being fired was really a very present fear. Keeping it that way is important — vitally important. Our organization lives and dies by the creativity and initiative of its people, engines of productivity that work through positive contact between individuals. As psychologist Robert Sardello told an interviewer, "Fear closes down our imagination. And by imagination I mean our social contact with one another."

If, as some contend, a little tension is a good motivator, don't worry. We all have more than enough to keep us going: deadlines, fear of losing face with our peers if we don't come through, relational frictions. Some pressures will always be there. But we can work on the rest. Sardello said in the same interview, "Remember, we cannot eliminate fear. We can lessen its impact on our lives."

At The Richards Group, demonstrating, as we have many times, that losing an account does not trigger a bloodbath has probably done as much as anything to keep the fear level low. Encouraging people to change jobs within the agency helps a lot, too; you don't have to worry that bad chemistry with your group head will be your downfall. And with our cultural aversion to office politics, you don't have to worry that some unseen enemy will have you assassinated.

Mr. Dithers, Dagwood Bumstead's boss, makes a great cartoon character, physically booting poor Dagwood right out of his office at the slightest provocation. His character resonates with office dwellers everywhere. Even in the most civilized companies, there's a little part of many people, way back in the deeper recesses of their brains, that secretly fears their own boss may morph without warning into a Dithers and give them the heave-ho for any little thing—jamming the copy machine or something. For the record (and for the benefit of any Groupers who harbor that secret fear) let me say that only once in all these years have I ever fired somebody in anger. Even then, it wasn't a capricious summary execution. The guy's work hadn't been up to snuff for a while, and when he finally copped an attitude one time too many . . . well, let me just tell you the story.

He was a designer we'll call Don, and he worked here back when the company was just a small studio. I saw one morning that Don was having trouble with the piece he was working on, struggling to make the design work. Do you ever have those moments when you look at a problem that's baffling someone else and, in a flash, the solution just hits you? That happened when I looked at Don's layout. I saw an obvious solution that was eluding him. "Hey, why don't you try this?" I said, and explained what I was seeing. He grunted something that sounded like "okay," and I went on about my own work.

Several hours later, in the afternoon, I noticed that he was still struggling. Upon investigation, I found that he hadn't tried my idea yet. So I went over it again, explaining in more detail how it would solve the problem.

The next morning, there he was, *still* struggling mightily, still not even trying my idea. "Hey, Don," I said, feeling a little prickly about this by now, "I'm sure if you'd just try what I suggested it would get you unstuck and you could move on."

"Look," he said, "if you're so sure it needs to go that way, why don't you just do it yourself?" Which is pretty much what happened, since by lunchtime Don wasn't around to finish the project. Even at that it wasn't an especially spectacular scene. I didn't go totally Dithers on the guy. Exclamation points didn't pop out of my head, and I didn't scream and call him a dunderhead or anything. Guess I just don't have the old killer instinct.

Nobody should have to live with the constant threat of being sacked. You've got to feel free to make honest mistakes. Creativity, after all, is largely a process of finding something worth keeping out of all the lame and ho-hum ideas—mistakes, if you like—that constitute the majority of your output. Lashing us creative people with the fear of making a mistake is like whipping dairy cows to try and make them increase production. It's likely to dry up the output instead. Besides, the boss who rules by fear can expect to find, sooner or later, that his little pet will turn on him.

Promote People before They're Ready

One advantage of a company without managers is that it vastly increases the pool of employees who are qualified for promotion. No previous management experience? Hey! Join the club!

In a traditionally structured company, custom, protocol, and formal credentials can play too major a role in determining who moves up the ladder, to say nothing of the part played by good old-fashioned political jockeying. Nearly every organization has its horror stories of terrible managers who looked terrific on paper. By contrast, in an open workplace, choice candidates just emerge as part of the natural order of things.

We value leaders with a track record of producing good work in their particular discipline—media buying, account planning, copywriting, what have you. In fact, that's just about *all* we look for. If someone has been coming through in their work for a while, weathering the battles, rising to some hard challenges, then chances are they're already inspiring people to follow their example. Clients start asking for people like that: "I sure hope so-and-so is going to be working on this." And you can pretty well figure they've got a solid work ethic or the weakness would have revealed itself. So let's see . . . good work habits, plays well with others . . . sounds like a candidate for promotion to me.

Not that they would necessarily agree with that assessment. When first tapped for the role, many of our best leaders felt less than fully qualified to lead a group. But that's a good sign, too. Shows they're not too cocky.

Dennis Walker, Doug Rucker's partner in heading up one of our creative groups, was one such reluctant leader. A veteran art director, Dennis quietly went about his business, doing exceptionally tasty work. A print campaign that he and writer Kevin Swisher did for Neiman Marcus is still being shown in retrospectives of the agency's work nearly 10 years after they produced it. Clients could count on him to come through for them. Younger creatives could count on him for smart input. So when a group head position came open, Dennis was, to me, an obvious choice. Not so obvious to him, though. He took a few days to think it over before taking the plunge (with a little nudging on my part). He quickly proved to be one of our key creative leaders, not because he had to transform himself into a bigshot manager type but because the gifts he was already exercising made room for him in a place of leadership.

I learned the basics of my craft through formal education, but I learned how to run a company through on-the-job training. That established the pattern for my organization. When promoted to leadership positions, solid practitioners of their crafts prove time and again that they can fill out the rest of their portfolio of skills through OJT. If the foundation is there in their craft and in their character, the rest will come. No one has to be perfect at this. It's not like we're working with live ammunition or something. Trial and error, hits and misses, even out-and-out clinkers — they're fine, even necessary.

I'm not sure I'd say that, however, in a tribalized company where every boo-boo is an invitation for somebody to take you down a peg and where you're not surrounded on every side by willing advisers. The innate support structure of an open workplace encourages the trial-and-error learning that's at the heart of creativity and innovation while, at the same time, providing a safety net against most of the really disastrous missteps.

In terms of style and personality, good leaders are all over the lot. Strength in their chosen discipline and diligence in their work are pretty much the only common denominators. Ironically, ability to give detailed direction isn't even something I particularly look for in someone who will be, in fact, giving direction. If someone has a gift for being able to articulate precisely what needs to be done, I suppose that's a bonus, but, especially in creative, it's not a necessity.

THERE ARE NO FASHION POLICE.

No fashion citations. No fashion laws, for that matter. In the end, all that matters this fall is you. What you like. What you wear. Yet, while you alone can choose

your look, you don't have to choose it alone. For there's one fall collection that's been custom-tailored to your needs. It's waiting for you at Neiman Marcus.

How to look.

Part of the Neiman Marcus campaign by art director Dennis Walker and writer Kevin Swisher, with photographs by Geoff Kern.

I, myself, when reviewing creative work, rarely give very specific guidance. As a classically trained right-brainer, my ways of managing my world—be it the arrangement of visual elements on a poster or the arrangement of functions within the agency—tend to be, at least initially, nonverbal. I'll do what I know intuitively to be right, then go back later, if asked, and supply the verbal interpretation.

That works because people need line-upon-line directions less than you might think. When I'm reviewing work in progress, I find it's usually enough just to call attention to a specific area that needs work, without trying to give an instant answer about precisely what to do differently. "I don't think *this* part is working." "I think you should do something different *here*." "I don't think this visual is really working with that headline." I give a lot of input like that.

Usually the team gets it and doesn't need to ask for details. Once they recognize where a weakness exists, they'll solve it their own way—probably different from the way I'd do it and very possibly better. Their project, their solution. That's not the only way to give direction, but it's what works for me. And I get to be delightfully surprised by all the ideas I never would have thought of in a million years. This is part of the curatorial aspect of leadership. If you're good at editing out wrong answers, you don't have to be the person with all the right answers.

Fearless Collaboration, Free Communication, and Other Unnatural Acts

Peaceful, and prosperous, coexistence with your fellow citizens of the peaceable kingdom.

FIRST PRESUPPOSITION: YOUR EMPLOYEES ARE GROWN-UPS

Someone has described the advertising business as junior high school with money. I don't see it that way. At least not here. The paradox of a company culture like ours is that the more freedom you give your people to act like big babies, the more they'll prove to you that they're nothing of the sort.

Sure, we have our share of headbutting, hurt feelings, misunderstandings—this is intensely collaborative work, after all, and people invest a lot of emotion in it—but I rarely, if ever, see it turn into a petty, ongoing conflict. With our well-established practice of getting all the parties in the same room as soon as trouble pops up, people learn to work out their differences, or at least accept their personality conflicts like professionals, without getting all snitty about it.

We have an understanding here that there's a bottom line none of us should cross, and that is to rob another person of his or her dignity. Disagree, debate, get a mediator if you have to; just keep it clean. And that's about all the company ever has to say about it. Like most everything else around here, conflicts usually happen in plain view, which encourages both an air of civility and the involvement of the rest of the team as a moderating influence.

Some bosses worry they won't get an honest day's work from people. They *must* worry about it, or nobody would make time clocks. But I've found that diligence is the rule. And not because we *make* it a rule. Given the tools and the freedom they need to use their gifts, people enjoy working hard. I can't remember ever having to put on my boss hat and say, "Will you people get busy?" What I do end up doing, and often, is walking around the office at six o'clock saying, "Go home, guys." My experience around here has been that if people are imbalanced in their approach to work they're usually imbalanced on the side of working too much.

Now, I don't know, there may very well be some Groupers with a disposition toward goofing off. Get several hundred people together and it's likely you'll have some slackers in the bunch. But the culture pretty well takes care of that. There's no place to hide, literally or figuratively. The diligent majority sets the tone and pace. That's the positive side of peer pressure. An open workplace is remarkably self-policing.

Small case in point: We have our custom (I won't call it a policy) of using the stairs instead of the elevators within our several floors of office space. Nobody demands perfect compliance, and you do see people making little two- and three-floor elevator hops. But they can pretty well count on a good-natured jab from a friend ("Say, how's that *trick knee* holding up, buddy?"). And if somebody shows up at work in a leg cast or orthopedic boot, it's a standard joke to accuse them of faking an injury just to get around the "stair rule." The culture perpetuates its unwritten customs quite efficiently, without the insult of a bunch of regulations handed down from on high.

Among the Groupers I have yet to see anything but a mature outlook when it comes to our understanding that you're free to move out of a group or off an account if it's just not working out for you. My guess is that there'd be a lot more kvetching—and probably more turnover, too—if the rules said you were stuck with an assignment until your boss let you move. It reminds me of the medical study that found, to the surprise of many observers, that patients after surgery who could take a painkiller any time they wanted it used less on average than patients who had to wait for the hospital staff to dose them. Same at work. Your employees will faithfully endure the inevitable discomforts when the system isn't making the discomfort worse.

In short, people work best when they feel that they're in control. And they should. They're grown-ups.

Second Presupposition: Your Employees Are Moral Beings

I would rather get burned now and then than to treat my employees like snakes.

For one thing, I don't like what it would do to my insides to operate on the assumption that the people around me are out do the *wrong* thing. I picture Old Man Potter, the building-and-loan owner from *It's a Wonderful Life,* glaring suspiciously across the desk at Jimmy Stewart. Who wants to be that way?

Besides, experience shows that I'd be wasting my time as self-appointed corporate hall monitor trying to keep people in line all the time. My Grouper colleagues are honorable men and women, and they prove it every day by their actions in a workplace where they're at liberty to run amok if they're so inclined. They're just not so inclined, that's all. The exceptions are so rare that to clamp heavy restrictions on the whole workforce just to try to control the actions of the potential bad apples would be a colossal self-sabotage. We'd be robbing ourselves up front of the potential that people at liberty have.

Maybe it's that positive group dynamic again, the fact that our open workplace and culture tend to encourage actions favorable to the team and discourage the other kind. There must be something to that because, heaven knows, The Richards Group is not *The Brady Bunch.* (From what I've heard the Brady Bunch weren't *The Brady Bunch* either, but that's another story.) We've definitely got our fair share of flaws and foibles, but so what? They haven't wrecked the company.

The last time I counted, the agency had roughly 600 employees. If I believe the National Institute of Mental Health's 1999 statistics about American workers (and, of course, I'd be crazy not to), then based on NIMH's percentages something like 120 of my coworkers have mental health problems, 50 or 60 are alcoholics, and 30 or 40 use illicit drugs. This assumes that our workforce is average. Some people think working at an ad agency is itself a symptom of mental illness.

You know what I do with scary statistics like that? Ignore them. Giving much attention to that stuff creates a mental health problem of its own: paranoia and suspicion—walking around the office with an Old Man Potter face trying to figure out who's nuts, who's a drunk, and who's a stoner. It's not our style to keep everybody under intense scrutiny all the time. Help whoever needs help, sure. But you're in a better position to actually know who that is if you lay off the Big Brother routine, give people a chance to be themselves, for better or worse, and just work together openly. As C.S. Lewis said, "You can't really study people, you can only get to know them."

We don't keep company secrets. I made the point earlier about how harmful it is to draw a dividing line between those in the know and those in the dark. The only information we ever really deal with on a strict need-to-know basis is personal compensation. People have proved wonderfully trustworthy with sensitive information. It's very rare for somebody to get sloppy with knowledge we'd prefer to keep within the agency.

Once, during a major new-business pitch, a trade publication (that I won't name just in case naming them somehow hurts their book division) printed some inside info about our presentation strategy. We'd had a leak. But we didn't hire retired Stasi agents to ferret out the blabbermouth or institute a policy of restricting information about a project to those with direct involvement. At our next stairwell meeting I simply cautioned everybody to please be prudent in the future. That's all it took. I don't think we've had a leak of any consequence since. And that was years ago.

The unity and productivity that come from sharing information are well worth the puny amount of risk. Authors Bennis and Biederman recount a story told by Richard Feynman, one of the lead scientists on the Manhattan Project team during World War II.

"The army," they write, "had recruited talented engineers and others from all over the United States . . . to work on the primitive computers of the period, doing energy calculations and other tedious jobs. But the army, obsessed with security, refused to tell them anything specific about the project. . . . They were simply expected to do the work, which they did—slowly and not very well." Feynman convinced his superiors to lift the veil of secrecy, and project director Robert Oppenheimer gave the technicians a special lecture on the nature of their work and how it could help bring an end to the war. " '*Complete* transformation,' Feynman recalled. '*They* began to invent ways of doing it better. . . . They worked at night. They didn't need supervising in the night; they didn't need anything . . .' Ever the scientist, Feynman calculated that the work was done 'nearly ten times as fast' after it had meaning."

Bottom line: You can trust your people. You're only hurting yourself if you don't.

HOARDING THE GOOD STUFF

Why is it so hard to get good help? Help from one's supposed friends, I mean.

In tribalized companies, you won't find many examples of one team/ group/department chipping in to assist another. Best efforts are always reserved for the tribe. There's competition there. But beneath the competition runs a suspicion: *If I lend a hand it's somehow going to end up hurting me.*

Where does that idea come from?

Now, if you work in an environment where backstabbing and subversion are common, I can understand feeling a little reluctant to say yes when somebody offers to help *you.* They could be like the "good Samaritans" that Americans traveling abroad are warned about, who offer to help you fix a flat, then steal everything in your car. Some workplaces warrant a bit of paranoia. But it's harder to understand how the same air of suspicion can keep people from *extending* an offer to chip in. And that happens all the time, too. How can helping hurt you?

I've seen people who act so suspicious when it comes to lending a hand outside the very narrowest tribal confines, you'd think it was a matter of vile treachery and high treason. "Help the account guys proof the leave-behind? Uh, I don't know . . ." You've probably seen the type— stingy and strangely distrustful about lending aid.

The real root of their suspicion (I suspect) is fear that the effort of contributing from their stock of knowledge or creativity will diminish them, empty them of whatever it takes to come through in their own assigned tasks. They see themselves not as a well of ideas, constantly replenished, but as a cistern—and a shallow one at that—continually in danger of running dry. Insecure about their abilities, they become miserly and overcompetitive. (This is a manifestation of the same insecurity that sends some creatives into a full-on snit when a client rejects one of their ideas. They're afraid they can never come up with another idea that's just as good and cannot conceive of having one that's even better. I wish they'd get some help for their problem because they're making our whole creative tribe look like big brats to all the others.)

It's just silly. Unless you're a complete moron and you *know* you're such a complete moron that your only chance of getting ahead is to hope you can make the other guy look like an even *bigger* moron than you— unless that's the case, then getting out of your little tribal box and giving away your best stuff is, in fact, the most self-interested thing you can do.

Think about it. If you have even a modicum of self-esteem, one iota of confidence in your abilities, then you know that offering ideas to another creative team, say, or helping another group put their presentation together isn't going to drain you of all your ideas and sap you of all your energy. You know you're not that finite. The exercise won't dull you; it will make you sharper. The more you give, the more you get. For yourself.

When ideas are your currency, thrift is not a virtue. Creative work rewards extravagance. Says Annie Dillard in *The Writing Life* (Harper & Row, 1989), "One of the few things I know about writing is this: spend it all, shoot it, play it, lose it, all, right away, every time. Do not hoard what seems good for a later place. . . . The impulse to save something good for a better place later is the signal to spend it now. Something more will arise for later, something better. These things fill from behind, from beneath, like well water. Similarly, the impulse to keep to yourself what you have learned is not only shameful, it is destructive. Anything you do not give freely and abundantly becomes lost to you. You open your safe and find ashes."

Secure people operate with the kind of enlightened self-interest she's talking about, giving away their best stuff, knowing that better will come. They don't feel smaller because they help someone else get bigger.

Still, it's a leap of faith every time. There's really no *proof* that you're going to find any water in the creative well the next time you go to draw a scoopful. And besides that, there's emotional risk every time out. Who's to say that you're going to be "on"? You could give your best efforts for the cause and find that your ideas are 100 percent lame-o. You feel exposed and vulnerable — you feel your fallibility. But that isn't necessarily a bad thing.

A study by social psychologists Justin Kruger and David Dunning revealed that the only people with an unflaggingly high opinion of their abilities were, in fact, perfect dodos. Complete incompetents. According to a wire service story about Kruger's and Dunning's findings, "when it came to a variety of skills — logical reasoning, grammar, even sense of humor — people who essentially were inept never realized it, while those who had some ability were more self-critical."

I don't know anybody who's any good in this business who doesn't approach each day with a certain understanding that *I just might not be all that smart today.* Some respond by being humble and self-deprecating; some come on with arrogance and take themselves way too seriously. Talented people, though, always sense their limited state, whether consciously or not. An oft-retold story about Bill Bernbach, one of my heroes in this business, is that he always carried in his pocket a laminated card bearing the words, "Maybe he's right." (The gender may be wrong in today's context, but the humility still works fine.) William Goldman, the screenwriter and novelist, has said, "I don't know how it is for others, but building up confidence is the single hardest battle I face every day of my life." Obviously, he gets over it. Somehow the good ones do. Or they take rank with those stingy souls who believe every idea could be their last, and they're sure not going to spend the last one on *you*.

"All right," you may say, "I'd be glad to offer a hand to the tribe over there, but they'd probably just say no anyway." That could be true; they might not trust you. But they also might be desperate enough (or if they're not all that sensitive to the political climate, naïve enough) to actually accept your help, in which case you've just struck a nice blow against tribalism.

Whether you save the day or even make a meaningful contribution to their cause doesn't really matter. The symbolic power of one small gesture could create the seemingly insignificant one-degree warmup in relations that ends up changing the political climate forever.

NOT-SO-STRANGE BEDFELLOWS

In Chapter 1 we touched on the notion of distinct tribal personalities and the potency they can bring to your workforce. In my industry, advertising, the classic pairing of creative with account management most often brings internecine warfare. At The Richards Group, though, we view the two as complementary aspects of one process: producing strong, original advertising.

If it's the job of creative people to afflict the comfortable with challenging new ideas, it's often the AE's job to comfort the afflicted. We had a health care account for a number of years that was a division of an extremely old, extremely conservative New England insurance company. In spite of that fact, we managed, when the job called for it, to do some pretty edgy, even wacky advertising.

One commercial that ran in a few test markets featured the greatest hits of bumbling daredevil "Super Dave" Osborne, who at the time was just becoming well known for his show on HBO. The general idea was, for the first 20 seconds or so we see the hapless Dave getting blown up, run over, slammed into walls, and squashed by a huge steel ball in a rapid-fire series of stunts gone terribly wrong. Then, in an on-camera stand-up, he tells us that he wouldn't attempt any of these stunts without a great health plan. It was one of the funniest commercials the agency had ever done. Consumers loved it. It tested great, which made the client love it. Certain influential doctors in the client's network, however, did not love it. "Hate" doesn't begin to describe their feelings. One of them actually said to the copywriter, David Longfield, "Have you ever *seen* a man who's been hit by a wrecking ball, Mr. Longfield? Well, I have, and I can assure you there is no humor to be found in it."

Could've fooled me. I thought it was hilarious. Nevertheless, chalk up one more great spot that didn't get out of test market. Still, considering the ultraconservative client, the fact that it got even that far is a miracle.

I think one reason the creatives were able, at least on occasion, to do work like that was because the client was so comfortable with the account team, who appeared every bit as straightlaced and old school as they. One of the account guys, Charles, was so conservative we figured he probably slept in gray pinstripe jammies with a well-thumbed

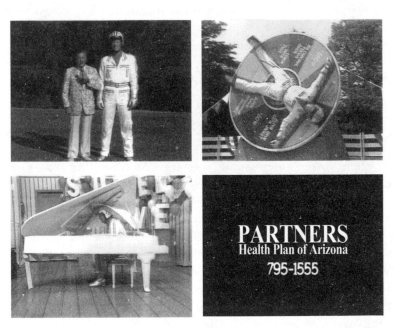

Our most slapstick commercial ever was produced for one of our most conservative clients—a testament to the trust that existed between the client and their account team. David Longfield was the writer; Jim Baldwin, the art director.

copy of *Robert's Rules of Order* for his night table reading. One look at the guy was enough to soothe any misgivings the client might have about what the agency was up to.

Then one night some people from the agency went to a concert at one of the punkier clubs in Dallas's Deep Ellum district. And there was Charles—the *real* Charles, as it turns out—decked out in black leather, wearing an earring (somehow we must have always assumed that the hole in his earlobe was the result of a freak mishap with a stapler) with a pale, waifish, black-clad girlfriend on his arm. Changed his image at the agency forever. All the while, as it turns out, Charles's conservatism was an act, a persona he put on every morning along with his Jos. A. Bank trousers. Charlie, we hardly knew ye.

Charles, to his credit, recognized that this particular client relationship—if it was going to work for more than about 10 minutes—needed someone with particular traits, distinct from the kind of agency folks the straightlaced client people might find a little too outrageous. Once again, wildly divergent types turned out to be a perfect blending, bound together by a common goal and mutual respect.

AID AND COMFORT TO THE ENEMY: WISE POLICY

I think I once helped a guy win an account that I wanted. You may know him: Gary Goldsmith.

Nowadays Gary is executive CD at Lowe Lintas, and I'm proud to say I knew him when. I first met him as a favor to one of my neighbors. This teenager they knew was interested in going into advertising, and they asked whether I would mind meeting him. Sure, no problem. So up to the office he came, toting a portfolio of art and writing samples. Lo and behold, my neighbor had sent me a keeper. I liked Gary immediately and recognized that he had the makings of a terrific adguy. So I recommended, as I often have over the years, that he check out Art Center College in Pasadena. He took my advice, went to Art Center, and kept in touch during his years there. So far, so good.

The idea, of course, was to keep track of a future star and then hire him before anybody else had a chance to horn in on my discovery. It was a great plan, and I'm sure Gary would have been *much* happier working at The Richards Group, but instead he headed to New York after graduation. Darn. Actually I don't blame him. He's from Dallas, and there's a lot to be said for making a career for yourself someplace other than your hometown. Besides, there was never any expectation on my part, nor any obligation on his. The world needs more good advertising people, wherever they may choose to land. We still kept in touch, though—even after he and Bob Jeffrey had launched their own agency, which quickly gained a reputation for doing some of the best work in the country.

Eventually, we did pitch against Goldsmith/Jeffrey. The account was EDS, based just a few miles up the road from us, in Plano. We were the only Dallas shop on the shortlist. Goldsmith beat us, won it right out from under our noses. So much for the home-field advantage. I guess it's some consolation—*small* consolation, but consolation nevertheless—that the business at least went to somebody I like.

When it comes to the professional group with the most abysmal public image, advertising people are in a neck-and-neck race with bootleggers and members of Congress. Maybe we could improve our image and at least give used car salespeople a run for their money if we'd spend a little more time sharing the legitimate tricks of our trade with newcomers—even those who may, on occasion, beat us old-timers at our own game. I'm not talking about swapping client secrets. Nothing reckless or unethical. It's just that the fences between people in the same industry needn't be quite as high and electrified as we tend to make them sometimes. If we'd be a little more willing to share the broad principles that could make us all more successful, we could raise the level of work our industry does and improve the quality of our contribution to the cultural landscape.

These days, as a creative guru in his own right, Gary devotes a lot of energy to just this sort of thing. He teaches classes, writes articles, and even cofounded a creative training program called Adhouse. In other words, he's giving away his knowledge just as fast as he can. We need more like him. Too many people, entrenched in their positions, are too insecure to reach across functional or generational barriers and share what they know—afraid they'll be diminished when in fact they'll be enlarged.

Others, however, are willing; they just need to be asked. You can't presume that the leader in the other department or the executive in the other company will look at you as the enemy. They won't come looking for you, though, to share what they know; you've got to ask them. See somebody across town or across the country whose organization you'd like to emulate in some way? What the heck. Call them up. That's what Gary did. And I've done it, too.

Back in the early 1990s, when The Richards Group made the shortlist for Mercedes-Benz, I realized that all of a sudden my little agency had moved up to a new league. The accounts were bigger, the pitches more elaborate, the competition more formidable, and the stakes higher than we had ever seen. Frankly, we didn't know quite how this game was played, but the good news was, we knew people who did. So we called some of them up—old pros who had been around the block a few times when it came to high-stakes presentations and who could give us a frank, knowledgeable critique of the pitch we were planning for Mercedes.

Larry Spiegel, our head of media, recruited Dick Peters, who, as public affairs chief at Phillips Petroleum had been Larry's client for many years. I called Norm Campbell. Norm, a tall Texan with a disarming aw-shucks manner, had started out decades ago as a junior AE at the Tracy-Locke agency and worked his way to the upper echelons of the BBDO organization. He's seen it all in this business.

When I called him, Norm had recently retired and moved back to Dallas from New York. Given his close association with both our long-time local competitor Tracy-Locke and our potential national competitor BBDO, I guess he could have viewed my company as a rival. But his approach was that of an elder statesman. "Man, if y'all can bring the Mercedes account to Dallas, it'll be a tremendous boost to this whole community," he said. "I'd be happy to come help critique you guys." He did, however, think it prudent to clear the idea with his BBDO colleagues. They saw no conflict of interest, either.

So one day, as our presentation was starting to take shape—I'd say it was in the larval stage at that point—Dick, Norm, and our own Rod Underhill, a strong presenter and shrewd judge of creative, gave up an evening at home to meet with our pitch team in a large conference room at the agency. After a few minutes of initial chitchat, we treated it just like a real pitch. They, the "clients," sat on one side of the table. We, the presenters, lined up opposite them and gave it our best shot. It was a great drill, very realistic. With a couple of heavy hitters from outside the agency there to judge us, we even had some genuine butterflies in our stomachs.

After we pitched our little hearts out, our panel of friends tore into us. Nothing unkind, mind you. On the contrary, we *wanted* them to be unsympathetic, to cast a jaundiced eye upon us and hold us to the toughest standards of this new league we were in. They didn't disappoint. We showed way too many ads, they said. We buried our strongest strategic insights. We belabored some points and skipped too lightly over others. We went too fast, or too slow. We looked too much like deer in the headlights. In short, we needed a *lot* of work. And, boy, am I glad they told us.

Without their help, I doubt we would have gone on to make the best presentation in our history (a proud moment even though we didn't win the account). I don't know that we would have made the right impression on M-B's Steve Cannon, who, as I'll detail in Chapter 7, would eventually become our client at DaimlerChrysler's giggo.com. Don't know that we would have done as well in who knows how many presentations after that. Don't know that we would have entered a new phase of our company's development with anywhere near the confidence we did. We didn't win that particular pitch, but we came out major winners in the long run, thanks to the help of outsiders.

Seeking—and giving—help outside the boundaries of your tribe can test your sense of self. How much is your identity tied narrowly to your company, your department, your group, your function? Maybe a lot. Insularity feels like safety. So does extreme self-reliance. Modern business has taught us to beware anyone who appears too willing to help you. What looks like an open hand may, in fact, be about to slap you upside the head, right?

A lot of progress for our companies and ourselves is locked inside walls of fear and suspicion, just waiting for somebody to make the first move. And every time someone makes that move—connecting with an enemy who turns out to be no enemy at all—it makes business a little better for us all.

AN AGENCY THAT GETS TO WORK ON TIME

Ask any ad agency employees in the world and they'll tell you, advertising isn't a 9-to-5 job. Oh, some days it is. A 9:10-or-9:15-to-5 job anyway. Other days it's more of a 10-to-9 job (that's A.M. to P.M.). After which, for a day or two, it's likely to be a 10:30-to-whenever job.

You work late one evening, so you come in a little later the next morning. Which forces you to work even later *that* evening, and so on. I call this phenomenon "sliding the day." In my company we strongly discourage it, and the reason is this: Just because you weren't here at 8:30 this morning (our firm's official start time), that doesn't mean people didn't *need* you at 8:30 this morning. In our particular business, and in most others, if sliding the day ever gets started, one group can end up keeping a rock-star schedule, while another group gets bitter because the rock stars are putting them behind schedule.

Sliding the day is fine in some lines of work. I know a research engineer at one of the high-tech companies in town who sometimes goes into the office at 10 or 11 P.M. and works all night because that's when he can get undisturbed lab time. In his job, it doesn't matter when he works as long as he gets the work done on time. Our company isn't like that. It's a collaborative business. People can't get their own work done without you. (Doesn't that make you feel *good?*)

So here's what I've always said. I don't really care how late you worked last night. Be here at 8:30. Otherwise, you're holding up the whole team.

As someone who has slept on the floor under my drawing board on more than a few nights, I know that sometimes the hours in this business are onerous. We all go through periods when several projects hit at once. Or we have to stay several nights in a row for focus groups that aren't over till 10:30. Or *something* comes up that makes you practically live at the office for a while. If we couldn't handle that, we would've picked a different business. Still, those desperately busy spells are one of the less pleasant aspects of this industry.

We've tried to deal with that, to make up for the strain, through an unusual feature of Richards Group life known as the FRO—FRiday Off.

Sometimes the only way to fairly compensate people for their time is to give time back to them. So as often as every six weeks, if you've been working a lot of extra hours, you can take off on a Friday, free and clear. Catch up on your sleep or your errands. Reintroduce yourself to the family. It's a free day and doesn't count against your vacation time. You've been busting your back for the firm; it's the least we can do for you.

Thanks to FROs, we're able to address what can be a downside of working with exceptionally diligent people. I'm not talking about burnout, though it does help on that. I'm talking about the temptation to cheat on time sheets by fudging *in reverse*—recording fewer hours than actually worked.

Certain people, who shall remain nameless, feel such a burden of responsibility for the agency's profitability numbers that they'll record only 8 or 9 hours that day even if they actually worked 12 or 13. I'd like to say I appreciate the gesture, but the fact is that I don't. Tell the truth; don't varnish. If in order to serve a client we're consistently having to work a lot more hours than our fee from the client covers, then we should simply ask for a higher fee. But this is where FROs come in. Brad Todd did a little quantitative research with time runs for his account group and found that taking regular FROs virtually wiped out what some of his people *thought* was excessive overtime.

All of which makes the FRO a pretty nifty little system. It helps balance our lives and balance the books all at the same time.

E-MAIL LESS, WALK MORE

We used those words a few years ago as a headline for Cole-Haan shoes, but we use them every single day as our own corporate manifesto. Get up. Walk to the desk of the person you want to speak to. At the very least, pick up the phone and call the person on the intercom if you're really in a big hurry. But no internal e-mails.

You've got to get out of your electronic cocoon. Direct, nonvirtual contact breaks down barriers.

Now, I do like e-mail for certain things. We use it with clients and suppliers and friends just like everybody else. The text of this entire book has traveled all over the country by e-mail. So I'm no Luddite. It's just that I'm a believer in direct communication, in seeing body language, hearing inflections, reducing the distance between people in the company. And you can't really connect with somebody through an emoticon. Not even the kind that winks. ;-)

Here in Dallas and other cities, developers are rushing to build new urban neighborhoods that are like *old* urban neighborhoods: densely built with a mixture of functions—homes, shops, cafés, offices, parks, and other gathering spots. They've rediscovered that for all the talk

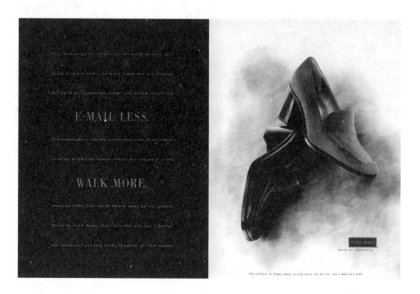

Good line for shoes, great idea for company policy. The writer was Mike Bales; the art director was Shane Altman.

about online communities, *real* community happens best through incidental contact with your neighbors. It's a pleasant way to live—and as we find in our open, mixed-use office, a pleasant way to work.

Direct contact is the only way to deal with *un*pleasantness, too. Our kingdom isn't 100 percent peaceable yet. After all, it's not that far from rubbing shoulders to butting heads. But one of the paradoxes of our company culture, and one of the secrets of its success, is how the open workplace confines conflict and helps us deal with it in a straightforward way. In close quarters, and with no possibility of firing off long-distance shots via flame mail, little irritations and conflicts must necessarily be dealt with pretty quickly, before they fester, by the parties involved. You've got to live together. There's no good place to hide from one another. So you might as well get it worked out and get it over with.

Getting all the parties to the conflict in the room together is an absolute necessity. Leave the shuttle diplomacy to Henry Kissinger. On the rare occasions when I'm called upon as the court of last resort, I don't even have to render a decision all the time. Once the combatants are gathered, I say this: "I suggest that you try one more time to reach some resolution. If you can't work it out, then, yes, I'll do it for you, and probably *neither* of you will like what I decide." Off they go and, more often than not, reach some kind of détente.

So maybe we're not yet perfect at this direct-contact thing, but at least we're trying to make sure we get plenty of practice.

"DEAR JOHN, PLEASE BE INFORMED THAT OUR PARADIGMS ARE NO LONGER SYNERGISTIC . . ."

It doesn't require many words to speak the truth.
—Chief Joseph

It's not enough just to talk to each other. The language you use can either raise or lower barriers between people.

Nearly every job has its tribal dialect, its codes and shorthand phrases. In my company, to overhear certain exchanges between, say, media planners or IT people, you might as well be listening to a conversation in Urdu. Nothing wrong with that. Specialists need special words to communicate efficiently with each other. The trouble comes when special vocabularies are used to obscure or to intimidate or to exclude people who aren't members of the club.

H.L. Mencken, in his 1936 book *The American Language*, wrote, "Nearly every . . . trade has its argot . . . some of them unintelligible enough to the general to be almost classed as cant, on higher levels." The problem of language as a divisive force has gotten worse since Mencken's day. There's no "almost" about it anymore. You hear a *ton* of cant these days—bombastic baloney intended to make the speaker sound smart and the hearer feel like an outsider. It's fast becoming our native language. Richard Saul Wurman, author of *Information Anxiety* (Que, 2000) and founder of the TED conferences on technology, entertainment, and design, writes that employees "are losing the ability to communicate clearly with their coworkers and clients."

Particularly in management ranks, where it's considered important to emphasize that one is smarter than the little people, straight talk has become so rare that it sounds as strange and anachronistic as something out of Chaucer. Sales never go up or down anymore; they're positively or negatively "impacted." Thinking and concentrating are passé; ideation and focus are where it's at. It's as if we're insecure, afraid that what we're saying isn't important enough all by itself, so we think we have to say it in an Important Way.

Never call a spade a spade if you can call it a manually operated terrain relocation system.

Even in marketing, a discipline that doesn't need a lot of technical language and that is supposed to be close to the person in the street, there's a growing tendency to become, in Woodrow Wilson's phrase, "intoxicated by the exuberance of our own verbosity." Not long ago Dave Snell, one of our senior account planners, gleefully exposed an example in a creative brief somebody was writing for Corona beer.

You've probably seen our Corona commercials. *Very* laid-back. What little action there is takes place at a languid, tropical pace. A typical spot features a guy at a rough-hewn table on a Mexican beach, thumping slices of lime between two Corona bottles in a south-of-the-border variation on the old game of paper football. You see only his hands, the limes, the bottles, and the water in the background. In another spot, a guy is skipping stones on a Mexican lagoon, when his pager goes off. So he skips the pager. Again, you never see the guy, just his arm and hand.

Never showing the guy is an important element in the Corona campaign, so naturally it needs to be noted on the creative brief. But simply saying "Don't show the guy" didn't *sound* important enough to whoever drafted the brief Dave saw. In the part of the brief titled "Are there any creative guidelines?" was written this lofty phrase: "Ambiguity of protagonist." Now there's one heck of a guideline. Fortunately,

Thought you were seeing just a guy's hand? Nope,
you were witnessing "ambiguity of protagonist."
Impressed? Art director: Jim Baldwin; writer:
Mike Renfro.

Dave had the brief rewritten before somebody came up with a new
Corona campaign starring Boy George.

BE UNAFRAID, BE VERY UNAFRAID

> *Our greatest foes, and whom we must chiefly combat, are*
> *within.*
>
> — Cervantes

Pressure, anxiety, stress — we've got those puppies by the litter at our
agency. Who doesn't? The emotional investment we put into the work,
the subjective nature of so much of it, the fact that half the time we
never really know whether a job's finished (you can *always* fuss with an
ad a little longer, try to come up with a better idea), the fact that we do
it on deadline — let's just say you could probably pick a profession more
conducive to your mental health. This is not news. We all knew when
we went into this business that it can mess with your head.

So it seems to me that we have more than enough to worry about as
we follow our bliss in this business without having to introduce another,
entirely optional emotional burden into the office. I'm talking about
fear. It breeds in ad agencies like rats in a grain barge. Fear of screwing

up. Fear of appearing vulnerable. Fear of looking bad. Fear of being bested. Fear of being squeezed out. Fear of losing an advantage. Fear of losing your meal ticket. Fear of nothing that you can put your finger on — just free-floating fear, gnawing away and having lots of loathsome little rat babies.

To use another, nonrodent, analogy, when fear gets into a company's culture it's like aromatherapy in reverse — a sulphurous, enervating vapor that moves through the ductwork, depressing creativity, agitating conflict, and in general just spoiling all the fun.

As I've discussed, knocking down doors and tearing out walls has done wonders for reducing one species of paranoia, the understanding that if that door over there is closed, then they *must* be talking about me in there. As for other forms of fear, they don't all go away quite so automatically, but our company culture has done a pretty good job against them, too.

One reason I survived my early years in business was that I wasn't afraid to try stuff, to implement ideas I hadn't seen before. Working solo, I had no other choice. It was all on-the-job training. I'd watch and try to learn from the example of others, I'd ask for advice when there was someone to ask, but mostly I had to just live by my own lights and fly it on out there. Sometimes I was wrong. I'd overcommit or underestimate or otherwise misjudge, and I'd have to pay the consequences. But it never killed me, never put me out of business. And I learned so much from the mistakes that I became unafraid to make them.

As my little company grew into a bigger company, I made a concerted effort to give the others their chance at OJT, learning by doing without fear of disaster. I tried to make this a place where it's okay to screw up.

Michael Eisner has said he wants Disney to be a place where "people feel safe to fail." That's what I want. If you play it safe, if all you do is try to *not fail,* then you'll never really succeed. Falling short of the mark, when it comes through risk taking and not through sloppiness or moral weakness, can be a gift to the organization. It builds wisdom and maturity, gives you something other than thin air to build from. As somebody has said, "Anything worth doing is worth doing poorly to begin with."

Look at the example of the creative process. I suppose it would be nice if all good advertising ideas could be born into the world full-grown and beautifully formed, like Botticelli's Venus emerging from her clamshell. But they just aren't. Practically every beautiful idea has really ugly parents. Take, for instance, the lame, stupid, misdirected, outrageously wrong headlines that you and your creative partner have to write before one of you hits on the brilliant, outrageously *right* line that somehow grows out of all that wrongness. We know that the creative process has to work that way, from not-right ideas (I really hate to call them wrong) to right ones. So why don't we cut the rest of our business practices the same break?

We make judgment calls all day every day. It's a fearful way to live if you think you'll be hammered for every wrong call you make. Who's always right anyway? You can't operate solo, not forever. The Lone Ranger can't be right often enough to produce consistently strong work. This has to be a collaborative business. Through collaboration we polish the rough edges off our work while it's still safely inside, before it's sent Out There, where the stakes are a whole lot higher. Doesn't matter if it's creative development, account management, research design, or media planning and buying. You won't get the best work out of the agency without a whole lot of give-and-take *within* the agency.

One practical payoff of our relatively barrier-free workplace is that it promotes constant, incidental collaboration. You're continually seeing and hearing what your coworkers are doing, and vice versa, so it's easy to simply put in your two cents' worth. We have little choice but to conduct the messy part of the process — the silly ideas, the intriguing but irrelevant thoughts, the abortive attempts, the *learning* — out in plain view. You're there with your awkward little featherless newly hatched idea — your baby — and there's a good chance somebody will be around to recognize its potential and contribute a nourishing tidbit to help nurture it toward maturity.

That's exactly what happened with the Chick-fil-A cow campaign. When I first saw the idea, it was practically just a doodle on a piece of layout paper. An art director named David Ring brought around a cartoon he had drawn, a cow holding a sign that said, "Eat mor chikin." There wasn't an assignment open in the Chick-fil-A group that it really fit; the notion had come up in the course of something else he and his writer partner, Gail Barlow, were doing for the client.

So he was showing this little cartoon around the agency and basically asking, "Okay, so what *is* this?" Well, besides the obvious answer that it was pretty funny, as we all talked about it we agreed that it was also relevant. In the previous year or year and a half, since becoming Chick-fil-A's agency, we had been positioning the brand against hamburgers as a more wholesome, higher-quality alternative. For example, a billboard from around that time featured a huge, delicious-looking close-up shot of a Chick-fil-A sandwich, with the headline "Don't Have A Cow."

Given all that, the little cow cartoon seemed to contain the seed of a big idea. So even though we didn't have a specific assignment, the creative group started exploring where the cow idea might take us. And where it first took us was a single billboard: two fiberglass cows with paint can and brush, tagging the board with their plea, "EAT MOR CHICKIN."

In a perfect world we would have had a lot of money. But we didn't, so we just made the most of what we had, and that was money to do one great outdoor execution. Getting to that answer required input from the whole account team: account management, as chief stewards of the budget, to help reconcile the desire for a splashy introduction with the need to find unbudgeted dollars to do it with; account planning to keep us grounded in the branding and to become the voice of the consumer in responding to the idea; media to figure out a way to make an impact with a tiny number of boards; production people to figure out how to fabricate the cows.

Starting with a single board in Chick-fil-A's home market, Atlanta, and expanding from there as dollars were available, the campaign grew and grew and became a phenomenal success for the brand and for us. The cows have become like a guerrilla insurgency, taking their radical

First ad of the now famous cow campaign. It came about only because the creative team of AD David Ring and writer Gail Barlow hit upon a funny, embryonic idea and weren't afraid to share it with others who could help find a way to develop it.

message of bovine self-preservation into radio, TV, and even packaging. One consumer wrote to tell us the campaign was so effective that every time he sees a field of cows he thinks of chicken. We co-opted an entire species. And it started with a doodle.

So back to fear. A common fear is that somebody's going to swipe your idea. Bosses do this all the time, of course. Subordinate comes up with a good concept or starts a worthy initiative; boss says thank you very much, cuts the junior out of the deal, has all the fun, and takes the credit. But the more open your working environment is, the less possible this kind of wormy behavior becomes. It's hard to steal in plain sight and get away with it. You *will* be asked to justify your actions.

If David Ring had been afraid someone was going to steal the cow idea, he never would have shown it around, never would have gotten help to turn a funny notion into a career-making campaign. He might have found a way to quietly gin it up on the cheap as a small-space ad, cajoled the account people into finding a few dollars to run it in a high school football program somewhere, entered it in some award shows, and felt lucky to have gotten it produced at all. Fortunately, he and his partner felt no such compulsion. They used the resources that were around them, the other people on the team, and scored big.

Here's our practice, ever since we started the agency. If you originate an idea, you get to follow it through. Now, as it happens, David and Gail, who got the cow campaign rolling, were seasoned creative people. But I don't care if you're brand new and totally untested. You get to present and produce your work. As for the rest of the agency — your group head, the other disciplines represented on the team, myself when needed — our job is to circle, in supporting roles, around the product, the idea, and help it achieve its potential.

Making you part of an ensemble is one way we address fear of failure. You have as much autonomy as you need, and maybe sometimes even a little more than you might think you can handle, but there's a whole team around to share accountability. You won't be put into the position of becoming a scapegoat when problems come up, as they almost always do, nor will you be muscled out of the position to receive the credit you deserve.

Another common fear is that the slightest mistake, especially if it costs the agency money, will get you zapped right into the title sequence of the old *Branded* series, with you in the Chuck Connors role, drummed into the center of the fort, stripped of rank, your cavalry sword snapped across the CO's knee, and then you're banished into the wilderness. And as you stand there in your humiliation, they play the theme song over the office paging system: "Branded! Marked with a coward's sha-a-a-me / What can you do when you're branded? / You must fight for your name."

But going back to the example of you and a partner concepting an ad, you don't punish or shame each other for tossing lame ideas out on the table, do you? Of course not. You write them all down, ridiculous though they may be, and treat them as potential parents of the good ideas to come. And that, I decided long ago, is the way to treat all the other less-than-lovely bits of output our workdays produce: Don't punish them; note them and build on them.

People need to *try* things. The newly hired account executive turned loose to do real work with the client on her first day, for instance. To her the assignment may feel like a real stretch, but chances are she's going to get the job done just fine, and in any case she's not working without a net; there's the rest of the account team.

It comes down to this. The ambient level of fear drops practically off the chart when you put people right out in the open and simply let them *solve something*, including letting them solve the new problems they create in their attempts to solve the original problem. Yes, it's messy; just go with it.

When you start cataloging all the stuff you can potentially get wrong today, if you're afraid of the consequences, then you'll never do *anything*. And as Wayne Gretzky says, "You miss one hundred percent of the shots you don't take." So the message I've always tried to send to my people is: Take the shot. And, thanks to the give-and-take and checks and balances of open collaboration, not once, ever, has a shot gone so wild that it flew over the glass, killed the league commissioner, maimed the team owner on the rebound, and put the club out of business. The consequences are never as horrific as one imagines they might be.

Fear of losing face, losing status in the agency pecking order, losing your future chances—those fears go away incredibly fast if you simply encourage shot taking and then prove you're serious by rewarding *all* the shots, even the ones that fly way wide of the mark. I don't mean you have to say, "Hey, you came up with some stinko ideas on that last project. Here's a raise." One of the best rewards is just to not make a big deal out of mess-ups when they're done in good faith.

The Gentleperson's Guide to Making a Killing

Clients, agencies, and some proposals for how both can conduct the dance more gracefully—and successfully.

HITTING THE BIG TIME WITH FOUR SIMPLEMINDED QUESTIONS

Some advertising trivia: According to industry scrutinists who are supposed to know these things, The Richards Group is the largest ad agency in the country with a single shareholder. (That would be me.) As of this writing, we're getting within Troy Aikman throwing distance, if not spitting distance, of a billion dollars in billings. Don't ask me precisely how close we are because, frankly, it's a little hard to know from month to month where we stand on that.

If you work for an ad agency, you know that it's just in the nature of the business for extremely busy spells to fall upon you and turn your life into a sleep deprivation experiment for a while. I noticed recently that our entire office had been in one of those spells, running at around 120 percent capacity for three months and bringing in new talent as fast as humanly possible. On one day alone I counted, lined up on a counter in the workroom, 25 of the new-employee fliers we put out with each new Grouper's picture, job function, and directions to their desk. We were as busy as I had ever seen us. So I asked our maven of money, Scot Dykema, to poll the account-group principals

and
total up the
projected billings of
all the new accounts we had
gained in the previous 90 days.
Then I called a stairwell meeting.

When the staff was assembled I selected four or five Groupers at random and asked them to take a stab at how much billing we had picked up in three months' time. Their guesses ranged from $14 million to $23 million, which, in my book, would still have made a pretty decent quarter's growth. The real number, however, was $121 million, conservatively estimated. They were astonished. It felt good to learn that all our stress and OT came with hefty dollar signs attached. Now, if one $121 million account had come in, we would all have been well aware of it. As it was, though, the billings were spread across something like eight different accounts and nearly every account group in the shop. Till Scot totaled it up, none of us had any idea the agency was on that hot of a hot streak. We were all too busy working to think much about it.

After reporting business results like that, I couldn't just say, "Thought you'd like to know. Now get back to work." So I announced a sizable bonus for everybody, payable immediately. We have a profit-sharing plan for spreading around the rewards of everyone's hard work, but at the time, year-end was still a long way off. If you're busting your back to produce results like that crowd was, you deserve some juice on the spot.

We haven't always grown at such a torrid pace. But if you start at, say, zero in 1976 and do the math from there, you'll get some idea of the steep growth track the agency has been on. Certainly we've done better than average. But what makes our history interesting for a lot of people is how we've managed to grow so much without losing the creative standards that got the ball rolling in the first place.

Want to know how we've done it? I'll tell you our new-business model. If it seems too simpleminded for you, then you can apply to grad school at Wharton or something. I'm happy sticking with this. Going right back to the beginning, we've always evaluated every prospective account with four questions:

1. Can we do good work?
2. Can we make a difference?
3. Can we have fun?
4. Can we make money?

That's pretty much it. And that's more or less the order of priority.

If we're doing good work and making a difference for the brand, chances are we're having fun. And profit usually follows as a natural consequence of the first three, although if it doesn't, that's not necessarily a deal killer. Lots of times we've stuck with unprofitable and break-even accounts just because we could answer an emphatic, resounding yes to questions one through three. And numerous times we've resigned big, lucrative accounts because something like meanminded brand managers, questionable ethics, or (as happened with Taco Bell) being pitted against a second agency militated against good work and internal satisfaction.

Motel 6 has been one of the agency's spectacular success stories. But as a new account in 1985, it could have looked like a real loser were it not for our four little questions and the order in which we took them. When we pitched their business, the answer to all four questions was, as far as we could tell through our limited, precontract involvement, a probable yes. Then we dived into the account in earnest, and it's a good thing we kept our four questions in mind because they helped guide us through what happened next.

The product, we learned, was terrible. When account planning did focus groups with past Motel 6 guests, the sessions turned into gripefests. Rooms were tatty and often dirty. The rooms had no phones; you had to walk to a pay phone in the office. If you wanted to watch television, you actually had to plug quarters into the TV set.

So we recommended to the client that Motel 6 not advertise. Better, we said, to take the time to invest in the properties, work out operational problems, make sure that if we do produce ads that convince travelers to try you, you won't alienate them with a bad experience.

In a way, as their agency we were shooting ourselves in the foot. The traditional agency thing to do would have been to keep our mouths shut, produce a big campaign, make a quick buck, and move on when the brand went in the dumper and the relationship went bad. But making money wasn't the immediate priority. Doing good work, first in the form of strong account planning and branding strategy, laying groundwork for making a difference in the future of the brand—these were the priorities.

Which, in itself, was kind of fun. It was satisfying anyway—even before the *real* fun of the Tom Bodett "We'll leave the light on for you" campaign.

Needless to say, we didn't exactly rake in the dough with a client that wasn't even advertising for a substantial period of time. But we stuck it out because we had our priorities straight. And the profitability straightened itself out quite nicely in due time.

On the other hand, on two different occasions I have resigned what was, in each case, the biggest account in the agency's history up to that point. Making money, while nice, is not as nice as being able to live with yourself, and with these accounts we were on the verge of feeling like sellouts.

One I mentioned earlier: Long John Silver's, whose marketing managers paid eloquent lip service to good creative until we had the account, then proceeded to badger us to produce the sort of stuff that any third-rate agency in the country could have done. With good work out of the question, making a difference in their business was beyond our powers, and we sure weren't having any fun. So it was *hasta la vista,* and we haven't missed them since.

The other time was a sadder situation: a good client for whom we had done spectacularly successful work. It did wonders for their brand, won a shelf full of creative awards for us, and built a tidy bottom line for all concerned. Then their two top guys asked us to do something so petty and base that any money we'd make on their business in the future would feel tainted. They had a personal grudge against a former associate of theirs, and when he became our client (as CEO of a company not even remotely in competition with their own), they issued an ultimatum: Resign their enemy's account, or they'd fire us. When they put that unethical demand on us, the fun was definitely gone. And so were we.

Sometimes when everything is firing on all cylinders, we can review the questions and say four big yeses. Our first client after the transition to full service, MBank, was like that. And so was another account that dropped serendipitously in our collective lap not long after.

Why *Time* magazine called us, a puny little agency in Dallas, Texas, is a mystery. It was either an inspired thought or an act of desperation. The results, fortunately, weigh in on the side of inspired.

The request was from *Time*'s circulation department. They were looking for some help with their direct-response television, something in which we had almost no expertise, but what the heck, if they were willing to call us we were willing to have a crack at it. After numerous experiments, *Time* had never succeeded in delivering an acceptably low cost per subscription with TV advertising. The best they had been able to do was around $30 per sub. At that rate, they would have done just as well to pick out people at random and send them the magazine free for a year. Still, their instincts said that TV could deliver new subscribers efficiently, if it was done right.

I guess we did it right, because our first spots brought their price per subscription down to $10.50. The circulation people couldn't believe it. TV was suddenly the most efficient medium in their whole arsenal, next to those blow-in cards that fall out when you open the magazine. News of *Time*'s TV success traveled fast around the big, open circulation floor of the Time-Life building in Manhattan. We got a call from *Sports Illustrated*. Then *Fortune*, then *Money, People, Life* — the whole Time-Life stable. We did their work for years, essentially inventing the now-familiar format of stirring music; pithy, clever copy; and powerful photos from the pages of the magazines.

You may remember some of the spots we did over the years. One of the last ones we produced, for *Life*, featured Ray Charles's sensational rendition of "America the Beautiful" against brilliant photographs of, well, life in America. Someone at the agency dug that one out not long ago. It held up pretty well all these years later. Not only did I still feel proud of the work, I felt proud to be an American!

So back to the four questions. Did we do good work for Time-Life? Yes, by a landslide. Did we make a difference? At $10.50 a subscription, you bet we did. Did we have fun? Lots. It's almost not fair to call it work — people would fall all over themselves to get in on a Time-Life project. Did we make money? Year after year. Our friends in New York rewarded us most fairly and stuck with us for over a decade.

For a new little growing agency, having a signature client such as Time-Life was like holding a handful of aces. And it launched at least one brilliant career. Our main writer on the Time-Life business the first few years was a guy named Larry Sons. Eventually he left the agency, went freelance, and became one of the reigning masters of direct-response TV, especially with his *Sports Illustrated* spots.

We love those four-big-yes experiences, love telling you about them. Plenty of times, though, we may not be satisfied with how we're actually doing on *any* of the four questions — not producing work as good as we think is possible, not making as much difference as we hope to, having less fun than we'd like, not bringing home a profit. Imagine, for example, a new account when you're still learning their business and working out the inevitable bugs in the relationship. But notice that the operative word

Nice-guy baseball star Steve Garvey and notoriously ferocious defensive lineman Lyle Alzado in one of our spots for Time-Life. "I gotta get me one of these!" Alzado says of Garvey's bat. Writer and art director: Larry Sons.

in the four questions is *can* we, not *are* we. The questions are an assessment of *potential.*

In looking over our four simple questions, one definition may be in order, and that is what I mean by "good work." That's a squishy term, for sure. Some advertising that I love, you might think is lousy. Some that you love, I might consider to be a blight upon the planet. On a case-by-case basis, you and I will probably never fully agree. So when we say "good work," we can't be talking about advertising that is universally lauded. It doesn't exist. So I will tell you what I mean by "good work," as we define it at The Richards Group.

Good work, ultimately, is advertising that is endearing to the people for whom it is intended. *Endearing* meaning relevant and rewarding of the time spent with it by the only people who really count. Not the client, the account team, the head of the agency. The intended audience. The people Out There into whose lives we come, mostly uninvited, with our hundreds of messages a day. (I once saw a conference report in which the AE had written, "Client responded that the concepts presented were too endearing." The creative team enlarged that part of the memo about 1000 percent and kept it pinned to the wall. I think we might have had a slight problem with our definitions.)

I preached "endearing" for decades, knowing by instinct and conviction that it's what we should aim for. After all, I'm a consumer, too, and I know how I like advertisers to treat me. Finally I got empirical evidence to back me up. Several years ago, a group of the largest, most conservative advertisers and ad agencies assembled a blue-ribbon panel and set out to establish once and for all what makes people respond to some ads more than others. They commissioned a massive nationwide study using every consumer research method short of vivisection. They interviewed 12,000 people. This thing took years. And at the end they reached a stunning conclusion. The single greatest predictor of how effective a piece of advertising will be *in generating sales* is . . . (drum roll, please) . . . whether people like the ad.

That's it. People respond, with their good, green dollars, to ads they find endearing. Of course, exactly what to do so that a particular audience will like the ad, how to make it endearing within their particular frame of reference, is up to you to figure out. And for Pete's sake, don't go off trying to devise some kind of Endearingness Score. Go with the fact that there's art to this.

"Endearing" is a moving target. It could be primarily factual, the breakthrough product feature. It could be purely in the tone and attitude. Most likely it's a combo of a lot of factors. In any case, "endearing" is going to mean something different for, say, expectant mothers with advanced degrees who live in A and B counties in the Northeast than it is for, let's say, adult males with household incomes of zero-plus, who have purchased custom motorcycle accessories in the past three months and index 180 and higher on upper-body tattooing. Our job is to put ourselves in their shoes (boots, slippers, Birkenstocks, whatever) and present our messages as an act of identification with them.

That's what we mean by good work. Getting there takes every discipline in the agency, from canny account planning to shrewd media placement. Do it well, craft your stuff with respect for yourself, your clients, and your fellow citizens, and your work can be a credit to our business. Get sloppy or greedy, get your priorities mixed up, and your work will be what most advertising, unfortunately, is: boring, wasteful, aggravating, and a cultural pollutant.

Heaven knows, my agency and I don't have a batting average of 1.000. This business is hard. Oh boy, is it hard. You can be the biggest talent since Leonardo da Vinci. It's *still* hard. And that, I think, is all the more reason to keep the basic questions as simple as we can get them.

HOW TO DEVELOP A KILLER NEW-BUSINESS PROGRAM

Step 1: Do great work for the clients you've already got.

There. Your new outreach program is complete.

You don't have to go out prospecting for new business if you're doing terrific work. The prospects will find you. Honest. In 25 years as a full-service agency and 20-some years before that as a freelance practice, that's the only new-business program The Richards Group has ever had. It has been as effective during recessions as it has in the fat years.

Oh, to be sure, our folks keep in touch with their webs of relationships, run down the leads that crop up, send out a reel, that kind of thing. Due diligence — but informal, and best left that way. As confident as I am that our side will knock 'em dead every time, as much as I believe that this agency is the *obvious* choice on *every* shortlist we make, I have a hard time feeling very sanguine about spending a quarter-million dollars or more on a major pitch that we had to beg or shoulder our way into.

Far and away our best results in winning new business have been when we've let our work cast the net for us. That includes our work behind the scenes, because in the tiny, talkative world of marketing, word gets around — even word about the functions in your company that you think nobody is paying much attention to.

So I really don't care what a cool house ad you've come up with or what a slick new-business team you've got running the traps. Doing enviable work for your clients is the best advertising you can do for yourself.

LET'S PITCH PITCHES

I propose a one-year moratorium on spec presentations.

One year. That's all I ask. A sabbatical for the dogs and ponies, a 12-month hiatus from one of our industry's most wasteful and least efficient practices.

Clients can still conduct agency reviews during the hiatus. Search consultants can still earn their money. And the agencies — well, we'll hardly be getting off light. Because without spec creative, we'll have to let ourselves be judged on the merit of the real work we've done for real clients and on the way we've gone about doing it. We'll have to explain our choices and defend our mistakes. We won't be able to beguile or dazzle an audience with the snow job that new-business presentations so often become.

"In a new-business pitch," to paraphrase a familiar line, "truth is the first casualty." I'm not suggesting ill intent. It's the nature of the process to obscure the very truths that are supposed to come out of it: What are these people really like, their weaknesses as well as their strengths? How are they to work with? Can we depend on them to make a difference for our brand?

How many times have we seen the trade papers report the awarding of a big account, only to follow up a few weeks or months later with a juicy story of how the client-agency relationship blew up? Clearly, in most of these cases the two had no idea what they were really getting when they entered the relationship. The review, almost always built around a spec campaign, didn't tell the two sides what they needed to know. Wittingly or unwittingly, each gave the other a false impression. That's the real trouble with spec presentations. They don't reveal the truth.

For years my agency wouldn't do spec creative. Capabilities, tours, preliminary marketing spadework, all that getting-to-know-you stuff—of course, gladly. But whenever a would-be client asked for spec creative, we always said a polite no, thank you.

Sometimes, after a pause lasting from several seconds to several weeks, they would say, "Ohhhhh . . . all right," and go ahead and give us the business anyway. Sometimes they'd mark us off their list. But I always figured that in any case this arrangement was yielding us a batting average at least as good as those of our competitors who were going through all the awful gyrations and histrionics of developing and presenting spec work.

There's a lot not to like about spec pitches. The process erects a tribal barrier right from the git-go, as we say in Texas. The client's over there. The agency's over here. There may be a search consultant in the middle. As forthcoming as all the parties may be, as cordial as relations may appear (and when are relations *not* cordial during a pitch?), the parties in question are most definitely in separate camps. Despite all the jolly bonhomie and fine promises, you're not on the same team, at least not yet. Nothing can take that factor—that barrier—out of the pitch process. In the short term at least, it's impossible for your fortunes to be shared.

There's a prize to be won. There is favor to be bestowed. There are money and jobs on the line. It's high stakes for the agency and the client. But there are *different* stakes for each. It's in the best interests of both parties to downplay flaws and play up attractive features, rather like the Saharan tribe whose courtship ritual is for the unmarried men to paint themselves with elaborate decorations and line up before the young women, displaying their shiny teeth and bright eyes with the most exaggerated mannerisms they can muster. Anything to be noticed and chosen.

To pitch a major account today costs so much that, as in major political campaigns, worthy candidates may be eliminated from contention because they are either unwilling or unable to gamble the obscene sums necessary to win. Or (and this may happen more often) enticed by the size of the opportunity, an agency may feel unable to say no and end up taking unwise financial risks. Two hundred thousand dollars, three hundred thousand, half a million—when you start conducting focus groups, producing a film, maybe shooting spec commercials, the numbers reach breathtaking size before you know it. Winning a high-profile account can catapult an agency into the big time. Failing to win can catapult it into serious financial straits.

A pitch is a "time cow," as one of our account guys once termed it. I never have liked the idea of taking people away from the accounts they're working on and putting them through the wringer of working brutal hours doing what is essentially guesswork for a client they probably know very little about.

It doesn't make a lot of sense. Spend untold hours putting several agencies through the process of creating campaigns, based on incomplete information and insufficient contact. Then hire one of them (while abandoning, in all likelihood, the campaign the agency developed at its own expense), and embark on a relationship, knowing that your new partner starts out in a deep financial hole—a hole they can best crawl out of by sticking it to you every chance they get.

Call me a grouch, but that's how I see that process. So we always said no to spec pitches. And it worked out fine. Our clients grew. Their success helped attract others. Our dinky little agency grew bigger every year.

But something happened when our billings hit $150 million or so. *We* started hitting a lot more radar screens. Bigger advertisers began to call and say, "We've noticed the work you guys are doing out there in Dallas, and we've heard good things about you. Now that you've got the resources to handle larger accounts, we're interested in having you do our work."

"Fantastic!" we'd say. "When can we start?"

"Well," they'd reply, "there's this pitch first."

Errgh. Frustrating words, but we knew we'd better get used to them. Saying no, thanks, wasn't really an option any more. We were now playing in a league where everyone is expected to be a pitcher. So we've been doing occasional spec creative ever since.

Now, don't think I'm complaining. Getting to do a lot of new-business pitches is a luxury problem, for sure. We worked hard for a long time to earn the privilege of vying for the kind of accounts we get invited to pitch.

And I do have to say this: Some of my proudest moments as the head of The Richards Group have been in new-business pitches. Some that we've won — The Home Depot, Continental Airlines, H-E-B grocery stores, 7-Eleven — but, strangely perhaps, just as much in big ones we've lost — Mercedes, Southwest Airlines, Porsche, Volkswagen. The teamwork, dedication, leadership, and sheer fervor that I've seen from the men and women of the agency during those times have amazed and humbled me.

When you win, the glory of victory sweeps everyone up in celebration and you don't tend to immediate introspection about the process that got you there. But sometimes in the somber mood of a loss, the glory of the energy and sacrifice that went into the effort are more plain to see.

In terms of billings, the Home Depot pitch was our biggest win ever, and we had knocked ourselves out to get there. In retrospect, though, it's hard to remember how arduous the pitch was at the time because, as it turned out, it was merely the first hard push into what has become a long and satisfying working relationship with The Home Depot, with *many* intense periods of hard work along the way. Maybe it's a little like what I've always heard about childbirth. It's horrible at the time, but the pleasure of the subsequent relationship makes you forget the gory details. With a big losing effort like we experienced with Mercedes-Benz, there's no baby to help you forget.

Mercedes was my dream account. I had been an unabashed M-B junky for years. If there was one product on earth that I aspired to make my own product like, it was Mercedes. Exhaustively thought out, exquisitely well crafted, but always restrained and never gaudy in its design. Nothing silly or extraneous. When they put us on their shortlist, I was elated. The whole agency staff went nuts. Nobody needs a pep talk to get excited about working for a brand like Mercedes.

A few days later, when the agency search committee from Mercedes-Benz of North America came to Dallas for a tour of the agency, they pulled into our parking lot and found, arrayed behind velvet ropes, examples of the top luxury cars on the American market. My own 500SL was there, representing the Mercedes brand. Next to it was a BMW, then a Lexus, a Jaguar, an Infiniti, a Cadillac, a Volvo — all showroom new. It looked like a car show, and in fact dozens of passersby had stopped to ogle these shining machines. A banner hung behind the cars asked,

"Ten Years From Now, Where Will They Be?" The committee members strolled around for a few minutes, looking over this formidable set of competitive marques, then came inside for the tour and a presentation of the agency's capabilities.

A couple of hours later, when the committee members reemerged into the parking lot, the 500SL was still there in all its gleaming glory. But behind the other velvet ropes, beneath the banner where all the competitors' cars had been, something had changed. You could still see the front grilles and chrome badges identifying their brands. The rich colors of their deep metallic paint jobs were still visible. But the cars weren't really cars anymore. They had been crushed—flattened and mashed into huge cubes, ready for recycling. The Mercedes stood alone. (By the way, we didn't really crush those new cars. Some unbelievably resourceful Groupers scoured salvage yards to find crushed wrecks of the right brands and colors, had them trucked to our office, and somehow managed to get them moved into position while the clients were inside the building.)

Over the next several weeks, nights and holidays included, the agency worked like men and women possessed. Account planning, marketing, media, creative—we all wanted this one bad, and had the bags under our eyes to show for it. Suppliers signed on as allies, helping us conduct research, produce a film, print a leather-bound keepsake book, and generally cram six months of work into one month.

We didn't win. Scali, McCabe, Sloves did. Right after taking the phone call with the bad news, I called everybody to a stairwell meeting and announced that we had lost. As I tried to tell the staff how much I admired what they had done and how proud I was to have been a part of it, I choked up. Several hundred of us stood there in silence, looking down at each other's shoes. It was a perfect crummy, gray winter day. Outside, drizzle ran down the windows. After a few seconds, I quietly said a final thank-you, and we all drifted away to try and resume our normal working life. No one had seen me get that emotional before; my reaction surprised even me. But it's deeply affecting to witness great sacrifice on a large scale. And pitches are a great sacrifice.

Glimpses of glory aside, the more pitches we do, the more I stand by my old assertion that asking for a full-boat presentation with spec creative, media plans, and the like is a dicey way to go about picking an agency. It's artificial, an eight-hour courtship with a wedding in Vegas. I wouldn't want to stake the future of *my* brand on the results of the heated frenzy that is a pitch.

The better way is so much simpler. If you're a prospective client and you want to know what an agency can really do, if you want some confidence that you're putting your money and your future in good hands, just do two things. Number one, spend as much time as you can (or as much time as the agency will let you) hanging around their office, getting a sense of what the place is really like for the people who would be doing your work. And number two, make them show you what they've done for their clients — all of them — the good, the bad, and the ugly. Don't let them trot out only what *they* want you to see.

Sure, it's important to see their high-water marks, the work that ends up on the reel, in the print book, in the awards annuals. But to have anything like a valid guess at how well they'd perform for you, then you really need to see their worst work, too, and hear them defend it. How low will they go? That's important.

How close together the high-water mark and the low-water mark are — that's the quality range within which they'd probably deliver work for you, too. Are all their creative groups (or, in the case of a multinational account, all their international affiliates) producing strong work, or just one or two? If there's inconsistency, why? How about their work in different media? Do they devote their best talent to TV and high-profile magazine campaigns and give short shrift to the lower-budget or less visible work?

I'm astonished, for example, at the number of advertisers who spend substantial amounts in radio yet never really investigate prospective agencies' work in that medium, assuming that if their TV and print are good, then they must be okay in radio. You'll probably have to ask specifically for radio in the presentation. Agencies often don't like to present it. Maybe one reason is that there's nowhere for people to look when the reel is playing; it doesn't make for good theater. But the more likely explanation is that, for reasons I've never fully understood, radio is usually treated like the ugly sister among the different media.

In any case, you've got to ask about this stuff. You've got to spend more time in the offices of your shortlist agencies than you would on the usual tour, when everyone is on their best behavior. Absorb as much of the agency's culture as you can. Call clients who aren't on the reference list. Peek behind the curtains. Open up the closets. You want reality. And you won't get it in a spec presentation.

Lately we've had some heartening experiences. Fruit of the Loom narrowed its field to us and a Minneapolis shop, then, after hearing our presentation, cancelled its meeting with the other finalist. Labor Ready, the industrial temp firm, invited several agencies to pitch their business.

After a thorough review of our capabilities, this client cancelled the rest of the pitch and hired us. You have to figure
a company called Labor Ready knows a few things about
not wasting effort. Scott Conklin was AD on this ad;
Chick Schiller, the writer.

But after a thorough review of The Richards Group's capabilities, they
cancelled the pitch and hired us. They saw all they needed to see in the
real work for our real clients.

I promise you this. If, for one year, we would conduct agency reviews
in the cold, hard light of reality instead of the frenzied unreality of spec
pitches, there would be better, more intelligent matchups between clients
and agencies, fewer strange mismatches, more client-agency relationships that actually work. And there would be more ad agencies paying
attention to 100 percent of the work they do for 100 percent of their
clients, knowing that failure to do so will cost them new business.

So let's set speculative presentations aside for a year. If we do, I bet we'll want to re-up for another year. And eventually, maybe—just maybe—we can all pitch pitches for good.

"REVIEW" IS ENGLISH FOR *SAYONARA*

We've talked about how work groups need to die sometimes. The same is true for some client relationships. It's painful to watch a company struggling in pathetic desperation to retain an account they either have no hope of keeping or no hope of doing their best work for. It's especially painful to watch when the company is mine.

That's why I've learned, in 9 cases out of 10, to say *sayonara* when a client tells us they're going to conduct a review. (The tenth case would be a client such as a government agency that's legally bound to hold a review at the end of each contract period.)

We may be in the minority on this. Most ad agencies, it seems, are willing to gamely pitch their little hearts out to try to win back a client who's threatening to leave them. Once in a blue moon one of them will pull it off and retain the business. But is it really worth it? How can an agency, after surviving a review, ever regain enough trust and enthusiasm to do a good job? And for that matter, how committed can the client really be to an agency they nearly split with?

I can't really answer the latter question, but I can say that the former question sums up why I've grown disinclined to participate in such reviews. We're in this to do great work, and doing your best work is nearly impossible after you've been told, in effect, "We don't really love you anymore." How can you *not* lose your enthusiasm for a client that has begun the process of replacing you? Once you've lost that loving feeling, as the song says, it's gone, gone, gone.

Think about it. Let's say that one evening after dinner you ask your wife to sit down for a little chat.

"Honey," you begin casually, "I've been noticing that there are some very interesting women at my office, and I've started to wonder if a relationship with one of them might be better than the one I have with you. Now, don't get me wrong, you *may still be the one for me*"—and here you chuckle lightly, just to emphasize that this is no big deal, no big deal at all—"but I've decided to, you know, go out—just on a trial basis, you understand!—with three or four of those women. You know, just to be sure you're the one.

"In the meantime," you continue in your most reassuring tone, "while I'm conducting this little, er, *trial review*, you and I can keep right on living together . . . just like normal."

Yeah, sure you can.

Now look me in the eye and tell me things won't be just the merest bit strained around the house after *that* family meeting. So what makes anybody think they can expect a committed, productive relationship with their ad agency after essentially that same conversation? I'll tell you this, if the relationship doesn't go sour in a hurry, you're dealing with an agency that has either a serious self-esteem problem or complete indifference to anything except the fat check you send them every month.

Here's something that happened not long ago. A company that had been our client for a long time, and with whom we continued to have a terrific relationship, was sold by its corporate parent. The buyer was an investment group that, while noted for making money by the carload, approaches business relationships with all the jolly comraderie and warm goodwill of the Spanish Inquisition. As is their wont, they immediately broomed the old board of directors; the lead investors in the group became the new board. We wondered how long before it started to affect us. About two weeks, was the answer, enough time for us to decide our response to what we guessed—correctly, as it turned out—was coming.

The lead marketing guy from the client came up to the agency one morning a couple of weeks after the acquisition and met with Brad Todd, who was the account management principal on the business. It says a lot that the client didn't call us down to his office, his turf. These are people we like a lot, and who like us; we've been partners for a long time. He came to our place as a friend, which we appreciated. Unfortunately, though, he came bearing, as we anticipated, some not-so-great news.

"As you know," the client began, "we've been working together for 12 years, and personally I hope we'll work together for at least 12 more. *However,* the new owners believe that 12 years is too long for any company to work with one agency without a review." There's a good indication there of how highly the new owners value relationships, and our friend shook his head sympathetically at the absurdity. "I'm sorry, but they've told us to conduct a review."

He paused and waited for Brad's reaction. Brad took a sip of coffee. "Nah," he said.

"Excuse me?" our friend asked, mystified.

"Nah," Brad repeated as casually as if he'd been asked if he needed more Cremora. "We won't participate in a review. We resign."

"Bu-bu-bu—" All the blood drained out of the client's face. He was incredulous. "But why?!"

So Brad explained our position, that it was impossible for us to do a wholehearted job after being told that the job we were doing, which already *was* wholehearted, was somehow inadequate. Specific criticism, areas in which they thought we could improve, a period to correct problems *before* a review might be considered—absolutely, we would welcome any of that. But this, of course, was not about any service issues.

If our clients, our old friends with whom we had been working to build the brand all these years—if they could have *their* way, we knew they'd conduct a perfunctory review of a few agencies' capabilities, confirm us as the best choice, and we'd all move merrily ahead. But their hands were tied. The board, whom we had never even met, insisted on a full review, just because. So we were out of there.

Don't misunderstand our cut-and-dried response as voiced by Brad. It was a pretty depressing day for us. To lose that way, through no fault of ours, a highly valued client—a partner with whom we had done so well for so long—leaves a bitter taste in our mouths. But while resigning was certainly a heavy decision, I can't say it was hard. It was the only thing we could feel good, in the long run, about doing.

Once your client drops the review bomb on you, it's best not to agonize over it. Just go on and leave with the same dignity you came in with. Sometimes, though, there's a happier ending. The client decides to recall the B-52s.

We've been the agency for The Home Depot since 1993, and it's been a marvelous experience. In their corporate culture they have a phrase for the most gung ho, passionate true believers in The Home Depot philosophy of service. Those people, they say, bleed orange, the bright signature color of the brand. And that, I think it's fair to say, describes us as their agency. We bleed glorious PMS 165 with the best of them.

So we were, to say the least, chagrined a few years ago when our marketing contacts at The Home Depot let us know that they were planning to solicit presentations of TV work from other agencies—just on a project basis, they said—for their official sponsorship of the 1998 Winter Olympics in Nagano.

Despite my sudden sick feeling, I managed to ask some basic questions. Had they lost faith in our ability to come through in the high-stakes situations? Absolutely not, they replied. The business was hitting new heights every day—in fact, it was now numbered among the great brands in America—and they valued our role in making it so. Okay, so why talk

The Gift Registry

Okay, it's not as traditional as china or silver. But for practical gifts you'll actually use for years to come, nothing beats Home Depot's Gift Registry. Tools, gas grills, lawn mowers. If you need it, your local Home Depot makes it easy for friends and family across the entire country to purchase it for you. In fact, it's a piece of cake.

Elaborate new-business pitches with speculative campaigns are *supposed* to lead to long, happy marriages like the one we enjoy with The Home Depot. But considering how seldom they actually do, it's time to try a different courtship ritual. The art director of this ad was Mike Gustafson. Mike Fisher was the writer.

to other agencies? They explained their thinking: It's a very high-profile, breakout event for the brand, the stakes are very high, let's make sure we're getting the absolute biggest bang for our buck, and so forth. You can see the reasoning.

Basically, it seemed to me, they were using their best customer-and-vendor thinking. However, they hadn't fully considered all the ways that a good client-agency relationship is more *intimate* than a simple buying-and-selling relationship with a vendor. They hadn't realized how it would dump every bit of wind from the agency's sails to pit us, their old partner, against other agencies now that, after years of growing the brand together, we were looking at our biggest creative opportunity yet.

Their decision to review agencies for the project was pretty firm, Dick Hammill, the marketing chief, told me, but I was welcome to state my case to their president, Arthur Blank, if I wanted. I definitely wanted, and Arthur was gracious to give me a hearing.

I described the agency's commitment to the brand and our sense of ownership, and explained how using another agency for the project — even if it was one time only — would effectively spell the end of our companies' relationship. We simply couldn't bleed the right shade any more. And, thankfully, he saw my point of view. Neither Arthur nor his associates had fully recognized the all-or-nothing commitment we had to their business and how, if we saw an erosion of trust, our ability to come through for them day after day after day, as an agency must, would be seriously compromised.

They called off the review, never contacted other agencies. We took the assignment and, sure enough, hit a creative home run like The Home Depot had never seen. You may remember the spot, in which a young Japanese girl sees a downhill skier appear from the kanji lettering on a banner hanging above a street in her town.

Hundreds of viewers wrote e-mails and letters to Home Depot praising the commercial. What they appreciated most was the fact that it wasn't really a *commercial* message at all but rather a tribute to the spirit of the Games and therefore worthy of a great company. Newspapers wrote stories about the grassroots response to the advertising. And our relationship with The Home Depot ended up stronger than

The Home Depot demonstrated their commitment to the agency by giving us their Olympics assignment. We responded with their most successful commercial ever, written by David Jenkins and Gregg Steward; art directed by Gary Gibson.

ever. Which isn't really surprising. After 40 years I've found that in this business, as in the rest of life, there are only two ways to go with a relationship. It's either all the way or no way.

TAKE IT LIKE A KID

I learned how to lose from a bunch of 10-year-olds.

It's one of the best lessons I've learned and one that I've faithfully applied every time The Richards Group has experienced a disappointment such as losing an account or coming up short in a new-business pitch. I learned it while coaching the peewee basketball team in our neighborhood, something I did for a number of years.

Whether it was because of my masterful helmsmanship or just some lucky concentration of athletic kids in the area, I don't know, but for 8 or 10 years we had a string of pretty hot teams. One squad, though, stood out from all the others. They were a well-oiled run-and-gun juggernaut and a lot of fun to coach. Several of the kids came from right on our street, so the sound of a dribbling basketball anywhere on the block was all it took to start an impromptu scrimmage. The practice paid off. The team mowed a swath through our North Dallas rec. league and came undefeated to the championship final.

The big game was on a Saturday, one of those bright, warm late-winter days we often get in Texas when everything seems right with the world. Spirits were high on our side of the gym, as parents and grandparents packed the bleachers, super-8 cameras at the ready, to witness the crowning achievement of the boys' glorious season. The only real question on anybody's mind was whether they'd have a good camera angle for the trophy presentation. This team was unstoppable.

Naturally, we lost.

It wasn't pretty. As the game progressed and the disaster unfolded, confidence turned to concern, concern to panic, and panic to abject horror until the final buzzer unleashed a veritable fugue of anguish. Boys were crying. Parents were crying. Grandfathers who hadn't shed a tear since 1941 were dabbing their eyes.

Stoically, like the great John Wooden of UCLA would've done it, I glued the boys together and sent them out to fulfill their duty as sportsmen and file past the jubilant winners, mumbling congratulations: "Good game, good game, good game." Humiliation hung in the air like a sweat-scented cloud.

The fall of Rome wasn't
as gloomy as this. Life — so
bright and good a mere 32
minutes of playing time earlier — didn't seem worth liv-

← NOTE THE
UNBRIDLED
SPIRIT AND
ENTHUSIASM.

ing anymore. That's how the boys and moms and dads looked, so awful
was their devastation. I gathered my sobbing charges for a final team talk
and reminded them how wonderfully they had performed, what a spectacular season they had had, what winners and great kids they were. But,
of course, it didn't help their feelings in that moment. So everybody went
home. As I recall, each kid had a perfect, personal-size rain cloud hanging over his head as he left.

An hour later, doing Saturday chores back at my house, I happened
to glance out the kitchen window and witnessed an amazing scene. In
front yards all up and down the street, those same kids were out with
bats and gloves, playing baseball and having a great time.

The season had changed.

So here they were, limbering up their fastballs and home-run swings
with every bit as much enthusiasm as they had for jump shots and bounce
passes just a few hours earlier. After all, these kids had some catching up
to do. While they had been working their way through the championship
bracket in basketball, most of their friends and rivals had moved on to the
next thing, baseball. Basketball, ignoble defeat and all, was ancient history.

In that moment I realized that those kids knew how to lose. And I
resolved right then and there to start following their example. They
didn't try to deny that it hurt. They didn't smile bravely and "take it
like a man." With childlike honesty they poured out their disappointment with all the tears they had to give, got it out of their system, and
went on to the next activity. It was a revelation.

Ever since then, whenever the agency goes down in defeat I gather
the entire staff at the stairwell, break the bad news, fill in as much
detail as I know, offer the always too-meager consolation of praising all
the jobs well done, and generally preside over a 15-minute collective
paroxysm of grief. Unashamed, we get to feel as bad, as crummy, as
low as we need to feel. And then we go back to work.

Never have we felt crummier than the day we lost our bid for
Southwest Airlines after what even the client acknowledged was a
spectacular presentation. It was a two-agency contest: us versus the
longtime incumbent, Austin's GSD&M. The whole agency wanted this
one badly. We killed ourselves for weeks to get ready.

On the evening of our presentation at Southwest's Love Field head-quarters, a sizable crowd of Groupers gathered nearby at Club Schmitz, a 1940s-era roadhouse, to await the pitch team. The first of the presenters to arrive was a carload of agency people garbed as Southwest baggage handlers. They had participated in a goofy little piece of theater (goofy theater is *very* Southwest) in the early part of our presentation. "It's going *great!*" they shouted as they burst through the doors. "We're knockin' 'em dead over there!"

When the rest of us got there later, we were equally exultant. I always try to play it cool until the client announces the outcome. With new-business pitches, you never know. But I couldn't help feeling excited about this one. We all went home that night with a very good feeling. We — and, more than that, the work we presented — had been terrific.

Terrific didn't win. For the coup de grâce of its presentation the next day, GSD&M bused its staff three hours north to gather before the clients' office and sing "Stand By Me." It worked. Herb Kelleher couldn't bring himself to fire them. We heard later that Southwest told them very sternly that they didn't retain the account because of the work they showed. On that, I suppose, we had them beat. But we couldn't beat sentimentalism.

I hope I never again see my staff as downcast as they were at the stairwell meeting when I told them the news. It was horrible — in part, because we knew that we could not have been better. It's one of the few times when I can say that with absolute certainty. We're better now, but for our capabilities and experience then, we were at our absolute peak. And that made losing an absolute bummer.

But we moved on — wailed and groaned for a little while, then put shoulders to the wheel again. (As I'll describe shortly, the pitch wasn't a total loss by any means. It led directly to one of our greatest suc-cesses, but, of course, we couldn't know about that at the time.)

Some leaders are reluctant to announce bad news. Maybe they don't want to bum out the whole organization. In fact, it's when you don't share bad tidings that you cause problems.

Colleagues have told me that at other agencies where they've worked they always knew right away when there was a win. The whole place got to celebrate. But when there was a loss, only the insid-ers, the people directly involved in the pitch or on the account, heard the news immediately. Everybody else had to ask an insider if they wanted to know anything (once again, that old division of people in the know versus people in the dark), or they could just wait till news got around by way of the rumor mill, as if it was a dirty little secret. That's what happens when bad news circulates by itself. It takes on a life of its own. An unwarranted sense of shame attaches to it.

Organizations, like individuals, need to mourn their losses freely. It's cleansing. And when the loss is simply one of the inevitable setbacks we all suffer in the course of competition, the period of mourning doesn't have to last long. It can be over before lunchtime. But the disappointment you don't express, the grief you stuff, the bad news you allow to disseminate in dribs and drabs—that can sour the atmosphere of the whole organization for a long time.

Get it out of your system. Take it like a kid. And then move on. Because no matter how disappointed you are, no matter how much you had pinned your hopes on the big win that didn't come, there's always a new season just about to begin.

My Favorite Losses

I've learned to appreciate a good defeat. And I'm not talking about all that character-building bull. (Oh, all right, maybe losing does build character sometimes, but that's still not what I'm talking about.) I mean that over the years, when we've gone all out, committed heart and soul to an account so that we felt like we'd die if we lost, and then lost anyway, those losses have had an uncanny record of turning into wins later—sometimes a really long time later, and usually in really unexpected ways.

When I talk about finding benefits in losing, this is in no way a recanting of my earlier remarks about spec pitches. You can still lose very gloriously without having to do spec work. So if you're a client thinking of reviewing agencies, don't think you'll be denying the second-place finishers some great good fortune by confining your review to credentials. I just wanted to be clear on that.

So a number of terrific relationships have grown out of "failures." The lesson here, where tribalism is concerned, is this: When clients reject you, try to resist the temptation to subtly vilify them as a salve to your company's hurt feelings. It's natural to resort to some version of the old "if they don't want us they're boneheads and we don't want their dumb old account anyway" reaction. But do that, wall them out of your company's camp, and you can cost yourself all sorts of opportunities later.

A relatively recent case in point is giggo.com, DaimlerChrysler's auto-financing site. Years before he hired us to handle the account, Steve Cannon, the chief marketer at giggo.com, got to know us when he was assistant to the then-president of Mercedes-Benz of North America and we were one of the finalist agencies for their account. He seemed to like us; we definitely liked him. So Dick Murray, who had headed our pitch team, simply kept in touch with Steve as he moved around the world on Daimler assignments. Circumstances were never quite right for us to work together, though. This went on for seven or eight years, until Dick got a call one morning in September of 1999.

"Hey, Dick, it's Steve. I'm in Dallas."

"Great! Are you in town long enough to get together for lunch?"

"Should be—they just moved me here, to giggo.com. I'm thinking of changing agencies. Would you guys be interested?"

Needless to say, we were, and we've been having great fun together ever since.

Our biggest account, The Home Depot, came through a similar circumstance, although it didn't take quite as long. Dick Hammill, their marketing head, invited us to pitch their business because we had come so highly recommended by a friend of his cohort Dick Sullivan. The friend was a senior marketer at Home Base, a home improvement warehouse (now defunct) that we had pitched unsuccessfully—or so we thought—a couple of years before. Lost the pitch but made a friend. I'll take a loss like that any day of the week.

You never know how they're going to bounce. A few months after losing our pitch for the Florida Citrus account, we ended up with ... the Florida Citrus account. At the end of a major review, the client, a state commission, voted to award the business to Ammirati Puris Lintas. We lost by one vote. But after five months their relationship was already going as sour as a certain yellow citrus fruit. Dick Murray happened, once again, to be the one who got the call one Friday afternoon.

"Dick, as it turns out, we might still be interested in working with The Richards Group—that is, if you're still interested."

"We are absolutely still interested."

"Good. Can you be here Sunday?"

By the time Monday rolled around, we were already at work on developing a new campaign.

Losing the Southwest Airlines pitch was, as I've described, a heartbreaker. But we made a good impression on Don Valentine, Southwest's marketing director at the time, and when he later moved to struggling Continental Airlines he hired us. We were Continental's agency partner for five years, through one of the most dramatic turnarounds in airline history—from the worst service record in the indus-

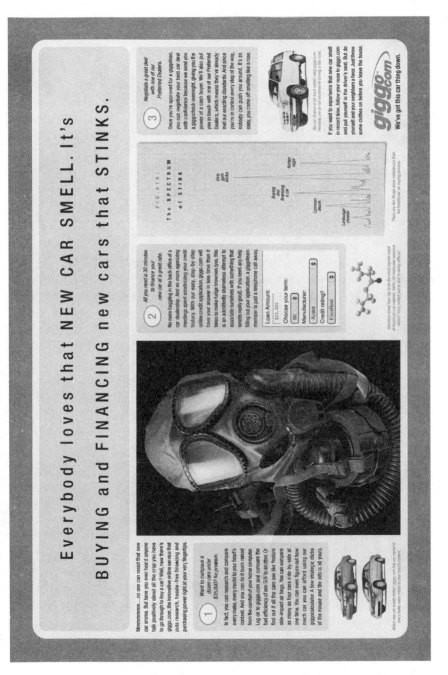

Our unsuccessful pitch for Mercedes-Benz led to a relationship with DaimlerChrysler's giggo.com financing site, and it only took about eight years. Art director: Lynn Fredericksen; writer: Doug Rucker.

Continental is pleased to be the official airline of Woodstock '94.

Some losses aren't losses after all. We got to know our future Continental client during our unsuccessful pitch for the Southwest business. The art director of this ad was Margaret Johnson. Vinnie Chieco was the writer.

try to the best. They canned us anyway (we won't get into that here), but it had been a terrific ride.

When we picked up Continental on the rebound from Southwest, it was actually a two-hopper. We owe our involvement in the Southwest pitch to an even earlier experience that had ended in disappointment: our brief but glorious tenure as agency for an airline called Muse Air. Muse was Southwest's bitter rival for a while, and we and Southwest came to know and respect one another on the field of conflict. While it lasted, it was a heck of a conflict, too.

It started with Lamar Muse. He was one of the most colorful characters I've known—irascible, profane, but when it came to running an airline he was, to borrow Darryl Royal's phrase, a rolling ball of butcher knives. Lamar was one of the founders of Southwest Airlines. He eventually split with his old partners at Southwest and, true to his cantankerous style, started his own airline and went into competition with them. Made a go of it, too, by matching their low fares while offering little extras like reserved seats instead of Southwest's famous "general seating."

I don't even remember who their agency was in those early days. It almost didn't matter because the product was so good, right down to the little breath mint they'd offer you as you deplaned. Before long, Muse Air's load factors (the airline term for the percentage of available seats that are actually occupied) were in the high 60s. When an airline's load factors are running above 65, the airline's ink is running black. Lamar, who by now was in the 60s himself, figured it was a good time to step down to spend more time — I don't know — probably toilet-papering Herb Kelleher's yard; he wasn't the type to spend his retirement mallwalking.

Lamar turned Muse Air over to his son, Michael. The nosedive started immediately. By the time Lamar came back to fix the mess a few months later, he had a full-blown crisis on his hands. Load factors were mired in the 30s. When your load factors hit the 30s, it's only a matter of time before your airline hits Chapter 11. Lamar didn't mess around. No sentimentalist, his first act was to fire Michael. His second was to hire Sam Coats, a seasoned airline hand with a history of successful turnarounds. Sam, in turn, hired The Richards Group.

What an experience. We attacked the challenge like it was the Battle of Britain and we were the RAF. The ad business doesn't get any more fun than this was. It was one of our great client relationships, a true partnership. Together we concocted new strategies to win back passengers from Southwest. One involved reconfiguring every Muse Air plane with big first-class cabins. You could fly first class for just $5 extra. Customers flocked.

Every morning we waited on tenterhooks for the previous day's load factors to come in, and daily they inched upward. Through the 40s, on through the 50s, 60 . . . 62. Then we passed the magic number, 65, and continued into solid profit territory — 66 . . . 68. Every point for Muse was a point *from* Southwest. The insurgents were winning. Southwest was scrambling. We were elated.

Then, early one Monday morning as I was pouring my Grape-Nuts and thinking ahead to the weekly creative-staff meeting, the phone in my kitchen rang. It was Lamar.

"Sorry to call you at home," he said — an uncharacteristically civil opening — "but I wanted you to be the first to know."

He sounded pretty happy. I guess what I expected to hear next was some spectacular news like "our load factor hit 70 over the weekend." What he said, though, was the *last* thing I expected.

"Stan," he said, "I just sold the airline to Southwest."

I nearly dropped the phone. It was like hearing Pepsi announce that they had decided to stop all the competitive nonsense and sell the brand to Coke. I was dumbfounded, but managed to stammer a few words — something really intelligent like, "Uh . . . what?"

"Yeah," Lamar said breezily. "Sold it to Kelleher and them. I wanted to tell you myself because when you guys came on with us, Muse Air was fixing to go under." I remembered well. That had been just a few exhilarating months earlier.

"And today," he said, "that SOB had to pay me 30 million dollars for this dog."

With that, The Richards Group's first great airline experience unceremoniously ended. It was over before breakfast. But not *completely* over, because we had made the right impression on our client's rival, Southwest, who years later would invite us into their pitch.

So here we are. Bounce-bounce-bounce . . . from the Muse account (lost) to the Southwest pitch (lost) to the Continental account (lost). And the ball keeps bouncing. Thanks to the reputation we gained through those earlier experiences—and the fact that we burned no bridges along the way—we got back in the airline fray yet again. As of this writing, it looks like this latest outing may be over as well, as our client, Legend Airlines, seeks the financing they need to keep flying. But so far, at least, it's been the same sort of competitive dogfight that got us hooked on the airline business in the first place, with Legend playing David to American Airlines' Goliath.

Legend is the brainchild of a team led by Allan McArtor, a wily airline veteran and former head of the FAA. Frustrated with the way airlines have become little more than "taxicabs with wings" for businesspeople, Allan and his cohorts started looking for ways to bring some style back to the industry. They found their answer at Dallas Love Field, the convenient old in-town airport.

Nobody had flown long-haul trips out of Love since DFW Airport opened on the prairie west of town in 1974. Nobody *could* fly long-haul from Love, thanks to the Wright Amendment, passed by Congress when they appropriated federal money for DFW. Under the amendment, airlines can fly from Love Field only to destinations within Texas and adjacent states. But Allan and friends found a loophole. The law, for some odd reason, applies only to planes with more than 56 seats. Legend flew right through that loophole, and the way they did it was ingenious.

For an airline, the real money is in those last-minute business travelers who buy full-fare tickets. Legend set out to serve no one *but* those travelers, many of whom would prefer to fly from convenient Love Field instead of DFW, where American has its hub. And "serve" is definitely the right word. Legend acquired DC-9s, stripped out the interiors, and refurbished each one into a single, giant first-class section with exactly— you guessed it—56 luxurious seats.

Travelers on Legend would pay the regular coach fare—same as American would charge on a plain-Jane plane—and get not only acres of room and the best food, drink, and service in the sky but also the convenience of Legend's stylish new private terminal. From day one, Legend started flying away with some of American's bread-and-butter business. Naturally American howled with indignation. Howled, but also outfitted their planes with new first-class seats as fast as they could.

Sadly, soaring fuel costs and tight financing may spell the end to Legend's audacious experiment. But at least for a while, air travelers have enjoyed a welcome choice of airports and styles of service in the Dallas market. Meanwhile, as Legend's agency partners, we Groupers have once again been having the time of our lives in the air wars, waiting for each day's load factors like kids at Christmas, grateful for the way things really do seem to work out—sooner or later—when you just give it your best shot.

Bizarre Practices of the Financial Kind

How we handle and discuss money is at the heart of our open workplace.

MONEY: A FORBIDDEN TOPIC

If you want a can't-fail formula for sowing discontent and division in your company, you can't beat this one: Encourage idle chatter about salaries.

Chances are you don't have to encourage it; it's already going on. Speculating about who makes how much, comparing salaries and bonuses with your buddies, kvetching about perceived inequities— they're favorite games in nearly every organization. It helps you know who to hate, who to envy, who to commiserate with as your fellow victims. And nothing productive comes from it, ever.

At The Richards Group we don't explicitly ban a whole lot of things, but we definitely ban this one. Talking about compensation— your own or anyone else's—with anybody other than your group head is one of the few acts that will bring immediate dismissal. We put it right up there with stealing. It's incredibly damaging to a collaborative effort. We cannot work as equals if, in our minds, we are divided along lines of pay scale. And once pay information is voiced abroad, that division happens instantly. It's just the way people's minds work.

A Notre Dame management professor named Matt Bloom studied professional baseball teams and found that the greater the pay spread, the worse the team did, both in their win-loss record and in the club's financial performance (in *Across the Board*, November-December 1999). The problem, in my estimation, is not the pay spread per se. The problem is that, in baseball, every player knows exactly what every other player is making. It's public information. Contract negotiations often receive more media coverage than the games. So, *of course,* teams with vast pay spreads are going to have performance problems. Everyone, on the field and in the stands, is just a little preoccupied with how much one player is worth compared to the next guy.

Such comparisons are deadly for teamwork. Think about it. If you're playing second and the guy next to you at shortstop is pulling down three times your salary, when he's a split-second late throwing to first on your next double-play opportunity, are you *really* going to cut him the same slack you'd cut yourself? How about the fans, or the front office? Every player is running around out there with a little price tag supered over his head. Don't look for harmony in an organization like that.

This notion may sound hopelessly outré in this day of tell-all books and the E! channel, but intimate information ought to be *kept* intimate. And a person's salary is very intimate. Work partners shouldn't talk about it. At the moment we have one art director–writer team that is a married couple. Presumably *they* know each other's salary, but beyond their special case we draw the line. Group heads shouldn't even talk to other group heads about their respective team members' salaries unless there's an obvious reason for doing so, like when somebody is switching groups.

Speaking of baseball player salaries, we do like to pay well. Salaries, bonuses, profit sharing—these checks are the ones I most enjoy signing. And when it all adds up, we want you to feel really good about your total comp. As for where you stand in the salary market, there's plenty of basis for comparison without comparing notes with your coworkers. Magazines publish salary surveys. Headhunters are calling all the time. You're always free to shop yourself around and see if there's a better deal for you elsewhere. Our company's position is that, if you're not happy with how much you're paid, by all means talk about it. *Just talk with the people who are in a position to do something about it.*

Each person has a legitimate interest in receiving all that his or her work is worth. All we ask is that it be handled in a legitimate way.

MONEY: AN OPEN TOPIC

Other than compensation information, where money is concerned let it all hang out. Budgets, group P&Ls, how the clients are doing, bad news, good news—sharing it all is a terrific unifying force.

Companies get unnecessarily reticent with their own people when it comes to anything with a dollar figure attached—and not always out of mere conservatism, either. What's often couched as confidentiality is actually just tribalism in disguise. As we've discussed, because information is a tool of power, even unimportant information divides the people in the know from everybody else—the cognoscenti and the ignorati. Most of the financial information that managers take pains to reserve for themselves is just really not all that important or even interesting. It's the withholding that gives it weight. "I know something you don't know" is a powerful phrase, regardless of how dull the information.

Some of the information you might be holding back would provide valuable perspective and context for the workforce. Take, for example, a creative group's P&L. Does the newly hired junior art director really need to know that the group was in the hole on one of her accounts for the first six months of the year? No, says one argument. That's her group head's responsibility; she should stick to her assigned work.

But really, what's the harm? For one thing, this new AD could be, as far as we know, a group head herself within a few years. Why wait till later to let her learn some of the ins and outs? Lots of accounts start the fiscal year in the red because of intense up-front creative development, then quickly catch up once the work is running in the media. She might as well know that. Besides, creative people are still *business*people. A little dollars-and-sense context can do wonders for their productivity, just like those Manhattan Project engineers who became vastly more productive once they knew what their tedious work was producing.

You may gather from the foregoing discussion that we actually know at any given point in time whether The Richards Group is making money, and you would be right. If you know much about ad agencies—particularly some of the ones with reputations as "creative" shops—you might find this surprising.

A friend working at a hot agency in another city—a brilliantly successful shop from a creative standpoint, where the creative tribe is definitely the ruling junta—told me that the owners could hardly ever tell whether any given account was profitable because they couldn't accurately account for the work the team was doing. They're a latter-day example of Fred Allen's old line that advertising is 85 percent confusion and 15 percent commission. (The 15 percent isn't so accurate anymore, but the confusion figure is still right up there.)

Theirs is a common problem. Never been a problem here. We don't always make money on every account ("Can we make money?" is not our highest priority, remember), but we always know exactly which color the ink is. And whatever color it is, the topic is open for discussion.

Creative people, I find, can be reluctant to discuss financial matters, fearing that much attention to filthy lucre will pollute their art. But ours is, after all, *commercial* art. It's good now and then to provide positive reminders of our collective responsibility for the company's and our clients' financial performance.

I think, for example, of Scot Dykema, who, as designated money guy, got the job, some years ago, of negotiating our lease in the building we occupied at the time. So here he is, going over the documents with the leasing people, and they read through the clause that says when the lease comes up for renewal the rent will go up to reflect the prevailing market rate. Standard stuff. Boilerplate. So they read this clause and keep right on going, but Dykema stops them. "Hold on," he says. "What if the market rate goes down?"

This is the funniest thing the leasing people have ever heard. The guy's a regular comedian. Office rents in Dallas don't go *down*. (We're in the early 1980s when this story takes place.) So the leasing people enjoy a good laugh at Dykema's little joke. Then they notice that he's serious. "Well," they say, "a *lower* market is really not very likely, and this is the standard language in our leases."

"Humor me," he says.

So they humor him. Still chuckling, they write in a clause stating that at renewal time the rent will match the market rate, higher or lower.

Well, you know what happens. Ten years go by, during which oil crashes, dragging a lot of overbuilt Dallas real estate in its greasy wake. The whole cocky city gets a dose of humility. The big banks go under, J.R. and Miss Ellie get cancelled, the Cowboys fall from grace, and our lease comes up for renewal at roughly half as much per square foot as it cost when Dykema got big laughs from the leasing people with his silly question.

Good for us, of course. But I would guess that in most closely held companies this sort of good news would not be heard too far beyond the ownership ranks, which in our case would mean me. We, however, have a profit-sharing plan. So on the afternoon of our lease renewal I called the whole staff to a stairwell meeting.

"Let me tell you," I began, "about the value of asking dumb questions." I told them the whole story of Dykema's lease negotiation 10 years before, then got to the punch line. "By asking one dumb question, which was really a very smart question, Scot Dykema saved the agency about half a million dollars a year." Low whistles and murmers of "wow" went through the group. "That's money," I continued, pointing randomly at folks standing nearby, "that goes in your profit sharing, and your profit sharing, and your profit sharing."

The whole staff gave him a big standing O. In that moment, people who had never had more than the vaguest idea what Dykema does all day found that he was forever endeared to them. And we all went back to our desks a little more aware that the way we handle money — whether it's commissioning a photograph, booking a radio session, negotiating a media buy, or ordering copier paper — has tangible consequences.

THESE ARE THE DAYS (IN 15-MINUTE INCREMENTS) OF OUR LIVES

We know whether the company is making money because we're absolute lunatics when it comes to keeping track of our time.

Every living soul in the agency fills out a time sheet every single day. No one is exempt. Longest-tenured principal and newest trainee, we're all co-owners of the company's financial performance, and we're reminded of that fact every day when we fill out our time sheets. It influences the company culture in another important way, too. It helps us maintain an awareness that time isn't just time, it's our clients' money. We're obliged to fill our working hours with activity that's worth paying for.

Your time sheet accounts for your previous day's work in quarter-hour increments, coded by function. Time sheets have to be in by one o'clock each afternoon. Fail to turn yours in by then and it will cost you $8.63 (a figure I will explain later).

You would not believe how fastidious we are about time sheets. If you're fiddling with a rough cut in our in-house Avid suite, you use a different function code than if you're at an outside edit house. If the cut you're working on is a revision requested by the client, you use another code entirely. It sounds complicated, but it's no big deal, really. Write down a job number, fill in what you did on the job that day and for how long, and that's it. I doubt that we spend more than about five minutes per person per day on time sheets, and, boy, does that small investment of time ever help manage the bottom line.

We know, for example, exactly how we come out compared with the estimates we give clients, and as a result we learn how to do a better estimate next time. Advertising work almost invariably takes more time than you'd probably tend to estimate, often double or triple the time. Agencies that don't learn this—the ones that do supposedly tight estimates without then tracking their time very closely—sometimes go out of business and never really know why; it *seems* like they should be making money.

Groupers become pretty good at estimating. It's still more art than science since you never really know when a machine is going to go on the fritz or you and your creative partner are going to be infected with a particularly severe case of the stupids or revisions are going to pile up, but you eventually learn to do a pretty good job of accounting up front for Murphy's Law. In estimating time expenditures, wisdom is usually on the side of pessimism. Any client who's ever worked with an agency that was constantly lowballing estimates and then coming back begging for more money appreciates this.

I discourage group heads from analyzing individuals' time too closely. If the monthly numbers clearly reveal an extreme situation— a fairly recent one involved an account person who stoically worked crushing overtime hours without asking for the help he deserved— fine, then let's address that. But overbearing micromanagement of everyone's time would run completely counter to our culture. The last thing, literally, that I ever want to do with our time records is to start telling responsible, spectacularly productive people how they should have used their time last month or could, in someone's opinion, use their time better next month. When you're all sharing space as we do, daily action, not monthly time numbers, tells the real performance story.

I wouldn't recommend our kind of time sheet zealotry in a control-oriented company. Somebody's going to abuse it—guaranteed—to "identify the slackers." And if there's fear of harsh judgment, then people won't do honest time sheets anyway. You will have defeated the purpose. In an open workplace with an emphasis on relationships, not controls, the team knows soon enough if people aren't pulling their weight. You don't need a time sheet Gestapo to rat them out.

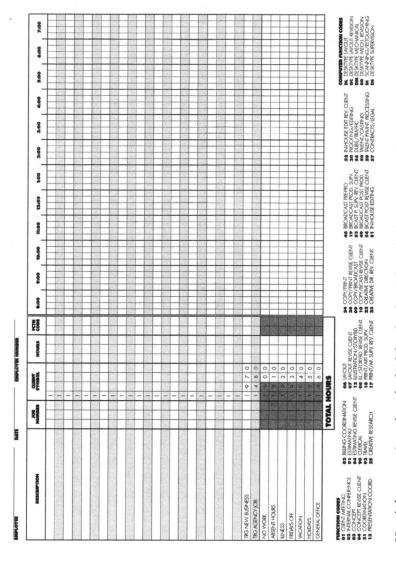

Here's how my time sheet looked for the day I described on pages 55 through 57. (The half of the page devoted to the time line doesn't have to be filled out, by the way; it's just there to help you track your day as you go.) You can also do your time sheet on computer, if you prefer.

The $8.63 Solution

The biggest trick with this whole time sheet business is simply getting people to turn the darned things in every day. And I do mean *every* day. Weekly or monthly time sheets wouldn't be worth the paper they're printed on. With as many projects as most of us have going all the time, you'd have to have the memory of a Vegas card shark to accurately remember what you did yesterday morning, let alone two weeks ago. You've got to fill one out daily.

The task of getting everybody's time sheet in on time wasn't so bad when the company was very small. When you're all practically in the same room together, a little bit of nagging covers a whole group pretty efficiently. But as the company grew, so did the delinquent-time-sheet problem.

For a while, back in the 1980s, a woman from accounting had the unhappy chore of visiting all the transgressors and coaxing the day's time sheets out of them. Eventually it was taking up most of her work-day. Hardly the best use of someone's time, nor the most satisfying. It's hard to achieve self-actualization when your full-time job is being company noodge. Fortunately, she kept scrupulous time records herself, so some clever person was able to crunch a few numbers and figure out how much it was costing the company to chase down all those delin-quent time sheets. The figure was exactly eight dollars and sixty three cents per.

With that intriguing figure in hand, we instituted a new system. Everybody is allowed up to five late time sheets per year, free. Starting with the sixth, for every tardy time sheet, you forfeit $8.63 from your year-end bonus. All the late-time-sheet money goes into a pool, to be divided equally among all the Groupers who came in under the six-tardy limit.

Voilà! Problem solved. Although not completely, of course. It's amaz-ing how much some people are willing to spend on their procrastination habit. An annual feature of our year-in-review stairwell meeting is our reading of the Top 10 Time Sheet Offenders. A check of the records reveals that the top single-year contributor in recent history donated $560.95 to the pool. Most years, several profligates finish with three-figure forfeitures. On the whole, however, the system works beautifully in spurring us to timeliness with our time sheets. Over the past several years, the faithful, who make up the vast majority of our workforce, have taken home an average of only $15 to $20 extra per person.

You might expect the worst offenders to be the staffers who travel a lot, but such is not necessarily the case. Some people go on lengthy film shoots overseas with never a late time sheet. They just e-mail or phone in their time sheet information to their coordinator each day. In any case, at home or abroad, doing time sheets is not an onerous task, and for the vast majority it's second nature.

Surprisingly we've never had to up the ante for delinquent time sheets. Adjusted for modest 3 percent annual inflation, the penalty should be somewhere around $14 or $15 by now, but $8.63 still seems to keep us all moving just as well as it did when we started.

CONSENSUS STARTS WITH A DOLLAR SIGN

You probably heard this old bromide from your high-school coach: *There's no "I" in "TEAM."* Well, I'm sorry, coach, that's not entirely true. Every Grouper has a very personal, unabashedly self-interested reason to put aside shortsighted personal agendas, pull together, and help the company do well. It's called The Richards Group profit-sharing plan.

By the time you've been here a year or so—long enough to become eligible—you've got a stake in the financial consequences of your work. It's a significant stake, too. Historically, the company has done well enough to pay nice year-end bonuses and still contribute the legal maximum, or close to it, to profit sharing nearly every year. Profit sharing isn't like a 401(k). You don't have to contribute part of your salary. It's funded 100 percent by the money we earn for the agency through our collective effort.

Profit sharing has influenced the company culture out of all proportion to the amount of attention we usually devote to it. (Making money is not our highest priority, remember. It tends to follow as a natural consequence of pursuing the higher ones.) You don't have to talk about it all the time or frame all your decisions in terms of their impact on profits. When you do your job with a vague awareness somewhere in the back of your mind that you'll participate directly and materially in the success you help create, you become more than a mere servant of the company. You become a citizen.

On issues large and small, consensus can be remarkably easy to reach. Take the little fact, often reported about our culture, that we never have an office Christmas party. That's not because we're (a) a bunch of stiffs or (b) an obscure ascetic sect, as some have speculated. Trust me, there's never a shortage of Grouper-instituted yuletide merriment. We just don't spend each other's money on it, that's all. Whenever the question comes up—do we want to have a Christmas party this year or keep the money for bonuses and profit sharing?—the answer every year so far has been virtually unanimous: *You kiddin'? We'll take the money.* True, if there's a recent hire in the room, he or she might say, "Hey, wait! I want an office party!" But some fully vested old-timer is usually there to counsel, "Wait a year. Get your profit-sharing statement. You won't want a party."

In larger endeavors like a new-business pitch or the push to develop a major new campaign, the promise of abstract rewards such as team spirit and prestige and a sense of accomplishment is fine as far as it goes, but it sure helps build resolve for the hard toil and personal sacrifice when you know the potential rewards include everybody's favorite thank-you notes, the kind with dead presidents' pictures printed on them. And as for your colleagues who aren't participating directly as members of the project team, knowing that they'll reap some of the benefits of your efforts makes them a most supportive cheering section.

To profit sharing we owe a lot of our success in keeping good people. Competitors offer nice-looking raises sometimes, but then they usually have to break the news to you—couched in the most salesman-like terms, of course—that you'll have to chip in a sizable portion of your salary for the 401(k) plan if you want to have any retirement money. That's why Groupers considering offers elsewhere often find that when it comes to total compensation, their best move is to stay put. I always tell new employees that I want them to stay here 40 years and go away rich. I mean it. And it's possible.

I want this to be a company that's hard to leave and easy to come back to. Profit sharing helps. Robin Ayres, principal of RBMM and The Naming Center, notes that she timed her return from full-time motherhood to get her back in the studio just under the wire, when the plan rules would have made her start her vesting over from scratch. Smart move on Robin's part. And a good deal for the organization; we got a key player back a little sooner than we might have otherwise.

Participation in profits is powerful incentive for hard work, cooperation, and efficiency. That's just Capitalism 101. But among our industry peers it's getting harder and harder to find anyone practicing it. Could our company still offer this benefit—and reap the rewards of doing so—if, like most of our competitors, we had given up our autonomy? I doubt it. Few indeed are the organizations that can distribute the bulk of profits to employees when there are absentee owners standing in the wings, waiting for their generous piece of the action. That's one more reason, when offers come along, that we'll just be planning to remain independent, thank you very much.

Doing the Unthinkable: Giving Back Money

There's a standard business practice in the advertising world, seldom mentioned but almost universally observed: When you can make money on an account, milk it for all it's worth. It helps make up for the duds you lose money on.

Agencies keep mum about this, of course, because you certainly don't want a client to know you're profiteering on their business. This plants yet another seed of secrecy, which you can bet will not be confined to the clients' books. It's bad for the company culture. Plus, it just ain't right.

At The Richards Group, what we do with excess profits may be the most bizarre of all our practices. We give the money back.

In our contract with a client, we agree to a profit goal, a percentage that the agency and the client both agree is fair. The client is free to check our books anytime to see how we're doing against the goal. At the end of the year, if the agency has exceeded the goal, we send them a check for the difference.

Usually we wind up right around the target. But sometimes unexpected events—say, a boost in media spending or a lower than anticipated expenditure of agency hours—create a windfall. As a business owner, I have to admit that there have been times when the pen has hesitated for a second or two before inking my signature on a check returning several hundred thousand dollars to a client, but I sign because it's the right thing to do. And besides, it's in the contract, so I can't lose my nerve for long.

Giving back money certainly helps cement strong relationships. Some clients get downright misty-eyed when you hand them a hefty sum of money that they know just about any other agency in the world would have kept without a second thought. I don't think a client has ever actually hugged me, but at least one confessed that he had a fleeting impulse to. (For the record, I didn't say, "Oh, go ahead." Richard Simmons, I'm not.)

Once, after giving money back to a client, we agency people were the ones who felt the impulse to do the hugging. It was back in our days with MBank. Our graphic design group, RBMM, operates, you'll remember, as a unit independent of the ad agency. Well, one year RBMM—which, unlike the agency, didn't have a signed contract with the bank at the time—did a number of à la carte design projects for MBank and finished the year with a $42,000 surplus above their estimates. In today's dollars, that would probably be close to a hundred grand. With no formal letter of agreement, the design group wasn't bound to return that money. But Dick Mitchell (the second "M" in RBMM), financial guy Scot Dykema, and I talked it over and concluded that, as a matter of principle, we should give the money back. Case closed, so Dick sent a check to Mark Bishop, our client at the bank.

The next day Dick got a call from the appreciative client. "Believe it or not," Mark said, "Jim McGhee [whose group handled the MBank advertising business for the agency] was short $42,000 on his profit goal. So I'm just going to send that money right back over to him." From RBMM to MBank to The Richards Group—it was even steven almost to the penny.

It's amazing how things work out when you do the right thing.

Branding: The Secret to a Business without Barriers

Some discipline in managing your most valuable asset can turn your company into a single, unstoppable interest group.

BIGGER THAN MERE METHODS

Attention, relativists. I am about to make an absolute statement. The ideas I have outlined in the first eight chapters of this book will help you make your organization more efficient, more productive, and happier. Count on it. It's like Newtonian physics. There are certain underlying principles here, and if you initiate certain actions, you can count on certain outcomes. "One thing leads to another," as someone (the British band the Fixx, as I recall) once said.

But I'm going to assume that you're after something bigger than mere performance-enhancing methods, something more valuable than just a slightly better version of what you've got now. I'm going to assume that you want to bring something into the world that will be more transforming, that will wield more long-term influence on your various constituencies and in your marketplace.

Getting there takes thinking beyond the methods by which you run your business. It takes thinking about your brand.

Your brand—even more than your mission statement, if you have one—can provide a galvanizing vision for all your company's diverse tribes to share. It's the banner at the center of the company that everyone can turn and face, the badge that gives meaning and authority to each job function. The more clearly you define your brand and institute a disciplined program for expanding its influence in the marketplace, the better everyone will see their place in the organization and how their function within the company relates to all the other functions and to your customers. In short, nothing can tear down the walls of tribalism like branding.

SO, JUST WHAT IS A BRAND?

As I've talked about branding with clients and associates around the world, I've found that the word *brand* is kind of like the word *sexy:* Everybody's conversant with the concept, but they all define it in their own ways. So let me tell you what *I* consider a brand to be.

I'll start with what it is not. A brand is not a person, not a company, not a product, place, or method. It's nothing so temporal. Founders die. Companies are bought and sold. Factories burn down. Products become obsolete. Patents expire. Technologies evolve. But a brand never expires. It's the one thing you have that really lasts. Western culture understands this durability that brands possess. Remember the Coca-Cola sign in *Blade Runner?* In the postapocalyptic vision of that film, a brand is the only thing that seems to have survived the desolation unscathed.

You can choose what you want your brand to represent, or you can abdicate the choice. It's going *to be* whether you choose or not. Because here's what a brand is: A brand is a promise.

It's a promise that you're going to fulfill certain expectations. Good ones, hopefully, but maybe bad ones. That's where the power of your choices comes in. Branding, as a business discipline, is the process of coming to a conviction about the expectations you want established, understanding every mechanism that affects those expectations, and managing

those mechanisms to deliver a consistent, positive promise at every point of contact.

Consistency is the key. If The Richards Group produces a wonderful product but treats its employees like pond scum, I haven't got a mere operational problem. I've got a branding problem—different promises at different points of contact with the brand.

And just look at how many points of contact there can be, all affecting the promise your brand embodies. Some are obvious: your product; your advertising and other brand communications; employees and other company representatives; franchisees or dealers and their employees; physical assets like factories, stores, vehicles. I'm sure you can think of others. But what about all the other, less obvious influences on the promise the brand conveys? The appearance of a customer seen wearing your label or coming out of your store can affect the observer's perception of your brand. For retail brands, even the smell of the hand soap in the ladies' washroom subtly influences a customer's perception.

With so many influences affecting the outcome, deciding what you want your brand—your promise—to be and then achieving any-where *near* consistency in delivering it takes some serious conviction. Of course, that's not easy. But the good news is, companies that gain that conviction have found the most powerful cohesive force in all of business.

A SINGLE, UNSTOPPABLE INTEREST GROUP

Show me a company with factionalism, infighting, political ferment, and I'll show you a company that's presenting an inconsistent face to the world. Think, for example, of the advertising agency with strong marketing types and a weak creative product, or the manufacturer with intriguing designs that are poorly executed. Or consider the case of a company that makes a terrific product and promotes it with stupid or shrill advertising. Inevitably in companies like that you'll find competing agendas, dispirited employees, castes of lordly heroes and despised pariahs, and assorted levels in between.

Somehow in cases like these, people have come to pursue differing visions of what's supposed to be happening at work. Without some overarching, unifying, reconciling tie that binds the activities and groups of the company together, factionalism and inconsistent perfor-mance are inevitable. Tinkering with your company's internal practices will never unite all your various tribes into a single interest group and propel your company to the place of influence you want. But done right, branding will.

Writing in the 1920s, political philosopher José Ortega y Gasset considered how disparate groups within a territory can be united. "The state comes into being," he wrote, "when naturally divided groups are obliged to live together. The unifying obligation is not one of brute force, but rather implies an initiating project, a common purpose offered to dispersed groups. Before all else, the state is a plan for action, a program for collaboration."

Think of your company's physical presence—a number of people gathered into physical facilities—as the territory. Then substitute the word *brand* for the word *state* in Ortega's assertion, and you have the point I want to get across: Your brand—or perhaps more accurately the strategy behind it—can embody your company's "unifying obligation" and "program for collaboration." It can be the common rallying point for all the diverse groups within your organization.

Even for some who aren't really *in* your organization. My colleague Doug Rucker saw this recently when he bought a Trane central air conditioner for his house. He purchased it from a local independent Trane dealer, who sent a service technician out to install the unit. The technician was obviously very proficient and clearly serious about making sure the new equipment was properly installed. Doug was impressed and said so. In response, the serviceman quoted our theme-line, "It's Hard To Stop A Trane," and talked about how the brand's emphasis on quality helps give him direction for his own work. He has a *promise* to uphold.

Keep in mind, this was a blue-collar good old boy talking, not some slick marketing type. He's not an employee of the Trane Company. He works for an independent dealer. Trane isn't even the only brand they carry. Yet it's the brand that he, as a craftsman, could proudly identify with.

Companies that work as a single, unstoppable interest group, expanding their sphere of influence and repelling competitive assaults, are distinguished by a clear vision for their brand and a zeal for presenting it ever more consistently. As a body of people, they attack inconsistency like the debilitating virus that it is. They strengthen the weaker or more distant parts of the organization (for instance, Trane's network of dealers, who are free to pursue their own business agendas), supporting and edifying them, not tearing them down as politically charged companies do.

A shared vision for your brand—a clear branding strategy—is the only axis around which your company can rotate without some dizzying wobbles. It establishes priorities. It illuminates areas of inconsistency. And it gives greater meaning to everyone's labors. Grand-scale branding strategy, not cultural rehab for its own sake, is the best way to build a business without barriers.

BRANDING FOR GENIUSES, AND FOR THE REST OF US

I know of two ways to build a powerful brand, a brand that delivers a consistent promise, growing ever wider in influence.

One way is pure intuition. Some of the true brand juggernauts have been built by great visionary figures—a company founder, usually—gifted with an innate, gyroscopically sensitive instinct for turning an idea into a killer brand. These intuitive geniuses see the brand, *feel* the brand, craft the brand, and jealously guard its every point of contact. I recently had a chance to meet one of these intuitive master brand builders, Ralph Lauren.

I would bet that in the instant you saw Ralph Lauren's name on the page, your brain received an info-burst of images, perceptions, associations related to his brand. Whatever you registered about the brand—its place in the world of fashion and décor, the quality of manufacture, the kind of people who buy the products, the price relative to other brands, the entire lifestyle the name evokes—that's the promise the brand holds for you. And I'd be surprised if your general perceptions aren't nearly identical to mine or those of just about anybody else reading this. We bring our own tastes and interpretations, of course. To people with certain preferences and aspirations, the Ralph Lauren brand represents the pinnacle of gracious living. If you live at the bleeding edge of avant garde, it may strike you as hopelessly bourgeois. But regardless of whether your taste runs to Ralph Lauren products, you *know* what the brand represents. And the reason for that consistent promise is Ralph Lauren, the guy himself.

We met at his office on Madison Avenue. From the street you enter a small, spare, almost stark lobby—no overstuffed club chairs or English concierge—a coolly modern sort of building. But ride up the elevator to the Ralph Lauren suite and you step into a different world, a clubby, comfortably upper-crust, just-so place of old wood and rich fabrics and genteel manners. Except for the stack of storyboards I was carrying, I could easily have imagined that I was arriving for a spot of tea and an afternoon of grouse shooting. Outside, the office towers and taxicabs of Manhattan seemed incongruous; you expected a croquet lawn and gillies loading spaniels into the Rover.

I was there because my client The Home Depot had just begun marketing a line of Ralph Lauren paints. The agency developed several TV directions and had already presented them to our clients at the Depot. But under their agreement with the Lauren organization, before we could proceed with production a storyboard had to be approved by R.L. himself. He's the guardian, the chief zealot, the one with the branding radar, and he doesn't lend his name to anything that doesn't feel right to him.

Dressed in boots, faded jeans, and a fringed cowboy jacket, he was gracious and *very* soft-spoken. We went over the boards—one of which he felt worked well—then discussed in more detail various matters of tone and manner in the commercial and reviewed the procedure for working with his art direction staff. He gives no rubber-stamp approvals. Every point of contact matters deeply, down to the last little tchotchkes on the back table in the far corner of the picture. And his instincts for what supports the brand promise are almost preternatural. You can tell in five minutes with the guy why his brand is so consistent.

Unfortunately, most of us aren't Ralph Lauren. There's got to be a way for those of us who aren't brilliantly intuitive brand builders to achieve conviction for our brands and gain consistency in delivering the brand promise.

There is. Call it brand building for the rest of us. The things those charismatic, visionary brand builders do by instinct can be done by ordinary smart people who are willing to work at it the right way, as a business discipline.

At The Richards Group we've developed, over the course of many years, a formalized, proprietary strategic planning process, an ordered brand-building discipline. The process even has its own brand name, a genuine circle-R trademark. We call our process *Spherical® branding.*

Because a brand is a promise, each contact with your brand either strengthens the promise or erodes it. Hence, you can see the necessity of being consistent at all points of contact. But consistency requires conviction and consensus about certain of the brand's qualities—qualities that *all* individuals with influence on *any* point of contact should strive to convey. Spherical branding is designed to get you there, to the consensus that will make your organization into a house undivided.

SPHERICAL BRANDING: BRAND BUILDING IN THE ROUND

Turn the page for a second and look at the illustration. You see now where we got the name *Spherical*. The idea of our little strategic planning regimen is to actively manage the whole universe of influences that constitute your brand, your promise. A sphere, I've been told, is the strongest form in the universe because it's capable of withstanding more external pressure than any other. That's the kind of brand strength we're trying to construct—resilient no matter what.

Returning for a moment to our theme of building a peaceable kingdom, you'll notice that the brand components addressed by Spherical branding are, by and large, externally focused. Our eyes are directed outward toward the consumer, not inward to examine in isolation the company's culture and procedures. Yet pursuing consistency in your points of contact with consumers will inevitably work cultural change within the organization. The process exposes relational barriers within the company that impede the brand's progress, and it provides a meaningful, relatively objective framework for addressing those barriers. Changes you make, then, are *about the brand*—in service of the grand, consensus agenda—and not about personalities, whims, or the agendas of petty kingdoms within the organization. Spherical branding gives the whole company a common rallying point.

Let's look at the sphere. We've broken the Spherical branding process down into three distinct and sequential parts:

1. At the core is correctly defining the highest calling of your business. This may not be as obvious as you think. We'll get to that shortly.
2. Around that core we wrap the most advantageous brand positioning, personality, and affiliation strategies. I'll discuss these in more detail as well.
3. To convey these branding strategies, we then develop communication briefs for every point of contact between the consumer and the brand and even between internal audiences and the brand. You can carry this step as far as you deem necessary. If you want to develop a ladies'-room-hand-soap-scent brief, you can.

The Spherical® Branding Discipline

Brand
positioning

Brand
personality

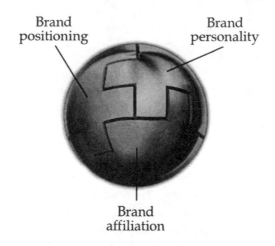

Brand
affiliation

The three strategic components of Spherical branding.

Once these three components of Spherical branding are in place, then you execute your strategy. Simple! Well, okay, maybe not all *that* simple. I never promised that this branding thing would be an easy job. But here's a reason to persevere. Once in place and properly executed, these three components of branding constitute the intrinsic value of your brand. And the higher its value relative to other brands, the greater the profit margin you can command. That's a concept Wall Street understands quite well. Just look at the price-to-earnings ratios of companies with strong brands versus those of companies in the same categories but with weak brands. Your brand is the most valuable asset you've got, because it's the most enduring. With Spherical branding you'll increase its value all the more.

So let's go through Spherical branding point by point, beginning, as great things often do, with a dumb question. Do you know what business you're in?

YOU MIGHT NOT BE IN THE BUSINESS YOU THINK YOU'RE IN

Back when typing was just typing and not "keyboarding," the machine of choice for millions of people was made by Underwood. Nothing else compared to the silky yet solid action of a big Underwood desk-model typewriter. It gave your words *force.* Offices, newsrooms, classrooms, homes — Underwood machines were ubiquitous.

So where's Underwood now? They're gone. Say "Underwood" today and your listener is more likely to think of deviled ham than office equipment. A great brand, dead. And why? Because they defined their business as typewriters rather than, say, word processing.

And look at the railroads. They used to carry passengers. Now they carry coal. Why? Because they thought they were in the railroad business instead of, for example, high-speed transportation. If they had defined their business differently, Santa Fe might be the world's dominant passenger airline or package delivery service.

Now contrast those examples with another venerable old brand, Arm & Hammer. They started selling baking soda for recipes sometime in the late Cretaceous period. But things changed in our generation. People stopped baking from scratch. So was it bye-bye Arm & Hammer? Could have been if they had gotten hung up on the fact that their product is called "baking" soda. But their business definition was bigger than that, and now they provide natural deodorizers and healthful products like toothpaste that *contain* baking soda.

So, you might say, Arm & Hammer did what any smart company must do. They adapted; they showed agility, and those other brands did not. Well, yes, obviously they did adapt well, but placing your reliance on your company's ability to do likewise is risky business. Tom Johnson of Toffler Associates and Alan White of MIT put it this way: "Though much vaunted, adaptability is *not* all you need to succeed; it is inherently reactive and relies on luck. Strategy is what you need — and if you don't have one, you will become part of someone else's." Your business definition is the first thing to strategize — *before* you find yourself forced to adapt under duress.

Let's look at one organization's clearly strategic approach to their business definition. Think about the Walt Disney Company. What business would you say they're in? Let's see, they've got studios, theme parks, TV and radio networks, web sites, Broadway . . . would the answer be entertainment? Well, their definition clearly encompasses that — and they do call themselves an entertainment company, for obvious reasons — but what about Celebration, that town they built in Florida? If the whole business definition is entertainment, how does that fit? Okay, so . . . maybe the town's an aberration, something they got excited about and built before they realized it was off the spine of the story, as screenwriters sometimes say. Could be, but doubtful. And what about the mall stores and catalog business? That's not really entertainment, either.

So how do you make it all fit within the brand? Intuitively you know it does—there's some kind of unifying idea here—but no traditional business-category term springs to mind to handily describe just what Disney *does*. Well, when I asked the question of a knowledgeable source, here's how it was described to me. Disney defines its business as *keeping alive the magic of childhood*.

That's brilliant. It's tightly definitive yet enormously expansive at the same time. Just like that, you can see how all those enterprises tie together conceptually. An experimental town? Absolutely, if the concept is to create that ideal Fred MacMurray/Dean Jones burg we all sort of remember without ever having really experienced it. A grown-up-targeted movie from Touchstone? Sure, as long as it delivers the magic of escaping into imagination for a couple of hours. *Nightline* with Ted Koppel? Um, well, when you put it up against the business definition, maybe it's not so extreme after all to suggest that the news division should be spun off and given its independence.

See how it works? A good business definition gives you plenty of room to exploit new opportunities and adapt to threats, along with the discipline to know where to draw the line on the businesses you'll engage in. In our Spherical branding process, we say that the correct definition of your business will satisfy six criteria. It will

- Be specific enough to influence the strategic and resource-allocation decision making within your company.
- Focus on the satisfying of customer needs rather than on the current physical characteristics of the product being sold.
- Reflect the essential skills of your organization and signal when those need to be expanded.
- Enable the organization to recognize future threats beyond your normal set of "blinders" (e.g., "What will happen to a product called 'baking soda' if home baking declines?").
- Be attainable but with difficulty.
- Be brief and memorable (so everyone in the company can be inspired by it).

If you asked several higher-ups in your company to define the business you're in, would their answers be alike? Try it. Find out if the answers meet the preceding criteria. When you're done, we'll move on to determining the three interrelated strategies that wrap around your business definition.

A Triple Dip of Strategy: Positioning, Personality, Affiliation

Once you know what business you're in, you can start thinking about just who you're going to be in the world. Getting to that answer takes three strategies. Brand positioning, brand personality, and brand affiliation reach your target at three levels: intellect, emotions, and, deeper still, ego.

Positioning Strategy: Intellectual Appeal

What do you want consumers to think about you? Your brand's positioning is the most basic of all strategic statements. Once you've noodled this one out, it should be the dominant consideration in your choice of all substrategies: product, pricing, packaging, creative, media, merchandising, promotion, point-of-sale display, shopping environment, PR, direct marketing, sales staff, phone operators, and so on.

To do you much good, a positioning statement needs to define three things: (1) a target audience, (2) a competitive category, and (3) the most meaningful point of difference for your brand. Each of these is a major decision in its own right, but because the three are interdependent, arriving at the best positioning can get *really* complicated. One particular shortcut may seem tempting, so let me warn you:

> *Do not attempt to construct your positioning statement by mere management consensus. The positioning will last only as long as the people who originally agreed on it.*

Done properly, the process requires primary research and rigorous data analysis. In the end, the positioning strategy is expressed in one simple sentence in this format: "For (target definition), your brand is a (competitive frame of reference) that provides (your most meaningful point of difference)."

Let me give you an example of a positioning strategy. It's for our client, Motel 6, and it says: "For frugal people, Motel 6 is a comfortable night's stay at the lowest price of any national chain." That's it. Like I said, it's a simple sentence. And therein lies another temptation. Your statement comes out so, well, *flat*-sounding, and you spent so much *money* on it. You'll be tempted to make it sound eloquent and grand. Don't. Your positioning statement is a ruler that you'll be measuring a lot of decisions by, not a piece of filigree to decorate the building. You want it nice and straight and easy to use.

Back to Motel 6. Their guests can be segmented into three distinct groups: seniors, vacationing families, and self-paying business travelers. The target definition, "frugal people," represents the common denominator that predicts their behavior regardless of their age, income, reason for traveling, or any of a hundred other things that make each guest different.

Notice that in our positioning Motel 6 isn't a motel, it's a comfortable night's stay. We used to think the competitive frame of reference was "motels," but over time we realized that the word narrowed our perspective to only the predominant source of new guests. Now we also attract visitors from their relatives' spare rooms and sofas. In other words, Aunt Doris's hide-a-bed is an important part of the competitive set.

As for the third point—a clean, comfortable room—of course, we provide that as the price of entry, but the most *meaningful* point of difference (to the target of frugal people) is having the lowest price of any national chain. We know that because we researched it. Exhaustively. Same with the target definition and competitive category. No matter how much you know, or think you do, only painstaking research can help you refine your positioning.

What's the real aim here? To develop a positioning strategy that optimizes your brand's appeal by being relevant to the largest possible customer segment for which it has unique leverage. Got your head around that? Okay, let's get emotional.

Creating Brand Personality: Emotional Appeal

In many categories, a brand's personality may be the only factor that can consistently separate it from look-alike competitors.

Take beer, for instance. The old saying in that business is that people "drink the advertising." For our client Corona, we didn't create a campaign around claims about the grain, hops, water, or calorie content. The campaign is all about personality, an attitude of laid-back, unhassled *tropicalismo*. And it has helped Corona become the best-selling import in the country, knocking off Heineken, which had been number one since the end of Prohibition.

No matter what category you're in, you've got to portray a likable

:60 Radio - Comparison Spot

```
Hi.  Tom Bodett here for Motel 6 with a comparison.  You know, in some ways,
a Motel 6 reminds me of one of those big fancy hotels.  They've got beds,
we've got beds.  They've got sinks and showers, by golly we've got 'em too.
There are differences, though.  You can't get a hot facial mudpack at Motel 6
like at those fancy joints.  And you won't find french-milled soap or avocado
body balm.  You will, however, find a clean, comfortable room, and the lowest
rates nationwide.  Under 21 bucks' in most places.  A lot less in some, a
little more in others, but always the lowest price of any national chain.
And always a heck of a deal.

Motel 6 has 400 locations from coast to coast.  And we operate ever darn one
of 'em, which means they're always clean and comfortable.

Oh sure, it'll be rough to survive one night without avocado body balm or
french-milled soap, but maybe the money you save'll help you get over it.  It
always works for me.  I'm Tom Bodett for Motel 6.


'Alternate Texas - Under 19 bucks.
```

Solid positioning provides a basis for long-running campaigns. This radio commercial was produced in 1986, but, except for minor details such as the number of locations, it could easily run in rotation with spots produced last week. The copywriter was David Fowler.

(to your target audience) personality if you're going to establish an emotional relationship between the brand and its customers. Without brand personality, you only have transactions; you're not cultivating customer loyalty.

Before we talk about creating your brand personality statement, it's important to understand what the brand personality is *not*. It is not the same as the tone of the advertising, although the tone of the advertising must be consistent with the brand's personality. And it is usually not the most meaningful point of difference in the positioning statement for the brand; however, when all the alternative brands provide a similar benefit, it may become the customer's key reason to connect emotionally and prefer a brand.

So here's what it is. A personality statement is the set of human traits that the brand should portray in its relationship with its customers. When you know someone's personality, what does it tell you?

Corona became the top-selling imported beer largely on the strength of its brand personality. Creative team for this spot: writer Mike Renfro and art director Jim Baldwin.

It gives you a good idea of what that person is likely to do or say, or not do or say, in any given situation. Can't you predict this with people you know well? To a customer or prospect, your brand should be just like a person in this respect. Integrity in character and personality establishes expectations.

Like Corona, Motel 6 provides a great example of the far-reaching impact of a strong personality strategy. The strategy we developed with Motel 6 states that the brand is to be "honest, simple, fun, humble, unpretentious, and a trustworthy source of good-humored common sense."

Pick any of the commercials with Tom Bodett and this statement obviously applies. Here's one way we've applied it outside the realm of advertising to deepen the brand's emotional connection with customers. At other lodging choices, you'll get a wake-up call that, more than likely, is impersonal and a bit on the cold side. At Motel 6, you hear the cheerful voice of Tom Bodett: "Congratulations, you've just won a lottery for 20 million dollars. Just kidding, but you did save money last night, so you can still feel good about getting up and getting back on the road."

If we weren't concerned about delivering the brand's message at every point of contact, wake-up messages like that might never have even occurred to us. A brand's personality should become a strategic cornerstone. Only when you give it such a high degree of importance, placing it right alongside your brand positioning, will your personality come through with every customer, every ad, every human contact, every communication channel.

Managing Brand Affiliation: Ego Appeal

As humans, we tend to affiliate with people like ourselves, people we admire or people we aspire to be like — the old "birds of a feather" principle. Which brings us to the next principle of Spherical branding: brand affiliation. A strong brand should intentionally convey an image to its users that evokes and capitalizes on this basic human behavior of affiliating with people who are like us or whom we want to be like. Simply put, brand affiliation is how people come to believe others will perceive them as a result of being a known user of your brand.

What club does the use of your brand make consumers a part of? Associations will exist whether you try to manage them or not, so to prevent a negative or limiting perception it just makes sense to actively convey the affiliation you want for your brand.

To illustrate, let's stick with the Motel 6 example. Like all brands that occupy a low-price position, if Motel 6 doesn't actively manage their brand affiliation they face a real risk: Prospects and users will be embarrassed, fearing that others will view them as cheapskates or, worse, unable to pay more. Clear positioning and an appealing personality alone can't overcome such a strong ego issue. That's why we consistently portray guests at Motel 6 as people who are always smart with their money. Staying with us is a badge of membership in that virtuous group.

We strive to make frugality a distinction to be admired and emulated. It's a virtue that crosses all lines of age and income. In a Motel 6 parking lot you'll see everything from a primer-colored Chevy Citation with the hood wired shut to a new Mercedes S-Class. The smart/frugal person realizes that when your eyes are shut (which, after all, is what you're there for — shut-eye) all motel rooms are alike, and it's better to spend five bucks extra on a nice dinner or a souvenir for Mom than to spend it for amenities you don't need. And here's the fun part. By implication, people who stay someplace else must be either uninformed, foolish, or just plain ostentatious.

For the record, here's the official Motel 6 brand affiliation statement: "People who stay at Motel 6 are solid citizens with enough common sense not to throw away their hard-earned money. Regardless of how much they make, they always take pride in finding ways to save a

For reservations call
505-891-6161

Voice-over: Hi, I'm Tom Bodett for Motel 6 with some insight for the traveler. This is what one of our rooms looks like when you're sleeping. And you know, it looks just like those big, fancy hotels. Only difference is, ours won't cost you nearly as much money. In fact, Motel 6 always has the lowest prices of any national chain on a clean, comfortable room. Makes you sleepy just looking at it. Well, I'm Tom Bodett for Motel 6, and we'll leave the light on for you.

Motel 6 doesn't have to show pictures of customers—or anything else, for that matter—to portray their guests as people who are smart with their money. Writers David Fowler and Thomas Hripko and art director Brian Nadurak were the team behind this frugal spot.

buck." When you write yours, if you can keep it that simple, clear, and true to the brand personality, you'll give your brand communications a good running start.

COMMUNICATING THE STRATEGIES: HOW YOUR BRAND APPEARS IN BRIEFS

You've nailed down your business definition and honed your positioning, personality, and affiliation strategies. It's time for the third major step in Spherical branding: creating a strategy brief for each aspect of your brand communications. That's one brief per. You need a brief for *every* form of contact with your constituents. Here's a by-no-means-complete list of briefs you might need to develop:

- Advertising
- Public relations
- Web site
- Relationship and direct marketing
- Sales promotion

- Logo and packaging, shopping bag design
- Signage
- Collateral, selling, and display materials

- Salespersons' recruitment and training
- Operator and phone contact
- Billing statements and inserts
- Catalogs
- Employee attire (e.g., hotel staff uniforms)
- Internal communications such as newsletters, intranet

In each case you'll be writing a paper that tells how the conceptual, strategic core of the brand should be given voice in a specific means of communication. This shouldn't be a piecemeal process. It's critical for the role of each and every form of communication to be *simultaneously* articulated. Obviously every communication device doesn't have to convey the same message; however, each must establish or reinforce one or more of the three branding strategies.

Take a prosaic example: billing statements. Think of this usually dull and often unwelcome piece of communication in light of your positioning, personality, and affiliation strategies. What surprising and endearing wrinkles might you introduce to your billing statement? It's more than a chance to say, "Hey, here's how much you owe us." It's a chance for *branding,* just like Motel 6's wake-up call became an opportunity to say much more than just, "Hey, wake up."

Now, when I say "write a paper," I mean write *a* paper—one side of one sheet if you possibly can. It's easy to amass so much of your knowledge, insight, and indoctrination that you end up with a binder that looks like the owner's manual for a nuclear submarine and that no one ever uses. Give the people executing your strategy a page they can tape to the wall next to their desks and refer to often. You'll have all kinds of backup materials—graphic standards, research findings, guidelines of every sort—but keep all that separate so the brief stays as lucid as you can make it. Be disciplined. Be brief.

Another thing: When you write a communication brief, use the language your customers use, not a bunch of business buzzwords. Remem-

Mt. Rushmore. One of the seven wonders of the modern world   The Black Hills of South Dakota

Developing a communication brief for each and every aspect of your brand communications will help you achieve the elusive goal of consistency, the key to expanding your brand's sphere of influence. This is a shot from the annual cow calendar sold at Chick-fil-A restaurants.

ber the Motel 6 brand affiliation statement, the one about "solid citizens" and "saving a buck"? The language of the statement itself was true to the brand. Try to make your communication briefs like that.

Maybe this will inspire you. Chick-fil-A has built a terrific brand around the imagery of those highly self-interested cows. Earlier I told the story of how the campaign began with a doodle that became a billboard and then quickly took on a life of its own. As the phenomenon grew, the agency team handling Chick-fil-A realized that it was prudent to codify what makes the cows work so well, so that years down the road future team members inheriting the campaign could maintain the charm that made it a hit in the first place. In other words, they saw the need for something of a bovine brief.

The account team could have written a list of dry and—forgive me—*bossy* guidelines for how to use the cows, but they didn't. Like the good brand builders they are, they considered the brand personality's emphasis on fun. Here are a few excerpts from what they titled *The Chick-fil-A Moo Manifesto*.

The cows always act in a renegade manner. These aren't your garden variety Holsteins. These guys pop up in places where you least expect them: up on a billboard, taking over the air-

DONKEES. ELEFUNTS. CHIKIN.

Vote Chicken at Chick-fil-A

Outdoor that ran during the 2000 presidential campaign.

waves, or even on the city's water tower. They know that if they don't continue to surprise us, they become boring and expected. Which is one step away from becoming burgers.

The cows are not on the Chick-fil-A payroll. . . . The cows must never be shills, which means they should remain free of Chick-fil-A logos. In fact, they would be offended if we gave them money. Besides, they have no pockets.

The cows have a fairly simple sense of humor. They don't believe in elaborate productions. Theirs is a "grassroots" effort, so they always opt for the simplest, most economical way to get their point across. . . . And their humor is marked by naïve silliness. Some would say stupidity. But that's not very nice.

The cows can't spell. Oh, they give it their best shot. But cows aren't the smartest creatures in the world, especially when using someone else's language. Their grammar isn't so hot, either. And they smell funny.

The cows are not always politically correct. . . . For example, they have no problem pointing out that people might not have such big butts if they didn't eat so many hamburgers.

Isn't that better than a bunch of pinch-faced thou-shalt-nots? One lesson here is that even though your brand represents the future livelihood of you and perhaps thousands of other people, you don't have to be so blasted serious about it all the time, unless, of course, being stiff is part of your brand personality.

CHIKIN. 4 MOR YEERS.

Vote Chicken at Chick-fil-A

Frequent Eater's Card

Branding to the nth degree. Items from the catalog of merchandise Chick-fil-A makes available to the operators of its restaurants.

You'll have to figure out how to craft your own brand-appropriate communication briefs, but let me give you one more example to help get you thinking. At The Richards Group, every creative assignment starts with a one-page brief. Doesn't matter if it's a massive multimedia campaign for a new client or the umpteenth pool-out in a long-running series; it gets that single-page brief. To challenge us and keep us humble, every brief has this statement at the top of the page: "People don't like ads. People don't trust ads. People don't remember ads. What will make this one any different?" From there the brief consists of short, plain-English answers to these seven questions:

- Why are we advertising? [For real. No fudgy answers like, "The client has budget they must spend by year-end."]
- Who are we advertising to?
- What do they currently think? [We write this answer and the next as if they're really quotes from a consumer, meaning we need to actually *know* what consumers think.]
- What would we *like* them to think?
- What is the single most persuasive idea we can convey? [It must be singular. *One* idea, no cheating.]
- Why should they believe it?
- Are there any creative guidelines? [This simply means any of the usual mandatories like using a certain piece of music or putting the Web address at the bottom of the page.]

Go for clarity. Go for brevity. And remember, do all your communication briefs simultaneously. They become like points of color that, viewed together, form a complete picture of your brand. Leave one out and the picture will be incomplete.

"My Brand Can Kick Your Mission Statement's Butt"

Quick review. Spherical branding clarifies the business you're in. It defines your brand's positioning, personality, and desired user affiliation. These strategic decisions build conviction. Conviction leads to consistency at every point of contact between your brand and its customers and prospects. The results are a comprehensive communications program, not just advertising, and enduring campaigns, not just ads. And (here's where we get back to the peaceable kingdom idea) everybody in your company will understand their responsibility to keep your brand's promise.

Through branding you will have transformed your workforce into a single interest group, participants in a clear, shared agenda that eclipses any personal and departmental agendas. If you've got tribal barriers you're trying to remove, you'll have a lot more willing participants in the process as a result of your branding efforts.

On the other hand, considering how much work brand building takes, you might prefer to go the route of drafting a nice, hollow, corporate-sounding mission statement and just make *that* your rallying point for the troops. That's what most companies do. Even that can be pretty time consuming, though, by the time all the major players fly in to Hilton Head or some other suitably neutral location for the big ideation session and get in their rounds of golf. So let me help you. I developed the following statements using the handy Mission State-ment Generator at www.dilbert.com—much faster than a Mission Statement Task Force and every bit as effective. I'm sure one of them will work just fine for you.

> "Our mission is to competently facilitate cost-effective infra-
> structures and globally simplify high-quality technology to
> stay competitive in tomorrow's world."
> "We have committed to proactively fashion ethical products so
> that we may authoritatively revolutionize value-added tech-
> nology while promoting personal employee growth."
> "Our mission is to globally provide access to high-quality intel-
> lectual capital as well as to professionally integrate enter-
> prise-wide benefits to set us apart from the competition."
> "It's our responsibility to seamlessly utilize emerging products
> while maintaining the highest standards."

So take your pick. Personally I recommend that last one. The kicky lit-tle contraction in "It's" will make you seem very approachable and with-it, while the weightiness of that word "responsibility" demon-strates that you won't be having *too* much fun.

I don't mean to completely dismiss mission statements. Once in a while a company actually will develop a solid one. But even in those cases the mission statement alone can't do what the discipline of branding can do. It can't provide the same clear focus for the efforts of the workforce. The Chick-fil-A people understand this well. Although they developed not one but *two* statements—of corporate purpose and of mission—to define what the company is about, they knew that even these aren't enough to produce consistency across every point of contact.

The Chick-fil-A statement of corporate purpose, which clearly reflects the beliefs and attitudes of founder Truett Cathy, is about as high-minded as one can imagine: "To glorify God by being a faithful steward of all that is entrusted to us. To have a positive influence on all who come in contact with Chick-fil-A." Wow. If it's our first day on the job with Chick-fil-A and those are our instructions, about the only response we could give is a low whistle. How are we going to do *that* at work today? Fortunately, Truett and friends don't leave us to figure it out on our own.

The mission statement narrows the focus a bit: "Be America's best quick-service restaurant at satisfying every customer." Okay, now we're starting to understand the job a little better, starting to see a more specific goal. And it's measurable. That's important. We can do consumer research and learn whether we're attaining it. Good so far. But still missing is the crucial element of *how*. Show that mission statement to 20 employees and you could get 20 different interpretations of how to pursue it. They might even be 20 pretty *good* interpretations, but they won't be consistent. So Chick-fil-A gives us more.

See how much better we understand our job with this positioning statement: "To choosy people in a hurry, Chick-fil-A is the premium fast-food restaurant brand that consistently serves America's best-loved chicken sandwiches." Aha. Now we know more about our customer. She's got high standards, but when she comes to see us she hasn't got all day. We know we're competing with fast-food places—no pretensions of "destination dining" here—but by the same token we're *premium;* we won't play the three-for-a-dollar discount game. And that means we've got to make sure we're worth every penny we ask. We know we *serve* food, not merely sell it. And while we may have great lemonade and waffle fries, we know who the marquee stars of this show will be: chicken sandwiches.

See what branding does that even a good mission statement doesn't? It instantly gives us a huge leap toward consistency. And that's before we even articulate the brand personality, which, for the record, is "caring; genuine; dependable; clean-cut, yet unexpectedly fun." The affiliation strategy and communication briefs take us still further.

So go ahead, by all means, write your mission statement if you feel you must. You might even hit on something not unlike the business definition at the core of Spherical branding. That would be a good start. But remember, without the clarifying and defining strategies of positioning, personality, and affiliation, and the specific marching orders of the sort our communication briefs provide, nobody will know

quite how to pursue that mission of yours. You'll get too many interpretations, too much inconsistency.

Besides, a brand is *bigger* than a mission. A mission, by definition, is
finite, closed-ended. A mission, if it really is a mission, can be accomplished. A brand, however, is enduring. Its influence can continue to
expand and expand and expand. And just how far it can go, the world
has yet to see.

Turning the Barge

Some final thoughts before you set off to change your company's culture. As long as you're not expecting an instant turnaround, you might actually enjoy it.

JE M'APPELLE POLLYANNA

Giddy, I ain't.

Like to have fun? Absolutely. Enjoy a laugh? You bet. Even so, you probably wouldn't mistake me for Rip Taylor.

When the newspapers and trade press do profiles on the agency, they often portray my demeanor as somewhat reserved. I suppose that must really be how I come across; who am I to argue with the ladies and gentlemen of the Fifth Estate? And, in fact, The Richards Group as a whole has something of a reputation for sangfroid compared to a lot of our brethren in the ad business.

I will say this, though. Beneath this supposedly stoic exterior beats the heart of a complete cockeyed optimist. I'm talking about the whole agency, not just me. Some of my colleagues may even disagree with this assessment, arguing that, by and large, we are clear-eyed realists fashionably accessorized with a dash of world-weary cynicism from life in the trenches of advertising.

Bosh. We're a bunch of Pollyannas. Always have been, might as well admit it. And looking back, I think that's one of the secrets of the agency's success.

In their interesting study of Great Groups,
the once-or-twice-in-a-generation sort of
world changers the rest of us hold in awe,
Warren Bennis and Patricia Ward Biederman looked at groups like Disney
Feature Animation, the Skunk Works,
Apple's Macintosh team, the Manhattan Project—groups that created a legend along with whatever else they were
creating. The missions couldn't have been
more diverse—singing dwarfs and atomic bombs—but Bennis and Biederman found some common traits, one of which is this: Great Groups are
slightly out of touch with reality.

Bennis and Biederman write: "As psychologist Martin Seligman has
shown, realism is a risk factor for depression and its attendant ills, including an inability to act and the loss of self-trust. Great Groups often show
evidence of collective denial. And 'Denial ain't just a river in Egypt,' as
twelve-steppers like to say. Denial can obscure obstacles and stiffen
resolve. It can liberate. Great Groups are not realistic places. They are
exuberant, irrationally optimistic ones."

At my company, we've got a streak of that same irrational optimism.
We haven't taken it to the same mythic proportions ("At least not yet!"
the voice of Pollyanna chimes in), but that collective, quixotic insanity
is in there.

It was in there when, at the ripe old age of 20, I headed for L.A. "to
work for Saul Bass" and ended up in Dallas to find fortune in some booming design community that didn't even exist yet. The insanity was there
when every person in our studio dived into the cockamamie idea of kiss-
ing off every client we had just to *try* to become a full-service agency. It's
been there for I don't know how many new-business pitches—the laugh-
able long shots, some of which actually came in. And even when they
didn't and we saw how crazy the quest had been, the goofy Pollyanna
insanity was still there for the next one.

Pollyannaism, I realize as I look at our choices over the years, is one
of the main distinguishing features of this agency's culture. Maybe I
have a natural sanguine streak that has rubbed off on the agency. That
could be part of it. But I do know for sure that for us, exuberant, irrational optimism has been, at least in part, a learned behavior.

Years ago I read *Worlds in Collision* by Immanuel Velikovsky, the
crank or possibly visionary scientist who studied myth and folklore

and posited some new theories about cataclysmic events in human history. He asserted that whenever an ancient culture went through a massive catastrophe such as being decimated by a plague or clobbered by an asteroid, a gap ensued in the historical record. Silence. Nothing to tell us how they got back on their feet, just highly unjournalistic folktales about wild cosmic events. Then, said Velikovsky, after a few decades or centuries of recovery, the record begins again — starts right over as if the bad stuff never happened. It's as though cultures respond to collective trauma by developing mass amnesia.

"You know," I thought, "that's not a bad idea."

From that day on, I have consciously chosen denial. Not denying that a setback occurred but, rather, conveniently forgetting about it as an obstacle to further action. Whenever we experience a disappointment, as soon as we've had our 15-minute mourning period, we've learned to induce organizational amnesia by simply not talking about it anymore. Abracadabra, back to work. There's no stupid rule that states, "You may never mention the Foonman account again." Mention it if you want to. Learn from mistakes, sure; those lessons come in handy. But it's most convenient not to dwell on the disappointments themselves. Move on, that's all.

It's not just the big events, either — the plagues and asteroid hits. Being a Pollyanna who forgets past disappointments and denies present obstacles is at least as important in everyday office life, which can seem dangerous enough in itself. Bennis and Biederman write that "many workplaces have become angry, anguished, poisonous places where managers are abusive and employees subvert each other." In a world like that it takes a true Pollyanna to believe that you can let down your defenses and live to tell about it.

Ask one of the account executives to help you work through a copywriting problem? Or if you *are* the account exec, encourage "your" client to call the creative team direct, without having you on the line? Rewrite the creative brief because some wet-behind-the-ears art director hit on a brilliant idea that's "off strategy"? "No way." That's what business-culture-as-usual tells us is the wise answer if we have a hundredth of an ounce of self-preservation in us. "And don't even *talk* to me about dropping officer titles, abolishing departments, taking away everybody's office. . . . What are you, nuts?"

Yeah, a little.

You'll need a measurable dose of insanity, the Pollyanna spirit of the Great Groups, if you're going to build a business without tribalism.

Reality's been driving you nuts anyway. You might as well try something else. And if you end up tilting at a windmill now and then, well, at least the exercise will do you good.

To be sure, transforming a company culture can feel, to borrow writer Anne Lamott's phrase, "like trying to level Mount McKinley with a dentist's drill." It's going to take a while, building a company without factionalism, fiefdoms, fear, and the rest of the harsher realities of modern business. Mere temporary insanity won't do. You've got a long road ahead of you. But believe me, as one who has headed that way, it's a good one.

And, as Mr. Quixote himself reminds us, "The road is always better than the inn."

DEPOSING THE EVIL GENIUS

> *I'm telling you, these walls are funny. First you hate 'em.*
> *Then you get used to 'em. Enough time passes, you get so you*
> *depend on 'em."*
>
> —"Red," Morgan Freeman's convict character in
> *The Shawshank Redemption*

Live long enough inside the walls of tribalism and you can forget how to live any other way. Sure, you know another way exists, that there's life on the Outside. But it's one big unknown out there, beyond those familiar barriers. "It may be dysfunctional in here," you'll say, "but at least it's *our* dysfunction."

Freedom can be a pretty scary concept. That's true not only for individuals but also for bodies of individuals. Organizations—which, after all, wouldn't *be* organized without some vital energy or dynamic system holding them together—resist anything that would mess with their fundamental structure. Try to alter the basic social framework of a company and the company will resist—seemingly all by itself, almost apart from any human intelligence.

An organization has what in the old days—the *real* old days—was called a *genius loci*, the peculiar animating spirit of a place. It's what you're talking about when you try to describe the distinct *feel* of a workplace. That's the genius loci. And the old genius does not like to learn new tricks.

Forget grandiose, large-scale culture-change initiatives. Well entrenched, a spirit of factionalism and fear will not quietly submit to your attempts at instant exorcism. It enjoys its present lifestyle and has no plans to resign from its position. You can't give it the bum's rush. You can, however, displace it bit by bit, one sneaky little subversive act at a time.

As former Hallmark creative executive Gordon MacKenzie says in his book, *Orbiting the Giant Hairball* (Viking, 1998), for a company to make radical change it must "make room for something other than the narcissistic echoes of its own remembered past." If you've read this far, then chances are that process has already begun. *You* are that first bit of room for a different way to doing things in your company. Quietly, patiently, without any big announcements, you can start to make little changes within your sphere of influence. Begin with yourself. You don't even need anybody's permission to do that. Simply find ways to behave contrary to the prevailing politics, cliquishness, fear, what have you.

If your authority extends to others, if you're a boss, then maybe you can identify the department or group or individual most closely approximating the model of barrier-free work you want to see. Quietly fertilize them with the tools they need, the money, the protection from meddlesome outsiders. Reward the behaviors you want to see duplicated in other groups. But for goodness' sake *don't* announce a new policy of rewarding those behaviors. Just do it.

Lights will go on. Your employees' enlightened self-interest will start to kick in. They'll see where the path of greater success and satisfaction lies. And, trust me, they're smart enough to follow it without any of the coercive management that, frankly, was probably part of the cultural problem to start with. You can't change a culture by fiat. It's a person-to-person job. A movement, not a pronouncement.

And it's a freestyle event. What works in my company may not be right for yours. To borrow another thought from MacKenzie, you've got to adapt your approach and style to the medium you're working with. This is, remember, more art than science.

As people in your company—starting with you—catch on to the peaceable kingdom model, the old genius loci will find his power base eroding. He'll be squeezed into smaller and smaller quarters until finally, just maybe, he'll pack his American Tourister in a huff and shamble away, jerking at his Windsor knot and muttering about how he gets no respect, no respect at all.

As you commence your resistance movement against the genius loci, a couple of virtues might come in handy for you. One is patience. Culture change works through an organization like yeast through dough. There's no microwave-speed option. If you know that going in, not expecting quick transformation, you'll be fine. Humility will help, too. You're quietly subverting a system here, not leading a boisterous frontal assault. Don't expect to have an equestrian statue erected in your honor in the employee lunchroom. This is behind-the-scenes work.

So if you're okay with that, go ahead, take a deep breath, and let's get down to it. There's a genius to be deposed.

DOING WHAT COMES UNNATURALLY

> *The lion and the calf will lay down together, but the calf won't get much sleep.*
>
> —Woody Allen

It takes some getting used to, this idea of working without tribalism, of exposing our throats to people we've been taught to keep at arm's length. It can make you nervous. In the business culture that raised most of us, tribalism is so ingrained that to work without it takes conscious, counterintuitive effort.

I had a good lesson in conscious, counterintuitive effort around the time I turned 50. That's when I decided that it was high time I learned to ski. Today skiing is one of my passions. And now it's second nature—off the lift, straight down the mountain, the steeper, the faster, the better. Such, however, was most definitely not the case in my early attempts.

The basic idea was the same as it is now: down the mountain, whistling wind, thrill of speed, and hopefully no wipeouts en route. But the way of achieving that goal of exciting, controlled skiing was completely contrary to instinct.

No one ever died by falling *up* a mountain. You die falling *down* a mountain. Your instinct knows this. And it reminds you of the fact as you stand, white-lipped and laughing nervously, looking down a slope that seems a lot steeper now than it did when you were looking up at it from the lodge. The second you push off and start sliding down this precipitous incline, your instinct sends emergency telegrams: "Mountain steep. Headlong plunge ahead. Safety behind." So you do the natural thing. You lean back, weight on the uphill ski. And what happens?

Wipeout. The very thing you tried to avoid.

In those first few descents I had to learn, like every skier, to consciously lean down the mountain, shifting my weight in the direction of what seemed like certain death or, worse, ridicule by the spectators below. As long as I kept telling instinct to stick a sock in it, consciously putting my weight downhill, a marvelous thing happened. The edges of the skis bit the snow. I could turn, under control. I could pick up speed. I could feel the rush.

Soon, of course, caught up in the exhilaration, I forgot. I stopped thinking for a second and let instinct take over. And I found myself sliding pell-mell down the mountain with snow being power-injected down into my stylish new skiwear. But that's okay. I had felt the rush, and I was hooked for life. After that, progress came fast.

So here's what skiing has to do with killing off tribalism. In those first few runs down the mountain, before I ever attempted a carved turn or perfected a stem christy—before I could do much of anything—I had to learn to *stop* doing what came naturally. I had to lean into the thing that my instincts insisted would kill me.

Rejecting the life of tribalism is like that. It feels weird. Your instincts resist. And there's never a guarantee that you won't get snow down your pants. But once you find the exhilaration, once you see it work, even if briefly, you're hooked.

And it's downhill from there.

A PLACE TO START

Take a small risk. Do something subversive today.

Widely distribute information that you'd ordinarily keep within your tribe.

Divulge a strategy to people who don't "need" to know the strategy.

Have a conversation in a hallway that you'd rather have in a conference room.

If you'd ordinarily send an internal e-mail, make an internal phone call instead. If you'd ordinarily make an internal phone call, walk to the person's desk instead.

Tell an ambitious upstart a business problem you're trying to solve and ask her for ideas.

Keep your door open all day.

Little acts of defiance against the invisible barriers of tribalism—that's as good a start as any. You don't have to go charging in, realigning teams or rearranging the office. You don't have to abolish titles or chuck the policy manual. You don't have to do anything nearly so aggressive. Not yet.

For now it's enough just to start a flow, even just a trickle, of communication (and then resist the temptation to stop it up again). The more it flows, the more the structures of tribalism will be undermined. All it takes is one individual, unafraid, to get it started.

THE LAST WORD (IT STARTS WITH "F")

So, how was your day? Did you enjoy work today? It's a pretty good bet that I enjoyed mine. I feel very fortunate to be able to say that.

I went into the design and advertising business because it gave me a chance to make a living doing what I enjoy most. And now, lo these many decades later, I'm still having a blast at the office. Most of my coworkers seem to be having a pretty good time, too. We can, because we're not strapped with many of the constants of modern business life — factionalism, fiefdoms, fear — that would rob us of the pleasure of work.

Maybe that's not your situation. That's okay. Take heart. If you're not doing business in an open workplace yet, just doing your bit to move the organization in that direction is enough to make your job infinitely more interesting and satisfying. Put a few principles of the peaceable kingdom into practice and see what I mean.

Even if you don't transform your company, you'll encourage those around you — which feels pretty good in itself — and you'll enjoy your own days a lot more. You'll find that coming to work in the morning is something to look forward to. (Okay, maybe not *every* day, but most.) Heck, you might even get back in touch with a feeling you had when you started out, back when you were doing it for love. You might start to have . . . dare we say it?

Oh, sure. Why not. It might even be what we're all here for anyway, if only we thought it were possible. Well, I know that it is possible. And not just possible. I'd say you're entitled to it. So I will say to you now what I say to my fellow Groupers at the end of every little gathering at the stairwell.

Thanks very much. Let's go have fun.

Acknowledgments

Several friends and colleagues deserve particular thanks—none more than Doug Rucker, who initiated the conversations with John Wiley & Sons, Inc., that led to the writing and publication of this book. Throughout the process Doug remained the project's point man, communicating with the publishers; encouraging and, when necessary, prodding the authors; marshaling resources within The Richards Group; and being the first to read and respond to the manuscript, page by halting page. We, quite literally, could not have done it without him.

The chapter on branding owes much to the clear thinking and lucid writing of Rod Underhill, Richards Group principal and chief nuncio of Spherical® branding. Particularly helpful was his article "Who's Minding the Brand?" that appeared in the July 1999 issue of the Arthur Andersen Retailing Issues Letter, published in association with the Texas A&M Center for Retailing Studies.

If you want your project to be better looking and better thought-out, you talk to Glenn Dady, art director extraordinaire and, in many ways, the conscience of The Richards Group. That's what we did. He lent his considerable organizational and graphic skills to the project, as well as serving as a memory bank for everything that's happened around here in the past 20 years.

Special thanks to Andrew Jaffe of *Adweek* for his hearty endorsement of the project and the keen critical eye he lent us along the way. His suggestions and support were invaluable.

Ruth Mills, our editor, shepherded the team of rookie authors with an admirable mix of calm wisdom and, as deadlines loomed, firm prodding. We're especially grateful to Ruth for bringing much-needed organization and clarity to the manuscript itself. Thanks, too, to Airie Dekidjiev and Jessica Noyes at Wiley for somehow turning 500 pages of e-mail and assorted photographs, videotapes, ad reprints, and illustrations into the volume you're now reading.

Finally, I dedicate my portion of this book to my partner and wife, Donna, whose encouragement subdued my self-doubt and whose steadiness proved stronger than my neuroses; and to our son, Flint, whose joyful approach to life helped draw me away from the computer every night and home to watch *Cow and Chicken*.

—David Culp

Index